The Rough Guide to

Accessible Britain

Fully revised and updated second edition

ROUGH
GUIDES

www.roughguides.com

CREDITS

Reviewers: Emma Bowler, Vivienne Bush, Chris Cammiss, Douglas Campbell, Karen Darke, John Hargreaves, Andrew Healey, Dom Hyams, Joy & Nic Jansen, Sue Kelley, Carol Lawley, Phil Lee, David Livermore, Andy Macleod, Jane MacNamee, Glenys Mashford, Lara Masters, Eva McCracken, Gary McGladdery, James Rawlings, Mik Scarlett, Richard Shakespeare, Helen Smith, Rob Smith, Paul Talbot, Jeannette Travis, Gill Westcott
Additional contributions: Suzanne Bull, Jane MacNamee, Alf Alderson, Phillippa Greenwood, Martine O'Callaghan **Text editor:** Richard Trillo **Design and layout:** Diana Jarvis **Cartography:** Katie Lloyd-Jones **Proofreader:** Stewart Wild **Picture research:** Mark Thomas **Production:** Rebecca Short **Project manager:** Emma Traynor (Rough Guides), Delia Ray (Motability) **Account manager:** Sarah Mycock (Rough Guides)

This second edition published April 2009 by
Rough Guides Ltd, 80 Strand, London WC2R 0RL
in association with
Motability Operations, City Gate House,
22 Southwark Bridge Road, London SE1 9HB
© Rough Guides, 2009

ISBN 9781848362437

Printed in Italy by LegoPrint S.p.A

All photography © Rough Guides except for the following:

Colour introduction: p.1 National Botanical Gardens © Alistair Scott/Alamy; p. 4 Lara Masters © Jan Gamble; p.5 Family with car © Motability Operations; p.8 Eden project © John Warbuton-Lee/Alamy; p.9 Kensington Palace © Robert Harding/Alamy; p.10 Christ Church College © Mark Thomas; p.11 Samphire Hoe © Philip Dew/Alamy; p.11 Red Kite in flight © Andrew Walmsley; p.12 Old Trafford © Manchester United; p.12 Legoland © Tony E Teggot; p.13 Cairngorms © Realimage/Alamy; p.13 Pine trees © David Plummer/Alamy; p.14 Abbotsbury Swannery © Emma Bowler; p.15 Boats © Bob Caddick/Alamy; p.15 Pedalabikeaway © Pedalabikeaway; p.16 Lily Pond at Wisley Gardens © Peter Noyce/Alamy; p.16 Royal Yacht Britannia © Peter Titmuss/Alamy

Black and white images: p.23 Kensington Gardens © Diana Jarvis; p.26 The National Gallery © Mark Thomas; p.29 The O2 © The O2; p.36 Plane at the BDFA © Rob Smith; p.41 Dungeness beach © Tony Lilley/Alamy; p.46 Wisley Gardens © Wisley Gardens; p.50 Christ Church College © Mark Thomas; p.53 Henley on Thames © Jstock/Alamy; p.54 Roald Dahl Museum © The Roald Dahl Museum; p.55 Spitfire at the Shuttleworth Collection © Alan Spencer/Alamy; p.56 Child playing at the Thames Valley Adventure Park © TVAP; p.62 Blickling Hall © Stuart Crump/Alamy; p.65 Dunwich Heath © geogphotos/Alamy; p.69 National space centre © Roger Bamber/Alamy; p.73 Sheringham Hall © David Burton/Alamy; p.74 Sherwood Forest © Richard Naude/Alamy; p.81 Chatsworth House © Chatsworth House; p.84 Cromford canal © David Martyn Hughes/Alamy; p.89 RAF Museum Cosford © RAF Cosford; p.92 Warwick Castle © David Martyn Hughes/Alamy; p.96 Abbotsbury Swannery © Emma Bowler; p.103 Isles of Scilly © Hemis/Alamy; p.105 Orangutan © Tom Uhlman/Alamy; p.107 Sherborne Old Castle © Emma Traynor; p.111 Stourhead © Susan Beatson; p.113 Tate St Ives © Mark Thomas; p.117 Another Place © Diana Jarvis; p.118 Blackwell House © Blackwell House; p.119 Man shooting © Joe Fox; p.125 Birdwatching © Conrad Elias/Alamy; p.126 Man visiting theatre © Theatre by the Lake; p.127 URBIS exterior © URBIS; p.130 BALTIC © Mark Thomas; p.134 Fountains Abbey © Johnny Stockshooter/Alamy; p.137 Durham Cathedral © Mark Thomas; p.139 MAGNA © Barry Morgan/Alamy; p.141 Interior of the SAGE © THE SAGE; p.144 Yorkshire sculpture Park © Sandra Dorney/Alamy; p.147 National Botanical Gardens Wales © NBGW; p.153 Pontcysyllte Aqueduct © Rob Rayworth/Alamy; p.158 Cairngorm Mountain Railway © David Gowans/Alamy; p.161 Culloden Battlefield © David Gowans/Alamy; p.162 Culzean Castle © DG Farquhar/Alamy; p.174 Men in glider © Walking on air; p.177 Glens Glenariff Forest © Stephen Saks/Alamy; p.178 Grand Opera House © Christopher Hill/Alamy; p.179 Laganside Pier Belfast © Christopher Hill/Alamy; p.181 Nature Reserve © Simon Brown/Alamy

With many thanks to the following organisations for their assistance with this guide: Mobilise, Attitude is Everything and Direct Enquiries.

CONTENTS

FOREWORD

Welcome to the Rough Guide to Accessible Britain's fabulous second edition! After discussing user feedback from the first edition, Rough Guides' team of disabled writers and Motability Operations have ramped up (see what I did there?!) this new guide. Within these pages are the access details of over 175 accessible sites visited by a thoroughly exacting team of disabled reviewers who were unafraid to ask probing questions or politely point out concerns. We all know that offering to carry a wheelchair user up two flights of stairs does not make a venue wheelchair accessible, even if the website and brochure claim different. Access aside, our writers have also included their thoughts about each place, reporting on how they found the whole experience, as obviously there is more to a site than a hearing loop or wide doorway.

As a disabled person I know that despite the lofty DDA and its stipulations, venue owners are often surprisingly unaware of disability access requirements and what their responsibilities are. When out and about in my hometown of London, I am frequently given inaccurate information about venue access through websites or on the phone, so was particularly keen to get involved with this completely impartial guide knowing how useful it would be for many disabled people.

Our team of reviewers has put together a tantalising selection of the cream of Britain's accessible attractions, from wine tasting to sled-dog safaris, with detailed information that disabled readers can rely upon. This edition is bigger, covering a greater number and range of sites than before, plus has new features including reader reviews, tips on accessing festivals and outdoor adventures, and an extremely helpful listing section of useful contacts. Turn to p.21 to see my top tips for food and drink in London. So, whether munching or raving, we hope you enjoy using this guide as much as we enjoyed making it and again, we would love to hear any feedback readers may have to offer. You can give us your comments at www.accessibleguide.co.uk.

Lara Masters

Lara is a writer, actor, model, TV presenter and owner of burlesque fashion label *Kiss My Cherry*. Check out Lara's weekly diary blog for *Marie Claire* magazine at www.marieclaire.co.uk

THE ROUGH GUIDE TO MOTABILITY

This updated and enhanced Rough Guide to Accessible Britain is packed full of ideas to inspire you to make the most of your leisure time. The same spirit lies behind the Motability Scheme, which has been providing cars, powered wheelchairs and scooters to help disabled customers enjoy the freedom of the road since 1978.

As an early public-private partnership, the Scheme was established to enable disabled people to access affordable, trouble-free motoring. Through the Motability Car Scheme, customers lease a new car as part of a package that includes insurance, free tyres, servicing and breakdown cover. The Scheme now has over 500,000 customers and a reputation for close attention to customer service.

Motability is available to anyone who receives the Higher Rate Mobility Component of the Disability Living Allowance or War Pensioners Mobility Supplement – no other checks or assessments are required. Customers transfer this payment, currently a little under £50 a week, to Motability, as the monthly lease payment. Large or higher specification cars require an additional advance payment, although around 200 cars carry no further cost. A parent, carer, partner or friend can drive the car if the customer does not drive themselves.

There are over 4,000 cars to choose from, including favourite models by all major manufacturers. There are also Wheelchair Accessible Vehicles and drive-from wheelchair options. If required, a selection of common adaptations can be included at no extra cost.

The Motability Car Scheme is overseen by the charity Motability, who may also be able to assist people who require a financial grant in order to fund the specific car or adaptations of their needs. The charity also carries out various fundraising activities.

Motability Operations, the company that runs the Car Scheme, is happy to continue its support of the Rough Guide to Accessible Britain to inspire more disabled people to discover more of the world around them. In turn, Motability Operations hopes to create a better understanding of the Scheme, and reach more people who could benefit from what Motability offers.

- Over 4,000 brand new cars to choose from
- Insurance, annual car tax, servicing and maintenance all included
- Full RAC breakdown assistance included
- FREE replacement tyres and windscreen

Motability Car & Powered Wheelchair Scheme Telephone: 0800 093 1000

Feet

3000
2000
1500
1000
500
250
0

NORTH SEA

John o'Groats

Durness

Stornoway

Western Isles

Ullapool

Inverness

Aberdeen

Dundee

Perth

Kyle of Lochalsh

Mallaig

Fort William

Skye

Mull

Oban

Islay

Falkirk

Glasgow

Edinburgh

Berwick-upon-Tweed

Jedburgh

Dumfries

Stranraer

Carlisle

Keswick

Newcastle-upon-Tyne

Durham

Tyne

Tees

Whitby

Campbeltown

Ballycastle

Ballymena

Bangor

Belfast

Lough Neagh

Derry

Omagh

N

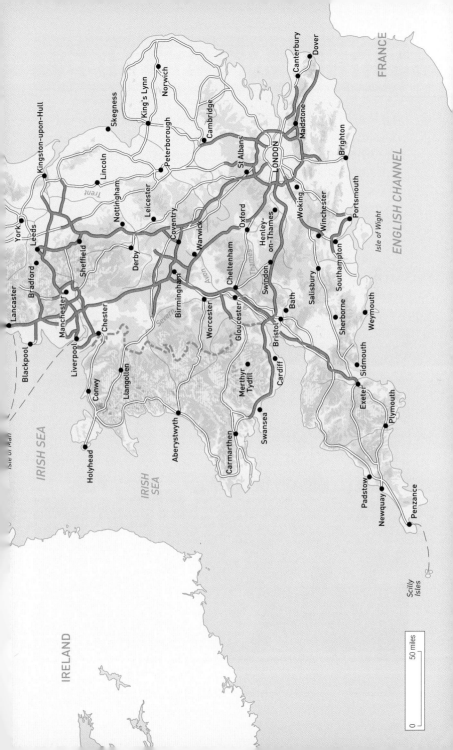

Things Not To Miss

The Rough Guide to Accessible Britain is packed with great ideas for inspirational and accessible days out all around the UK. What follows over the next eight pages is a taste of the highlights, whether you want to day-trip on a budget; brush up on your history; escape the tourist hordes; enjoy some family fun; blow the cobwebs away on an outdoor adventure; come face-to-face with tooth and claw (or beak and feather); get to grips with a new skill or simply spend some time celebrating your patriotism for these glorious isles. All entries have a page reference to take you straight into the regional chapter, where you can find out more.

The Eden Project ▶▶ The Southwest • p.102

① ▸▸ Free

The Science Museum ▸▸ London • p.31
The energetic Science Museum in South Kensington provides an enlightening experience for adults and kids alike. Spend a hands-on day here, and if you have any energy or time left you're conveniently right next door to the Natural History Museum.

Bolderwood Deer Sanctuary, New Forest ▸▸ The Southeast • p.38 With three accessible trails, Bolderwood Deer Sanctuary in Hampshire's ancient New Forest ticks all the boxes for anyone looking for a day of fresh air and exercise. Visit in the early afternoon in summer to watch the rangers provide lunch for the local fallow deer.

Kensington Gardens ▸▸ London • p.23 Although many visit Kensington Gardens whilst on a trip to the Serpentine Gallery, this classic London park is a must-see destination in its own right. JM Barrie was inspired to write *Peter Pan* during afternoon strolls in the garden, and during a similarly relaxing meander you're likely to come face-to-face with the famous statue of the boy who never grew up – not to mention the Albert Memorial, Kensington Palace, the Diana Memorial Playground and the glorious boating lake.

Buckfast Abbey ▸▸ The Southwest • p.98
Home to a community of Benedictine monks who have always welcomed visitors, Buckfast Abbey is a thriving monastery surrounded by tranquil grounds. Lose yourself in the sensory gardens, but before you leave, make sure to treat yourself to a gift of Buckfast tonic wine, handmade by the brothers themselves.

RAF Museum, Cosford ▸▸ West Midlands & the Peak District • p.88 Not just for aviation buffs; there are over seventy aircraft housed at the easily navigable and award-winning RAF Cosford.

Heritage

Sherborne Castles ▶▶ The Southwest • p.107 Moments from genteel Sherborne town centre, the "new" Sherborne Castle originated as the home of Sir Walter Raleigh. Thankfully his attempts to modernise the pre-existing "old" castle failed, so the picturesque ruins remain just over the lake.

Lincoln Cathedral ▶▶ East Anglia and the East Midlands • p.67 Once reputed as the tallest building in the world, Lincoln Cathedral clearly no longer holds that title, but dominates Lincoln's skyline nonetheless. Worthwhile guided tours of the imposing interior take place throughout the day, free of charge, but the cathedral is equally compelling as a spot for quiet reflection.

Blackwell House ▶▶ The Northwest • p.118 Just a short step away from the nearby tourist crush of the banks of Windermere, restored Blackwell House is an outstanding example of Arts and Crafts elegance.

Christ Church College, Oxford ▶▶ The Home Counties & Oxfordshire • p.49 Magnificent Christ Church college is a highlight of any visit to Oxford.

Fountains Abbey & Studley Royal Water Gardens ▶▶ Yorkshire & the Northeast • p.134 The majestic ruins of eight-hundred-year-old Fountains Abbey make up only a fraction of the eight-hundred-acre Studley Royal estate, which is complete with a sprawling Deer Park and formal Water Gardens.

③ ›› Hidden

Dunwich Heath Coastal Centre & Beach ›› East Anglia and the East Midlands • p.65 This lowland heath is a wonderfully remote-feeling area where you can blow away the cobwebs as you take in the tracts of heather, sandy cliffs and lots of local wildlife.

Samphire Hoe ›› The Southeast • p.45 Landscaped with small lakes and sown with wild local flowers, this magical nature reserve in Kent was constructed from the chalk that came out of the Channel Tunnel.

Walking on Air ›› Scotland • p.174 At the Scottish Gliding Centre based on Portmoak Airfield, this charity provides an opportunity for people with disabilities to soar the skies in a modified glider. Based right by Loch Leven, the stunning views add to an already spectacular experience.

Llangollen Wharf ›› Wales • p.152 Enjoy the serenity of a horse-drawn canal boat, admidst peaceful Welsh surroundings without even the noise of an engine to disturb the scenery.

Red Kites at Gigrin Farm ›› Wales • p.150 Settle in a viewing hide to watch as a quarter of a tonne of beef is fed to up to four hundred Red Kites.

④ ▸▸ Families

Magna Science Adventure Centre ▸▸ Yorkshire & the Northeast • p.139 Everything at Magna is done on a monumental scale – the museum itself is inside what used to be one of the world's biggest steel mills. Hugely interactive, Magna is a place where you can try your hand at blasting a rock face, all in the celebration of science and engineering.

Manchester United Stadium Tour ▸▸ The Northwest • p.121 Whether you're visiting for a match or a stadium tour, the access facilities at the Theatre of Dreams are first-rate and the atmosphere is electric.

Odyssey Arena ▸▸ Northern Ireland • p.182 There's no such thing as a bad seat at the Odyssey Arena. Treat the kids to a superb view of the ice rink as home team Belfast Giants battle their way through a match, or spend a fun afternoon at the bowling arena in the complex.

Thames Valley Adventure Playground ▸▸ The Home Counties & Oxfordshire • p.56 Gentle and charming, this adventure playground has been specially designed so that all children can take part in the fun of the zipwire and swings.

Legoland ▸▸ The Home Counties & Oxfordshire • p.51 Although firmly placed on the tourist trail, Legoland shouldn't be dismissed as a faceless commercial affair. With plenty of can-do staff and a scheme that allows kids who have difficulty queueing to effortlessly get on rides via the exits, the whole family will undoubtedly have a great day out. Take a trip on Brickadilly's Ferris Wheel that has a wheelchair-accessible gondola.

⑤ ▸▸ Outdoors

Cromford Canal Trail ▸▸ West Midlands & the Peak District • p.84 A gentle stroll along the Cromford towpath makes for the perfect low-key outdoor trip.

Cairngorm Funicular Railway and Ski Centre ▸▸ Scotland • p.158 An accessible funicular railway whisks you up to the fully wheelchair-friendly Cairngorm Mountain Railway and Ski Centre. If you want to get going on the piste, adaptive equipment is available from Disability Snowsport.

Peatlands Park ▸▸ Northern Ireland • p.183 Boasting the bizarre status of venue for International Bog Day, Peatlands Park is also rife with wildlife and is protected as a Site of Special Scientific Interest.

Mount Edgcumbe Country Park ▸▸ The Southwest • p.105 Fine countryside and dramatic coastline surround the stunning grounds of Mount Edgcumbe House.

Bedgebury National Pinetum ▸▸ The Southeast • p.37 Pick a nice day, bring a picnic and you'll find plenty to keep even the most active family busy at Bedgebury National Pinetum.

The Deep
▸▸ Yorkshire & the Northeast • p.132 With over forty sharks housed in a slick high-tech aquarium by the Humber Estuary, a day-trip to The Deep is a really satisfying experience.

Donkey Sanctuary at Sidmouth ▸▸ The Southwest • p.101 With countryside trails and sea views, this charity-run home for rescued and unwanted donkeys provides a charming day out.

Abbotsbury Swannery
▸▸ The Southwest • p.96 Although originally set up centuries ago to serve local monks with lavish banquets, Abbotsbury Swannery is now a much more compassionate affair – these days visitors feed the birds instead.

ZSL Whipsnade Zoo ▸▸ The Home Counties & Oxfordshire • p.58 One of Europe's largest wildlife parks, Whipsnade is home to more than 2500 animals. With the park dedicated to conservation, the majority of the freely wandering species you'll meet are endangered.

RSPB Loch Garten Osprey Centre ▸▸ Scotland • p.170 A mecca for birdwatchers and a favourite with Bill Oddie, this centre has comfortable hides perfectly appointed for viewing the osprey nests.

7 ▸▸ Hands on

Flying with BDFA ▸▸ The Southeast • p.36
BDFA say to date they've never turned
anyone away, whatever their disability. Try a
trial flight – you might end up training for a
pilot's licence.

**Horse-riding at Black Cat Equestrian
Centre** ▸▸ East Anglia and the East Midlands
• p.61 Located by the pretty seaside town
of Sutton-on-Sea, Black Cat staff are
experienced at providing horse-riding
lessons for people of all abilities. And you
can also try carriage-driving.

Loch Insh Watersports ▸▸ Scotland •
p.166 Loch Insh is an idyllic place to try
watersports, but be sure to warm yourself up
afterwards with a "nip" in a nearby bar.

Sailability, Rutland ▸▸ East Anglia and
the East Midlands • p.71 Sailability has
sites spread around the UK, all manned
by friendly, experienced sailors and fully
equipped with specialist kit. Rutland Water
is no exception with 23 boats to choose
from.

**Pedalabikeaway in the
Forest of Dean** ▸▸ West
Midlands & the Peak District • p.87
With a range of bikes catering
for visitors with disabilities,
Pedalabikeaway is ideally
placed in the Forest of Dean for
cyclists to enjoy scenic routes,
handy picnic spots and a
variety of routes with different
challenge levels.

Wisley Gardens ▸▸ The Southeast • p.45 Flagship garden of the Royal Horticultural Society, Wisley is unsurprisingly a fabulously designed public garden, with plenty for everyone to enjoy, experts and novices alike.

Cabinet War Rooms ▸▸ London • p.20 Buried deep under Whitehall, Churchill's Cabinet Rooms remain exactly as they were in 1945 when the lights were finally turned out.

RSC ▸▸ West Midlands & the Peak District • p.90 Early booking is advised for this popular venue, famed for keeping Shakespeare's work at the forefront of British theatre.

The Brit Oval ▸▸ London • p.20 Even without its refurbishment completed, this famous old cricket venue is fully accessible and an intimate setting to comfortably watch a game unfold. England will revisit their rivalry with Australia on home turf during the Ashes in 2009, and the Oval is booked as the venue for the final Test match.

Royal Yacht Britannia ▸▸ Scotland • p.169 One of Edinburgh's newest tourist attractions, a tour of the Royal Yacht *Britannia* can throw up many surprises – not least that it's not quite as luxurious as you might imagine a Royal residence to be. Perhaps most unexpected of all is that the ship is accessible – in fact many efforts have been made to make it so.

LONDON

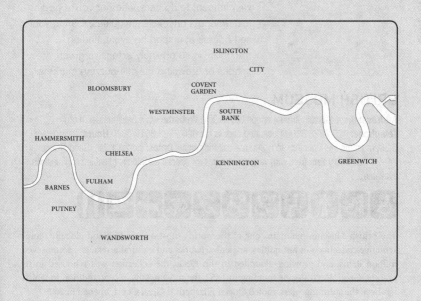

LONDON

Hectic and sprawling, yet full of life, history and culture, London is unmissable. Recent years have seen its institutions reinvented – from Wembley to the British Museum – increasing both their appeal and accessibility. There is a vast amount to do here, whether you're getting lost amongst priceless antiquities, roaring yourself hoarse at a sporting event, finding tranquility in surprisingly extensive green spaces or browsing the still-buzzing markets.

BRITISH MUSEUM

Address: Great Russell Street, London WC1B 3DG **Website:** www.britishmuseum.org
Telephone: 020 7323 8000 Dedicated access tel: 020 7323 8510/8850 **Hours:** daily 10am–5.30pm (some late openings to 8.30pm – call for details) **Dates:** closed 1 Jan, Good Friday, 24–26 Dec **Entry fee:** free, with variable charges for special exhibitions (disabled concessions available)

The British Museum maintains one of the world's most outstanding and globally representative collections of antiquities, ancient artworks and cultural artefacts – some seven million items, and growing. Founded in the 1750s, the collection was rehoused in its present, Greek Revival-style building in 1852, the most notable recent addition to which has been the stunning, glass-roofed Queen Elizabeth II Great Court, opened in 2000.

This jewel in London's crown provides for an amazing and – it's worth emphasizing – free day out, and it deserves at least a day's visit. However if time is at a premium, then one- and three-hour tour cards are available from the information desks and are extremely helpful. The Roman and Greek art collections are perhaps the greatest of all the exhibits here, and unparalleled anywhere in the world. You'll only see more impressive Egyptian exhibits in Egypt itself, while even more niche-interest sections, such as Hittite culture or medieval Southeast Asia, are impressively well-served. And visiting children are too, with free art materials and activity backpacks available, themed family trails to suit different age groups ready-mapped, and a family audio tour hosted by Vid the alien.

Parking can be arranged on the main forecourt (call ahead: 020 7323 8299). An open lift, to the left of the imposing main staircase, takes you up to the entrance and further lifts are available to all areas. Magnifying glasses can be borrowed at the desks and assistance dogs are not only welcome but, if you drop by the desk in the Great Court, will be given water. Access and what's-on guides and maps are vital accompaniments, not least because once you're through the doors and faced by the awe-inspiring Great Court and Reading Room, it's easy to be distracted. The temporary exhibitions are usually accompanied by tactile images and Braille. Touch tours and BSL-interpreted gallery talks are regular features, too, as are object-handling sessions and audio-described highlight tours.

The Norman Foster-designed Great Court at the British Museum

THE BRIT OVAL

Address: Surrey County Cricket Club, Kennington, London SE11 5SS **Website:** www.surreycricket.com **Telephone:** 08712 461100 (choose option 1) **Hours:** variable, see fixtures on website **Dates:** variable, see fixtures on website **Entry fees:** variable, see fixtures on website

This famous old cricket venue, home to Surrey County Cricket Club, has undergone extensive refurbishment over recent years. While the process is not yet complete (floodlights are the next step to allow evening fixtures), it already offers a relaxed and accessible environment to disabled fans, wherever you choose to sit.

At pitch level, a visit can be a remarkably intimate experience, as you're sitting just feet from the boundary rope. The playing area is slightly domed towards the centre, offering batsmen excellent opportunities for scoring fours. For a cricket fan, there is surely no better place to watch the game at its highest standard. More than sixty wheelchair-plus-companion seats are available, in four bays spread around the ground. But the higher up you can afford to go, the more spectacular the view.

Parking is available near or, depending on the fixture, in the ground itself (call to check availability 0871 246 1100). There is level access to the wheelchair bays (toilets here require a RADAR key) and lift access to everywhere else, including the recently-built OCS stand and sponsors' boxes. Here, if you can drag yourself away from the hospitality, seats are regularly removed to offer extra wheelchair access to the steep terraces outside. As part of a long-term relationship with Scope, low-level service points are being fitted at catering points and DDA-compliant pads help to open some of the stiffer doors. Induction loops are fitted in seating blocks 7–14, which includes disabled bays 12 and 13, while for the visually impaired, assistance dogs are welcome and free audio earpieces (available at the retail outlets) provide a running BBC radio commentary on the match.

CABINET WAR ROOMS

Address: Clive Steps, King Charles Street, London SW1A 2AQ **Website:** www.iwm.org.uk **Telephone:** 020 7930 6961 Dedicated access tel: 020 7766 0130/2 (advance bookings) Dedicated email: cwr@iwm.org.uk **Hours:** 9.30am–6pm (last entrance 5pm) **Dates:** closed 24–26 Dec **Entry fees:** [D]£7.50 [H]Free [A]£12 [under 16s] Free [C]£6–£9.50

Perhaps the biggest surprise is that the Cabinet War Rooms, buried deep under Whitehall in a warren of tunnels, are accessible at all. But here they are, and they offer a fascinating insight into how Prime Minister Winston Churchill and his staff managed Britain's day-to-day struggle during World War II.

Opened in 1938, when Nazi bombing raids were being anticipated, the rooms were used for meetings of Churchill's Cabinet for the duration of the war. The rooms remain exactly as they were in 1945, when the intelligence officers and map analysts finally cleared their desks and turned out the lights. As well as cabinet, map and communications rooms, Churchill's domestic quarters are now revealed – including his bed and a rather nice desk – and a new museum (adjacent to the War Rooms) celebrates the great man's life. A café selling British comfort food has also been introduced. You are supplied with a hearing-aid-compatible audio guide to hang round your neck. It's used like a phone, but an earpiece is available to improve the sound quality and leave your hands free. A transcript is also available.

For nearby parking, there's a single Blue Badge bay on Queen Anne's Gate. The best access is via Great George Street and the bunkers lie down a 20-step flight of stairs with a single handrail. However a lift beyond the ticket office can take you down to the start of the tour (and an accessible toilet). Although some of the passageways are quite narrow (minimum width 76cm), the tour is accessible to most wheelchairs. Owing to the cramped nature of the site though, there is limited seating: you'll find more in the café and Churchill Museum.

DONMAR WAREHOUSE

Address: 47 Earlham Street, Seven Dials, London WC2H 9LX **Website:** www.donmarwarehouse.com **Telephone:** 0870 060 6624 Dedicated access tel: 0871 297 5477 or 020 7974 4655 for parking info **Hours:** Mon–Sat 10am until curtain up **Dates:** closed Sundays and 24 Dec (variable) **Entry fees:** all performances [D]£12 [H]£12

This former Covent Garden brewery and banana warehouse is one of London's leading theatres, a multi-award-winning space, with a diverse artistic policy that takes in new writing, contemporary versions of European classics, British and American drama and small-scale musical theatre.

Formed in 1961, the Donmar (after the first names of founders Donald Albery and Margot Fonteyn) has only 250 seats and offers a particularly intimate experience for audience and performers alike, demanding an extra dose of chutzpah from actors performing less than two metres from the front row. Under the artistic directorship of stage and film

There are more bars, clubs, pubs and restaurants in London than anywhere else in the UK. With so many choices and a city clustered with contrasting architectural styles, it's not surprising that access standards vary. But there are lots of great options, even away from the generic chains. The perfectly accessible **Lounge Lover** (1 Whitby Street, E2 7DP; 020 7012 1234; www.loungelover.co.uk), with its baroque-burlesque decor and award-winning cocktail menu is a wonderfully decadent choice. If clubs are more your scene, **93 Feet East** (150 Brick Lane, E1 6QL; 020 7247 3293; www.93feeteast.co.uk) is a live music and dance club hosting eclectic bands, performance artists and DJs. Although largely accessible, the outside BBQ area is cobble-stoned so can be a little tricky, plus be aware that the disabled loo is serviceable if a little dilapidated. **The Drawing Room** (269 Portobello Road, W11 1LR; 020 7221 7696; www.drawingroomlondon.com) is a gem of a boutique style restaurant-cum-art gallery with a European menu. Expect to pay around £28 for three courses, and watch out for the live music nights. There is a small lip on the front door, but the airy restaurant is manoeuvrable for a standard-sized electric wheelchair.

director Sam Mendes, the Donmar became hugely successful in the early 1990s and his successor, Michael Grandage, has built on this reputation. Hit productions have included *Design for Living* (1994), *The Glass Menagerie* (1995), *Uncle Vanya* (2002) and *Frost/Nixon* (2006). 2009's high profile performances at the Donmar will undoubtedly include the restoration of the Tennessee Williams' classic, *A Streetcar Named Desire*, opening in July. Academy Award-winning Brit actress Rachel Weisz will be starring as the fragile and faded Southern beauty Blanche DuBois. And another big draw for 2009, again featuring a tormented female-lead taken on by a Hollywood star, will be the remake of Ibsen's *A Doll's House*. Gillian Anderson, best known for *X Files* and more recently the latest BBC *Bleak House* adaptation, is to play Nora in the story of marital strife, with the action brought forward into the twentieth-century world of British politics.

Given the infrastructure of the Donmar, access is good. There's a single, Blue Badge space outside the theatre, only available after 6.30pm. The main entrance from Earlham Street requires a temporary ramp: if for any reason it has not been laid, until 6.30pm you can get to the box office via the Thomas Neal shopping centre, twenty metres to the right. An 80cm-wide lift serves both stalls and circle: while the sole wheelchair space is at the rear of the stalls, the accessible toilet and only lowered section of the two bars are at circle level. Walkers will also find fewer, shallower steps in the stalls. An online audio brochure of the theatre and its productions also lists details of signed, captioned and audio-described performances. The latter are also preceded by free Touch Tours, on which patrons can explore the set and often meet members of the company. Braille and large-print cast sheets, and large-print brochures, are available on request.

ELTHAM PALACE

Address: Eltham Palace, off Court Yard, Greenwich, London SE9 5QE **Website:** www.english-heritage.org.uk/elthampalace **Telephone:** 020 8294 2548 **Hours:** 1 Apr–31 Oct Sun–Wed 10am–5pm; 1 Nov–21 Dec Sun–Wed 11am–4pm; 1 Feb–31 Mar Sun–Wed 11am–4pm **Dates:** closed 22–31 Dec **Entry fees:** [D]£6.60 [H]Free [A]£8.20 [child]£4.10 [C]£6.60

Entering Eltham Palace, you're transported back to the 1930s and immersed in the opulent world of former owners Sir Stephen and Lady Virginia Courtauld. The house is brimming with exquisite design features like the entrance hall's domed concrete and glass ceiling and wood-panelled walls depicting the couple's yacht and favourite holiday spots.

The original Eltham Palace dates from the fourteenth century and played a major role in royal domestic affairs – including being Henry VIII's childhood home – for more than three hundred years. In 1933, by then mostly in ruins, it was acquired by the Courtaulds, who redeveloped the interior of the Great Hall in Art Deco style, and lived here until 1944. This fabulous building is well worth exploring. By the time you've been through The Dining Room (pink leather), The Boudoir (where Virginia Courtauld devoted her time to the couple's social diary), and their bedroom suites, and paid your respects to the centrally heated quarters of their pet lemur, you start to get a feel for the privileged life of Britain's elite during the interwar years. Head into the nineteen acres of gardens and you're enveloped by quite a wonderland of flora and landscaping, including a mountainous rockery, a sunken rose garden and a medieval bridge.

Disabled parking bays are very close to the main entrance, which has two doors with small lips. The gift shop has many low shelves and the tearoom has movable tables and chairs but gets cramped when it's busy. In the house "blue shoes" (plastic shoe coverings) must be worn unless you use a wheelchair. There is a ramp to the Great Hall and a wheelchair lift upstairs. Some tight corners mean that a large electric wheelchair/scooter would struggle to explore the whole house, but if you can it is worth the challenge. The gardens have wheelchair-accessible paths with some uneven parts. Wheelchairs available to borrow are on a first-come, first-served basis. Signage throughout is clear and an audio tour is included in the admission price.

KENSINGTON GARDENS

Address: Kensington, London W2 **Website:** www.royalparks.org.uk **Telephone:** 07767 498096 to book Liberty Drives **Hours:** always open **Dates:** no closure dates **Entry fees:** free

Kensington Gardens offers everything you'd expect from a London park: formal tree-lined avenues, ornamental flowerbeds, a bandstand, a duck pond, a boating lake and fountains. But it has plenty more, too, which makes it a satisfying place to visit.

Perhaps most famous of the gardens' landmarks is the Peter Pan statue – JM Barrie was inspired to write *Peter Pan* during afternoon strolls through the gardens. You'll also find the Albert Memorial and Kensington Palace, most famous in recent years as the home of Diana, Princess of Wales. The gardens now contain a walk and fountain named in Diana's memory, while the Diana Memorial Playground was designed as a space where "less able and able-bodied children can play together". Much of the playground is indeed accessible, including a cleverly designed raised walkway giving access to sev-

eral slides, so it's a pity that the centrepiece, a huge wooden pirate ship, can only be boarded via tricky rope bridges. The café next to the playground entrance is a good place to get a hot drink or snack. Or if you want fancier fare choose The Orangery, famous for its afternoon teas. Many people come to the gardens purely for the Serpentine Gallery – one of London's best-loved galleries for modern and contemporary art. It's open 10am–6pm daily, and has level access.

Most of the gardens are easy to navigate, with mainly level ground or manageable slopes, but for those unable to undertake the full 260 acres of Kensington Gardens and Hyde Park, Liberty Drives provide a free mobility service around the park, accessible to wheelchair-users. Accessible toilets are available at Mount Gate.

The Diana Memorial Playground

THE LONDON AQUARIUM

Address: County Hall, Westminster Bridge Road, London SE1 7PB **Website:** www.
londonaquarium.co.uk **Telephone:** 020 7967 8000 **Opening Hours:** 10am–6pm (last entry
5pm) **Dates:** closed 25 Dec **Entry fees:** [D]£11.25 [H]Free [A]£13.25 [3–14]£9.75 [C]£11.25

The London Aquarium, tucked into County Hall by the Thames, is an underground
labyrinth of aquatic activity. There are fourteen zones of fish-filled tanks, from the slimy
bream that you can see in "Rivers and Ponds" to the far more exotic tiger shovel-nose
catfish in "Rainforest", and from shallow streams to multi-storey tanks like vast swimming pools. You should allow a minimum of two hours for your visit.

Displays include kid-friendly chunks of info along the walls – starfish only eat mus-
sels; manta rays grow to seven metres; some tropical fish have eye-markings on their
tails to confuse predators into snapping at the wrong end. The London Aquarium also

The London Eye

Address: Jubilee Gardens, London SE1 7PB **Website:** www.londoneye.com **Telephone:**
0870 990 8885 Dedicated access tel: 0870 990 8886 **Hours:** 10am–8pm (later in
summer) **Dates:** Closed 25 Dec **Entry fees:** [D]£14 [H]Free [A]£17 [under 4s]Free
[4–15]£8.50 [C]£14

Described as 'the landmark we never knew we needed', the Eye has become
so emblematic of the London skyline that it is hard to remember a time without
it. The graceful 30-minute 'flight' provides an unparalleled view over the city.
The pods are fully accessible, and can be slowed or stopped for easier access,
but wheelchair users are advised to pre-book, as capacity is limited. Disabled
visitors should take the side entrance into the County Hall ticket office and use
a dedicated ticket desk; those who find queuing a problem can access a Fast-
Track service.

charts the history of the once salmon-rich Thames and the cost to the river's wildlife of the Industrial Revolution. There is, in fact, a broad emphasis on conservation, not just fun, with information on how to get involved in the campaign to reduce over-fishing. Regular talks on topics such as the Rainforest and the Atlantic Ocean are entertaining and gently educative for adults as well as children. Activities include face-to-face encounters with the rays when peering over the open Ray Pool, while the ever-popular feeding-time in the shark tank involves the immersion of an intrepid diver equipped with steel-like nerves and a stash of shark snacks.

Blue Badge bays in Chicheley Street and Belvedere Road are a two-minute walk away. The Aquarium has level-entry, wide doorways and good wheelchair access throughout. Signage is clear and exhibits can be viewed from wheelchair height. There are lifts, accessible loos, a café with low counters and movable seating and a gift shop with some low shelves and helpful staff (but a high payment desk). There are often queues to get in but you can book online for discounted tickets that allow "fast track" entry. A wheelchair is available to hire.

MUSEUM IN DOCKLANDS

Address: West India Quay, London E14 4AL **Website:** www.museumindocklands.org.uk
Telephone: 0870 444 3857 **Hours:** daily 10am–6pm (last admission 5.30pm) **Dates:** closed 24-26 Dec **Entry fees:** [D]Free [H]Free [A]£5.50 [under 16s]Free

This bright and welcoming venue sits in what appears to be the only old building left in London's massively regenerated Docklands district. Happily, the rich history of the area is imaginatively described through a range of physical displays and audio-visual media, and the site itself has made great efforts to be as accessible as possible.

The city's story starts on the third floor, in the first century AD, where you're drawn into a well-lit, clearly signed maze of beautifully realised exhibits, telling the story of London's docks from their origins to the present day. You discover that London's reputation as a trading town was established under the Romans and grew to the point where it became the first port of the British Empire. There's a particularly evocative tour through nineteenth-century sailor town (though it has a slightly tricky cobbled floor). There are also some much less salubrious tales, such as the district's complicity in the transatlantic slave trade and – as exemplified by Jack the Ripper – decades of lawlessness.

While the museum is almost adjacent to the West India Quay DLR station, if you're approaching on the tube's Jubilee Line, you may find it more convenient to get off at Canary Wharf and follow the map (available to download from the website). If you come across steps, there will be a lift nearby. The footbridge immediately in front of the museum is bowed but negotiable. If you're coming by car, you can drive to the front of the museum, buzz through to security and park free of charge, with no need to book. Access is fine throughout the museum. Apart from the one cobbled area, most of the flooring is polished timber. Lifts help you work your way through London's history, back down to ground level. But before you leave it's worth stopping by the excellent and relaxed museum bar and restaurant, *1802*.

NATIONAL GALLERY

Address: Trafalgar Square, London WC2N 5DN **Website:** www.nationalgallery.org.uk
Telephone: 020 7747 2885 **Hours:** daily 10am–6pm, Wed till 9pm **Dates:** closed 1 Jan and
24–26 Dec **Entry fees:** Permanent collections are free; prices vary for temporary exhibitions

Britain's leading art collection, the National Gallery houses a vast range of paintings of exceptional quality. It's unrealistic to hope to cover everything in a single visit, so best to pick up a gallery plan on arrival and head for your favourites.

The steps leading up to the front of this iconic building are imposing and perhaps off-putting but never fear; there's level access via the Sainsbury Wing to the west or the Getty Entrance to the east. Once inside, life's a breeze. Most paintings in the permanent collection are on the main floor, linked to other galleries by large lifts with low-level buttons. Highlights of the permanent collection include Italian Renaissance masterpieces, with works by da Vinci, Uccello and Botticelli among many others; Velázquez's provocative *Rokeby Venus*; Dutch and German artists including van Eyck and Holbein; and some wonderful Impressionist art. In 2009 the Sainsbury Wing promises exhibitions including Picasso: Challenging the Past, an exploration of Picasso's life-long responses to the work of the great masters of European painting, and Corot to Monet, which will track the development of open-air painting.

Many of the individual galleries have benches and the Sainsbury Wing theatre and exhibition cinema have wheelchair spaces and induction loops. Toilets are on all levels and a wide variety of other access facilities are on offer, and detailed on the website. For example you can borrow large-print versions of the picture labels from the gallery assistants on duty. Excellent audio guides are available free of charge, as are guided tours twice daily. BSL interpreted talks and tours take place on the first Saturday of every month and some evenings, while Art through Words sessions for blind and partially sighted visitors are organised on the last Saturday of every month.

The National Gallery

NATIONAL MARITIME MUSEUM

Address: Greenwich, London SE10 9NF **Website:** www.nmm.ac.uk **Telephone:** 020 8312 6608 **Hours:** daily, 10am–5pm daily **Dates:** closed 25–26 Dec **Entry fees:** free

Greenwich lies at the heart of Britain's seafaring history and the National Maritime Museum, along with the Queen's House and Royal Observatory, are integral to it. The museum is a magnificent architectural set piece, overlooking the Thames, and its exhibits are full of appeal no matter what your age or preconceptions. You'll need to allow a good half-day to see all three sites.

The interior of the museum (which is housed in the old Naval Asylum) has recently undergone a major refurbishment and the collections, ranging from maritime art to model ships and Nelson memorabilia, are imaginatively displayed. Prized artefacts include Captain Cook's sextant, Shackleton's compass and Captain Scott's furry reindeer-hide sleeping bag. Plenty of hands-on elements will keep children occupied, though the child-specific All Hands gallery is perhaps a little difficult to navigate for a child with limited mobility. The royal apartments at the Queen's House, adjacent to the museum, are also accessible, though the Royal Observatory is a bit more tricky. The steep climb up the hill through Greenwich Park can usually be avoided by taking the accessible road train, but not all of the Observatory is accessible; among the things you can experience are the Meridian line and the brand-new Peter Harrison Planetarium, while access to other galleries is gradually being improved.

There's limited disabled parking at the museum itself (pre-booking advised), or you can park near the Royal Observatory at the top of Greenwich Park, where Blue Badge holders can stay for up to four hours free of charge. You can borrow a manual wheelchair, and all the galleries over the museum's three floors are fully accessible to wheelchair-users, and also have facilities for blind and partially sighted visitors and a programme of touch talks and sign-interpreted events. The museum's two cafés are wheelchair-accessible.

IDEAS ▶▶ London Market Shopping

Browsing the markets in London is one of the simplest, and not to mention less expensive highlights of a trip to the city. Whilst access predictably varies from site to site, the following two markets are surprisingly easy to navigate. **Spitalfields** used to be a small weekend market but has recently been modernised, without commercialising its selection of wares too far. Parking there is as easy as it gets in London – there are plenty of disabled bays available and there are disabled toilets on site. Fans of the alternative should head for **Camden**. Famed for its popularity with revellers, it might not seem an obvious place to visit, but the area can be surprisingly easy to get around. It is best to drive and use the disabled spaces at the rear of Morrison's car park – a lift takes you straight up to the Stables Market. Blue Badge holders can park for an unlimited time in the resident parking bays next to Main Street market (CA–F zones only). But do brace yourself for throngs of crowds and some less than well-maintained cobbled pavements.

NATIONAL THEATRE

Address: South Bank, London SE1 9PX **Website:** www.nationaltheatre.org.uk (access booking form on access information page) **Telephone:** 020 7452 3000 Dedicated access tel: 020 7323 8510/8850 Dedicated access email: access@nationaltheatre.org.uk **Hours:** 10am–11pm, Mon–Sat (some Sundays, noon–6pm) **Dates:** closed on bank holidays **Entry:** free to building and some exhibitions; performance prices vary: [D] half-price [H] half-price

The Royal National Theatre, to give it its full name, lies at the heart of the South Bank complex and its three auditoriums put on a wide range of drama productions, usually over relatively short runs. Under the directorship of Laurence Olivier, the theatre opened in 1983 with *Hamlet* starring Peter O'Toole. Since then the National has produced over six hundred plays, including the highly emotive and controversial *Jerry Springer – The Opera*.

The theatre publishes an access guide online and employs a full-time manager, who is charged with the continual improvement of access to all the facilities. A visit to the Olivier, the Lyttleton or the Cottesloe is, in fact, now such a seamless experience that the access office is turning its attention to improving life in general for disabled performers and staff. A nearby refurbished studio, opened in early 2008, offers fully accessible rehearsal and performance space. Catering is excellent, with well-prepared, if pricey, snacks and dishes at a range of spacious venues throughout the site.

While the National Theatre is well served by public transport, drivers who manage to penetrate London's Congestion Zone are also well catered-for: if you take your ticket to the underground car park and present it at the Box Office, with your Blue Badge and theatre ticket, the parking is free. The foyer area is flat and smooth – although some of the "sitting out" areas are carpeted – with lift access to all three theatres. The Olivier seats 1,100 people and offers three wheelchair spaces at the back of the Stalls (level 2). Seats at the front of each auditorium are set aside for visually impaired people. Touch tours, plus audio-described and captioned performances, are a feature of every National production and the schedule is available online.

THE O2

Address: Greenwich, London SE10 0BB **Website:** www.theo2.co.uk **Telephone:** 020 8463 2000 **Hours:** daily 10am–late **Dates:** no closures **Entry fees:** visiting free; exhibit, event and performance prices vary

That great white elephant by the Thames, the publicly funded Millennium Dome, has been reborn as the O2 – a vast and impressive entertainment complex run by the entertainment company, AEG. The familiar giant tent has been massively redeveloped and is now home to the enormous 23,000-seater O2 Arena, the eleven-screen Vue cinema complex, the 2300-seater IndigO2 venue, and the O2 bubble exhibition space.

You don't have to be attending a specific event to enjoy the O2. Entertainment

The O2

Avenue, which circles the main arena, has more than twenty cafés, bars and restaurants, mostly chain outlets – with all the usual suspects – but there's a great variety, with a Thai restaurant, sushi takeaway and tapas bar, among many other options. And once you're stuffed, you can indulge in a variety of other experiences, including a chill-out pod and a video "dance-oke" station – both accessible to wheelchair-users – as well as various seasonal offerings ranging from an indoor beach to an ice rink.

A state-of-the-art venue like the O2 should rate highly for accessibility and you're unlikely to be disappointed: staff are friendly and helpful and quick to show you to the lifts and disabled toilets. Even the small details work: cinema ticket collection machines and car park pay-points, for example, are at a good height for wheelchair-users. There's plentiful disabled parking but it's expensive on event nights, even with a discount (only for Blue Badge-holders: £10; book in advance on 0844 847 1655). Car Park 4 is closest to the entrance at 350m away. Visitors are encouraged to use public transport, and North Greenwich tube and bus stations are wheelchair-accessible.

THE ROYAL ACADEMY OF ARTS

Address: Burlington House, Piccadilly, London W1J OBD **Website:** www.royalacademy.org.uk **Telephone:** 020 7300 8000 Dedicated access tel: 020 7300 5732 (Access officer) **Hours:** Permanent collections Tues–Fri 1–4.30pm, Sat & Sun 10am–6pm, Mon closed; exhibitions daily 10am–6pm (Fri until 10pm) **Dates:** closed 24–25 Dec **Entry fees:** Permanent collections are free; Exhibition Fees [D] £8 [H]Free [A]£9 [C] £4–£8 [12–18] £4 [8–11]£3

The Royal Academy of Arts, or RA, tucked in a private, water-sculpture-filled courtyard just off Piccadilly, was founded by George III and has long been governed by artists – the present board includes David Hockney and Tracey Emin. Famous for its summer exhibition of some ten thousand works, to which any artist can submit a piece, it is one of Britain's premier galleries. Allow yourself at least half a day to visit.

Burlington House, home of the RA, is an elaborate piece of architecture which has passed through the hands of many patrons of the arts, many of whom have commissioned work on the house over the centuries. The John Madejski Fine Rooms were opened to the public in 2004, having been restored to their eighteenth-century glory. This collection of opulent salons is filled with design influences including Baroque and Neoclassical features, from gold columns to decorative ceilings. Artworks abound, including paintings by Sebastiano Ricci, and Kent's ceiling mural of Jupiter's blessing of the marriage between Cupid and Psyche. The Reynolds Room commemorates the fact that it was here that Darwin presented the draft version of the *Origin of Species*. Works from the Academy's collection are displayed in these rooms, and elsewhere, temporary loan collections are exhibited, always showing the works of internationally renowned artists, both contemporary and of historical interest.

Call ahead to book a disabled parking spot outside. The entrance itself is ramped and the ticket desk low. The restaurant has loose tables and chairs and low counters and payment desk, and the café also has loose tables and seating. The gift shop has some low shelves and a supervised lift. Available services include wheelchair-hire, large print information, large print labels for exhibitions, a tactile gallery map, one-to-one audio-described guided tours, BSL/lip-speaking tours, and audio guides with detailed descriptions of selected works.

SADLERS WELLS THEATRE

Address: Rosebery Avenue, London EC1R 4TN **Website:** www.sadlerswells.com **Telephone:** 0844 871 0090 Dedicated access tel: 0844 412 4300 Minicom 020 7863 8015 **Hours:** Box office Mon–Sat, 9am–8.30pm **Dates:** closed 25 Dec and occasional other public holidays **Entry fees:** performance prices vary [D] half-price [H] half-price

This renowned theatre, specialising in dance, especially modern dance, is now fully accessible not only to visitors with disabilities, but to disabled performers and staff as well. The new building, opened in 1998 (the most recent of six theatres to occupy the site since 1683), now offers a bewildering array of facilities and a visit here can be an inspirational experience, if only to see what is achievable.

From cutting-edge performance to mainstream contemporary dance, tango to tap and flamenco to family shows, the joy of movement and the celebration of dance lie at the heart of Sadlers Wells productions and many have won awards in recent years. Most shows only run for a few days however; if you think you might become a regular patron, the venue's Access Scheme can register your seating preferences.

There are fifteen spaces in the Sadlers Wells car park (call 020 7863 8000 or book online). Throughout the theatre, textured paths lead to significant areas on every floor and, as you approach the destination, the "feel" changes. The box office has low-level counters and sensory-impaired visitors can book tickets via Minicom or, if booking in person, ask to speak to a trained lip-reader or BSL interpreter. Audio-described performances are a regular feature. Wheelchair-users can enjoy the performance from dedicated spaces near the exits (companions' seats are slightly raised to bring them to the same level) or transfer to theatre seating (the outside arm-rests of several aisle-end seats can be raised). Walkers needing extra leg-room can specify seats in the same area. Patrons who can't easily sit up in the auditorium can even ask for the physio-bed. Seating in the bar and café areas has been designed to maximise contrast and all lifts have raised and Braille buttons, as well as voice announcements. To sum up, the theatre is a model of fantastic access provision.

SCIENCE MUSEUM

Address: Exhibition Road, South Kensington, London SW7 2DD **Website:** www.sciencemuseum.org.uk **Telephone:** 020 7942 4446 **Hours:** daily 10am–6pm **Dates:** closed 24–26 Dec **Entry fees:** free; charges vary for special exhibitions, IMAX cinema and simulators (reduced rates for disabled visitors)

The Science Museum in South Kensington is a buzzing, energetic place, dispelling the myth once and for all that science is boring. With more than two thousand hands-on exhibits, interactive displays and lively demonstrations, exploring everything from space travel to genetics, even the most reluctant visitors would be hard-pressed not to find something to engage them. Most people come away enthralled and genuinely enriched by the experience.

A meander through the spacious ground-floor galleries takes you from huge steam-powered machines in the Energy Hall, through the history of rockets in Exploring Space, to Stephenson's *Rocket* and other iconic objects in Making the Modern World. The Wellcome Wing is home to the IMAX cinema and two very worthwhile exploratory exhibits – Who Am I? and In Future. While the museum is a grown-up institution, there is plenty here to keep children occupied. The three specific children's galleries – The Garden (for 3–6 year-olds), Pattern Pod (5–8s) and the ever-popular Launchpad (8–14s) – are particularly appealing, with a mass of activities easily accessed by most children with limited mobility. Launchpad was relaunched on the third floor in 2007, and now boasts more than fifty interactive exhibits designed to quiz young minds.

If you're arriving by car, you'll find four disabled parking spaces right outside the

Natural History Museum and the V&A

NHM Address: Cromwell Road, London SW7 5BD **Website:** www.nhm.ac.uk **Telephone:** 020 7942 5511 (020 7942 5888 to book Blue Badge spaces) **Hours:** 10am-5.50pm **Dates:** closed 24-26 Dec **Entry fees:** free with charges for special events **V&A Address:** Cromwell Road, London, SW7 2RL **Website:** www.vam.ac.uk **Telephone:** 020 7942 2000 Dedicated access tel: 020 7942 2766 **Hours:** 10am–5.45pm (selected galleries until 10pm on Friday) **Dates:** closed 24–26 Dec **Entry:** free with charges for special events

These two institutions are located right by the Science Museum, so with a bit of stamina it is possible to visit all three sites in one culture-packed day. The NHM's appeal lies in its grandeur, never more evident than in the magnificent Central Hall with its 85ft plaster cast of a Diplodocus skeleton. But for sheer style you can't beat the V&A, with its stunning collections of art and design, where you can discover the extraordinary variety of the fashion collection.

museum and eight more further along Exhibition Road. If you can manage public transport it can be easier: there's a pedestrian subway (but no step-free access) from South Kensington tube station to the museum entrance. General museum access is excellent, with lots of manoeuvring space and low-level exhibits. At the information desk, you should ask for a map, which shows lifts, ramps and accessible toilets. The shop is spacious with most items within reach of a wheelchair user and the cafés all have some movable seating. One caveat: if you need to use the lifts, you may have a long wait at busy times, as you'll be vying with parents and pushchairs.

TATE BRITAIN

Address: Millbank, London SW1P 4RG **Website:** www.tate.org.uk/britain **Telephone:** 020 7887 8888 Minicom: 020 7887 8687 **Hours:** daily 10am–5.50pm; exhibitions 10am–5.40pm, last admission 5pm (1st Fri of every month open until 10pm, last admission 8.30pm) **Dates:** closed 24–26 Dec **Entry fees:** free entry except for major exhibitions

Tate Britain houses some of the greatest British art from the sixteenth century to the present day – touring the rooms gives you a pictorial history lesson – as well as some international modern pieces. Allow half a day to complete a tour of the gallery without hurrying.

Works by every influential British artist appear in the collection and a large space is dedicated to some three hundred paintings and thirty thousand sketches by JMW Turner – a riveting body of work covering an astounding range of subjects. The modern exhibits include pieces by Francis Bacon and Damien Hirst and displays are changed annually. But it's Tate Britain's historical story that is the most fascinating: when Henry VIII broke from the Catholic Church, devotional artworks were banned and there was an upsurge in portraiture; as London became prosperous, William Hogarth's painting offered a commentary on the new urban wealth; and, in the eighteenth and nineteenth centuries, John Constable was one of the first painters to popularise naturalistic landscape as a worthy theme.

You can call to reserve one of several disabled bays in the gallery's car park and take the back route into the gallery, but it's much easier to park in the Blue Badge bays outside the Manton entrance, which is ramped. Access throughout the site is good; information and ticket desks are low, disabled toilets don't need keys (and have grab rails) and there are several lifts. All gallery areas present the art and accompanying written descriptions at heights low enough to view from a chair. The gift shops have many low shelves. The restaurant and café have some movable tables and seating. Available services include: large print/Braille exhibition information, portable induction loops, audio guides, guided tours, touch tours and BSL interpreters.

IDEAS ▶▶ The Tate boat

The Tate boat connects both galleries. It's a smooth trip on the Hurricane Clipper but at some tide levels, a less accessible boat may be used, so it's best to call 020 7887 8888 on the day of travel. Boats run every 40 minutes during gallery opening hours. Find departure times at www.thamesclippers.com. A single ticket is £5, but concessions are available for travelcard holders and Tate members.

TATE MODERN

Address: Tate Modern, Bankside, London SE1 9TG **Website:** www.tate.org.uk/modern
Telephone: 020 7887 8888 Minicom: 020 7887 8687 **Hours:** Sun–Thurs 10am–6pm, Fri–Sat
10am–10pm (last admission to paying exhibitions Sun–Thurs 5.15pm, Fri–Sat 9.15pm);
seasonal variations: see website **Dates:** closed 24–26 Dec **Entry fees:** free, except for major
exhibitions

LONDON

Tate Modern, housed in the cavernous former Bankside Power Station, is filled with
post-1900 works of art from around the world. Modern art is awash with isms, and this
is where you'll get to grips with the motivations of the protagonists behind Surrealism,
Cubism, Minimalism and Vorticism, among other genres. And it's a thrill to enter the
vast turbine hall, which often features a stunning temporary exhibit.

Tate Modern's resident collections are: Material Gestures, featuring American and European artists in the postwar period; Poetry and Dream, exploring Surrealism and the
subconscious; Conceptual Models, dedicated to the role of the built environment; Idea and
Object, where bold 1960s Minimalism comes to the fore; and States of Flux which centres
on Cubism and reactions to the Impressionist movement. All the exhibitions are excitingly
peppered with celebrated names, such as Picasso, Monet and Matisse. But works by many
lesser-known artists bring their often radical messages to colour the gallery. Perhaps two
of the most striking installations are Paul McCarthy's combination of film and body art,
which comments on the impact of media sensationalism, and Jenny Holzer's *Inflammatory
Essays* – an imposing wall of brightly coloured political and religious statements.

Book ahead to reserve one of several disabled bays in the gallery's car park, only a few
metres away from a level-access entrance. Access throughout the site is as good as you
would expect in a modern gallery, with low-level information and ticket desks and care
taken to present work so that it is visible to wheelchair-users. The level 7 restaurant has
wonderful views, and there's also a café on level 2 and an espresso bar on level 4. All have
movable tables and seating. The permanent collections offer audio guides, guided tours,
touch tours and BSL interpreters at selected times and there are several wheelchairs and
two powered scooters available to hire.

VINOPOLIS

Address: No 1 Bankend, London SE1 9BU **Website:** www.vinopolis.co.uk **Telephone:** 0870
241 4040 **Hours:** Mon, Thurs & Fri 12pm–10pm; Sat 11am–9pm; Sun 12pm–6pm; closed
Tue & Wed **Dates:** closed 24 Dec–1 Jan **Entry fees:** wine tours, with tasting, from £19.50

London's South Bank doesn't instantly spring to mind as a wine-tasting region. At Vinopolis, however, you're transported to the world's vineyards to swill and spit a multitude of
vintages while learning the proper way to evaluate wine, beers and spirits. Allow a minimum of two hours.

After a concise wine-tasting class you're invited to meander around the world, sampling wine, champagne and spirits while learning about their production processes from the knowledgeable staff. You're given a notebook for recording the observations of your eyes, nose and palate. Try to avoid swallowing too much: if you ignore the spittoons, your tour may end earlier than you intended (fortunately, crackers and water dispensers are strategically placed). You can also sober up in the *à la carte* restaurant, *Cantina*, or continue your downward trend with more wine in *Wine Wharf* (which serves tapas), various beers in *Brew Wharf*, the microbrewery/gastro-pub, or with a cocktail in *Bar Blue*.

There are several Blue Badge bays near Vinopolis and while the local area is cobbled, it's possible to use the pavement to avoid most of the bumps. The venue itself is entirely wheelchair-accessible with a ramped entrance to glass doors where assistance is available. The wine-tour ticket desk is low-level and the entire venue is spacious with plenty of seating. There are lifts to all floors and six disability-friendly toilets. Most of the regions on the tasting tour present their wines from low-level tables, though some of the spirit stations are set at high bars (all are staffed, which is helpful, and tends to inhibit speedy drinkers). The *Cantina* has movable tables and seating, *Brew Wharf* has movable benches and long tables, *Blue Bar* is high but with low, loose tables and seats and *Wine Wharf* has steps but can be accessed through a back route.

WWT LONDON WETLAND CENTRE

Address: Queen Elizabeth Walk, Barnes, London SW13 9WT **Website:** www.wwt.org.uk/london **Telephone:** 020 8409 4400 **Hours:** summer 9.30am–6pm (last admission 5pm); closes 9pm Thurs and 29 May–11 Sep (last admission 8pm); winter 9.30am–5pm (last admission 4pm); early closing 24 Dec (last admission 2pm) **Dates:** closed 25 Dec **Entry fees:** [D]£6.70 [H]Free [A]£8.95 [4-16]£4.95 [C]£6.70

The Wildfowl and Wetlands Trust's London Wetland Centre, on a one-square-kilometre site, by a meander of the Thames in Barnes in southwest London, is a paragon of ornithological conservation, a mecca for birdwatchers and an internationally recognised Site of Special Scientific Interest. Even people who think they're not keen on nature visits come away having enjoyed the trip, and children invariably love it.

A maze of paths and boardwalks takes you around the marshes and over the lakes to view birdlife from Britain and migrants from around the world. Apart from the profusion of common mallards and moorhens there are plenty of exotic breeds, such as the orange-headed mandarins and the super-sized Icelandic eider ducks whose down has the highest thermal rating of any natural substance. Migrants flock here and on-site ornithologists protect rare species and help with global projects such as the reintroduction of the critically endangered Laysan teal back into Hawaii. Hides are scattered across the lakes, enabling you to watch the birds and other wildlife without being obtrusive. From the top of Peacock Tower, you can get out the binoculars and enjoy 360-degree views.

There are several disabled parking spots in the car park, adjacent to the main visitor centre. Some doors are heavy but staff do help. The *Water's Edge* café has movable seating and the menu is clearly displayed on a chalkboard. Outside, access is generally good although some walkways are uneven. The "Wildside" hide has no lift and some of the hide entrances are narrow. With many enclosure gates to get through, wheelchair users will need help.

THE SOUTHEAST

HAMPSHIRE

SURREY

KENT

WEST SUSSEX

EAST SUSSEX

ISLE OF WIGHT

- British Disabled Flying Association, Lasham
- Bedgebury National Pinetum
- Bolderwood Deer Sanctuary, New Forest
- Brighton Pier
- Brighton Royal Pavilion
- Dungeness RSPB Reserve
- Godstone Farm
- The Historic Dockyard, Chatham
- Leeds Castle
- Sailability, Frensham Ponds
- Samphire Hoe
- Wisley Gardens

IDEAS ▶▶ Special events
FOOD & DRINK ▶▶ Brighton

THE SOUTHEAST

As the region where Londoners weekend, the southeast can be prone to high visitor numbers, both from the capital and from nearby Europe. But steer clear of the obvious tourist traps, and you'll find a multitude of places offering respite from the crowds, with elegant tended gardens and broad tracts of unspoilt field and woodland proving this verdant region the deserved bearer of the title 'the garden of England'.

BRITISH DISABLED FLYING ASSOCIATION, LASHAM

Address: Lasham Airfield, Alton, Hampshire GU34 5SS **Website:** www.bdfa.net **Telephone:** 01256 346424 **Hours:** daily 9am–6pm **Dates:** all year round but weather-dependent **Entry fees:** flight experience in plane or glider £50 (approx 1 hour)

Flying a plane is something you might dream about, but never expect to do. One visit to the British Disabled Flying Association at Lasham will have you questioning your preconceptions, and realising just how easily the barriers can be broken down.

The BDFA charity enables people with disabilities to experience flying light aircraft and gliders. If you want, you can go on to gain flying hours and eventually get your pilot's

Preparing for a trial flight at the BDFA Lasham Airfield

licence. They own two light planes and a glider and the flights are heavily subsidised and have to be booked in advance. The planes have either two or four seats with easy access to the cockpit and full duel controls in the front seats. Once airborne, you're encouraged to take the controls to get a feel for how the plane handles: the qualified pilots, some of them disabled themselves, are always in full control. It's a thrilling, potentially life-changing experience, and even on your first flight, with the reassurance and simple explanations of your instructor about the dials and gauges, you'll get enough of an insight to want to go up again.

When you first call or email to book your flight, your instructor will let you know how to get through the entrance barrier and where to go. Disabled parking is adjacent to the clubhouse, which has an accessible toilet. There are two types of planes, giving options for cockpit entry for those with reduced mobility. The aircraft wings are strong, and low enough to step or transfer onto easily, followed by a few steps or a shuffle into the cockpit. For those with less movement, a hoist is available to lower yourself into the cockpit. If you have sight, hearing, cognitive or learning disabilities you can also participate: BDFA say they've never turned anyone away.

BEDGEBURY NATIONAL PINETUM

Address: Bedgebury Pinetum, Goudhurst, Cranbrook, Kent TN17 2SJ **Website:** www. bedgeburypinetum.org.uk **Telephone:** 01580 879820 **Hours:** Jan 8am–4pm; Feb 8am–5pm; Mar 8am–6pm; Apr 8am–7pm; May–Aug 8am–8pm; Sep 8am–7pm; Oct 8am–6pm; Nov 8am–5pm; Dec 8am–4pm **Dates:** closed 25–26 Dec **Entry fees:** £7.50 per car, £20 for a minibus; concessions by arrangement (Go Ape adults £25, 10–17s £20; booked in advance; height and weight restrictions)

In 2006 the Forestry Commission added additional species of trees to the forest to Bedgebury Pinetum, to make an "activewood" with 24 kilometres of trails. It's one of the largest family-orientated outdoor destinations in southeast England and much of it is accessible for disabled people.

Pick a nice day, bring a picnic, and you'll find plenty here to keep even the most active family busy. The visitor centre can provide you with trail maps and directions to the various activities – and a cup of tea and a cake in *The Pantry*. The trails are very well surfaced and fun to explore, and the pirate-themed play area is a real adventure for kids. The scenic Pinetum is more tranquil and has a unique collection of pine trees from around the world, including the tallest tree in Kent. Also on offer is archery, for all abilities, and "Go Ape", a high-wire forest trail, which takes you on a three-hour treetop adventure, including Tarzan swings and ziplines – not for the fainthearted – for which you have to book in advance.

On arrival, the disabled parking bays are on asphalt near the visitor centre – with a RADAR-key-accessible toilet and level-entry shower – as is the bike hire shop, which has adapted bicycles, tricycles, and an electric off-road scooter. The Pinetum Trail is mostly level with plenty of rest stops; the Forest Trail has fairly easy access but rougher paths; and the Family Cycle Trail is the most adventurous, but reasonably accessible, if somewhat hilly. If you want to book "Go Ape", phone ahead to discuss your needs. Participants are securely wired the whole time. Bear in mind that their general guideline for accessibility is: "if you can climb a rope ladder you should be fine", so if this is you, then give it a go.

BOLDERWOOD DEER SANCTUARY, NEW FOREST

Address: Bolderwood Deer Sanctuary, near Lyndhurst, Hampshire **Website:** www.new-forest-national-park.com **Telephone:** 023 8028 3141 **Hours:** permanently open **Dates:** no closures
Entry fees: free

Hampshire's ancient New Forest includes more than 160 kilometres of cycle tracks, many of which are suitable for wheelchairs. Approached via Lyndhurst through a drive of ornamental trees, Bolderwood Deer Sanctuary ticks all the boxes for anyone looking for a day of fresh air and exercise in this newly created National Park.

For those keen to explore beyond the grassy picnic area, next to the car park, three wheelchair-accessible trails meander through beautiful woodland. In summer the local fallow deer are fed by rangers daily (1.30–2.30pm), near to an accessible viewing platform just a few hundred metres down the Deer Watch trail (a podcast on New Forest deer can be downloaded from the website). Although still recovering from the ravages of the 1987 storm, some of the tallest trees in the forest – Douglas fir and Redwoods – can be found here amongst the native beech and oak. As well as the deer, New Forest ponies roam freely in the area and a huge variety of wildlife depends on the delicate environment being sustained.

Bolderwood car park has plenty of disabled parking and an accessible toilet. The information centre, situated in the picnic area, is staffed during summer weekends and school holidays, but there are no catering facilities. The accessible trails – Deer Watch, Jubilee Grove and Radnor – are finished with compacted gravel and start from the car park. They're of varying length and rated moderate, and feature some short 1:15 to 1:20 gradients. If you're tempted by the twelve-kilometre-long Bolderwood cycle trail, which also starts from the car park, be aware that it includes several cattle grids.

BRIGHTON PIER

Address: Madeira Drive, Brighton, East Sussex BN2 1TW **Website:** www.brightonpier.co.uk **Telephone:** 01273 609361 **Hours:** daily 10am–10pm, weather-dependent, individual attractions vary **Dates:** closed 25 Dec **Entry fees:** free access to pier, some charges for individual attractions

It's brash and tacky, the rides are overpriced and the food is the stuff of heart attacks, but for a few hours of unadulterated fun-seeking at its finest, it's hard to beat. Welcome to Brighton Pier, the archetypal British seaside experience.

There are theme-park rides – both traditional and terrifying – huge arcades of slot machines, penny-pushers and video games, side stalls, tin-can alleys, beer gardens, karaoke bars, candyfloss, fish and chips, doughnuts and, of course, Brighton rock. Despite the free entrance onto the privately owned pier, money is all too easily frittered away. If you can resist all the temptations, perhaps the pier's gentlest pleasure is just to sit and admire the view back over the beach and city. Most visitors don't know that Britain's most commercially successful pleasure pier is also an architecturally notable

THE SOUTHEAST

Victorian iron structure, not to mention Grade II listed.

Parking can be problematic. There is disabled parking for roughly fifteen cars just to the left of the pier. Otherwise, Blue Badge holders can park without time limit at a pay and display parking bay or voucher bay (indicated by a green tick). For wheelchair-users, navigating the pier is easy. A special strip of walkway minimises judder and entrance to all the buildings is step-free. Many of the arcade games and side stalls have low-level slots. The only wheelchair-accessible toilets are situated right in the middle of the Palace of Fun near the pier entrance, however, which does mean an often congested and noisy route to access them. There's plenty of seating and deckchairs are free.

Brighton Pier

BRIGHTON ROYAL PAVILION

Address: The Royal Pavilion, Brighton, East Sussex BN1 1EE **Website:** www.royalpavilion.org.uk **Telephone:** 01273 290900 Dedicated access tel: 01273 292822 **Hours:** daily 10am–5.15pm Oct–Mar; 9.30am–5.45pm Apr–Sept **Dates:** closed 25–26 Dec **Entry fees:** [D]£6.50 [H]Free [A]£8.50 [5–15s]£5.10 [C]£6.50

Built to impress by a bored Prince Regent, George IV, the Royal Pavilion in Brighton is a unique combination of eccentric architecture and sumptuous interior design.

From the outside the Pavilion looks like a cross between Buckingham Palace and the Taj Mahal, and the Chinese styling on the inside is as extravagant as George IV's lifestyle was scandalous. And while it may not be to your taste, you can't fail to be impressed by the opulence of the decoration – known as chinoiserie – the quality of the craftsmanship and the ambition of the design. Probably the most impressive example is the Banqueting Room. Here, suspended from the domed ceiling, a red-tongued silver Dragon clutches a nine-metre-long chandelier, weighing more than a tonne, from which extend six more fire-breathing dragons. Equally ostentatious in its own way is the Great Kitchen, where multi-course banquets were prepared. Even this domestic room is spectacular, with high ceiling lights and iron columns in the shape of palm trees.

BRIGHTON FOOD & DRINK

Slap-bang in the middle of Brighton's historic and lively Lanes area, family owned bar and restaurant **Fratelli** (5&20 Brighton Square; 01273 730355; www.fratelli.tv) couldn't be better placed for soaking up the resort's buzzing atmosphere. Traditional, hearty Italian dishes fill a reasonably priced menu. The toilets are navigable for wheelchair users and the ground floor is fully accessible. If the sun is shining, the tables outside in the square are a great place to sit back and relax with a cocktail.

The disabled parking is limited but bookable in advance and adjacent to the entrance. Inside, manual wheelchairs can be borrowed, and the ground floor is entirely level, with a roomy disabled toilet. The audio tour is free, and has a T-Switch for hearing aids, although there is no hearing loop as such. Unfortunately, the first floor is only accessible by a flight of thirty shallow stairs with a handrail. If you can manage these you can visit the bedrooms used by George IV's brothers, Queen Victoria's bedroom, and the Queen Adelaide Tearoom. An accessible tearoom can be found at the nearby Brighton Art Gallery and Museum, 100m across the Pavilion Gardens. Entrance to this is free, and on display are collections of fine and decorative art, local works, and world art of national importance. The building is very accessible and includes a lift to the first floor where you will find the tearoom, overlooking the main gallery, serving fresh cakes and warm scones.

DUNGENESS RSPB RESERVE

Address: Dungeness Road, Lydd, Kent TN29 9PN **Website:** www.rspb.org.uk/reserves
Telephone: 01797 320588 **Hours:** daily, 9am–9pm (or sunset if earlier) **Dates:** closed 25–26 Dec **Entry fees:** [D]£3 [H]free [A]£3 [5–16s]£1 [C]£2

Set on the largest shingle bank in Europe, Dungeness is a unique place. Being here feels like perching on the edge of the world, with the land as flat as a pancake in every direction. The fenced-off nuclear power stations (Dungeness A and B) seem to fit into this desolate scenery rather well. It all makes for a fascinating, and very accessible, day out.

In the marshes behind this remarkable landscape lies an RSPB nature reserve, home to more than six hundred species of plants and many unusual insects, and its gravel banks and small lakes are a haven for migratory birds. There's a three kilometre nature trail of packed shingle, which wheelchairs can usually manage (you'll probably need an assistant), with six bird hides on or near it, all of which are wheelchair-accessible. The area is famous among birdwatchers for frequent sightings of bittern and bearded tit, and for the marsh harriers spotted in 2007. Most famous of the windswept fishermen's cottages and artists' studios in the area is the former home of the artist Derek Jarman, Prospect Cottage (about one kilometre along the road up the coast, towards Lydd), with its inspirational shingle garden, made from hardy plants and beachcombed materials.

If you park at the RSPB visitor centre, you'll find disabled toilets nearby and the closest birdwatching hide just metres away. An enjoyable alternative means of transport in the area is the picturesque Romney, Hythe and Dymchurch Railway (www.rhdr.org.uk; 01797 362353), a narrow-gauge steam railway beloved of generations of children.

Wheelchair-accessible carriages are available, but there's a height restriction and they must be booked in advance, so call ahead to enquire (and note it's more than five kilometres by road from the station to the RSPB visitor centre). The station café at Dungeness – one of several local places to eat famous for huge portions of fish and chips – is accessible, and always popular, and you've also got the *Britannia* pub to fall back on.

Dungeness, the largest shingle bank in Europe

GODSTONE FARM

Address: Tilburstow Hill Road, Godstone, Surrey RH9 8LX **Website:** www.godstonefarm.co.uk
Telephone: 01883 742546 **Hours:** daily, summer 10am–6pm, winter 10am–5pm (last entry
one hour before closing) **Dates:** call to check for Christmas closure dates **Entry fees:** [D]£3
[H]£1.50 [A]£3 [1–2s]£1.50 [2–16s]£5.85 [C]£2.50

Godstone Farm is one of those places that reminds you that you really don't need expensive theme parks to keep kids entertained. It has a relaxed atmosphere and the children's experience is clearly very much at the heart of the place.

After you enter, either head down the hill to visit the animals or turn right towards
a huge adventure play area that almost justifies the entrance fee by itself. Older kids,
especially, love the zip slides, toboggan run, climbing frames and obstacle courses, and
there are sandpits and an under 3s area for toddlers. The farm itself provides plenty of
opportunities for getting up close to a variety of goats, ponies, pigs, sheep, cows, llamas
and chickens, and children in wheelchairs can participate equally in this. Children are
encouraged to be hands-on with the animals, and to try holding baby chicks and duck-
lings, or climb in and stroke the rabbits. At certain times of the year, it's also possible to
join the piglets and lambs in their pens. For rainy days there are plenty of indoor play
areas, too, including animal barns and sheltered picnic sites.

Note that there are no discounts for disabled children or adults, but that helpers pay
£1.50. The huge car park is indicative of just how busy Godstone Farm gets, but there is
ample disabled parking with sixteen dedicated bays. Access around the farm is variable,
with some steep slopes and a lot of pitted and uneven surfaces – wheelchair users will
probably need some assistance – but it's well worth it. The covered facilities are more
wheelchair-friendly, with wheelchair-accessible toilets at the adventure playground
and next to the shop. And the café is roomy, with staff who are happy to assist, and
movable chairs.

THE HISTORIC DOCKYARD, CHATHAM

Address: The Historic Dockyard, Chatham, Kent ME4 4TZ **Website:** www.chdt.org.uk
Telephone: 01634 823807 **Hours:** summer 10am–6pm, winter 10am–4pm **Dates:** open
Feb–Oct, weekends in Nov; closed Dec–Jan **Entry Fees:** [D]£11 [H]Free [A]£13.50 [5–15s]£9
[C]£11

The Historic Dockyard, Chatham, celebrates more than four hundred years of Royal
Navy shipbuilding. And, while a Navy dockyard might not seem an obvious choice
for an accessible day out, the museum's emphasis on the people who built these magnificent vessels, as much as the ships themselves, tells the dockyard's story on a human
scale. Tickets are valid for re-entry for a year, which is a good thing, because there is
much more here than you can see in one day.

HMS *Victory* was built here, as were some of the ships that defeated the Spanish

IDEAS ▶▶ Special events

The **Liberty festival** (www.london.gov.uk/mayor/equalities/liberty/index. jsp) is London's most accessible outdoor festival and was originally conceived as an annual chance to celebrate deaf and disabled peoples contribution to London's culture. A date has not yet been set for the 2009 event but expect it to be announced for around the end of August. Street art, live music and activities for kids are all on offer, complete with BSL interpretation, induction loops and free parking for Blue Badge holders as well as stewards on hand to offer any help you may need. Disabled performers have in the past included comedian Liz Carr and the Graeae Theatre Company. The Mayor of London, assisted by organisations including Attitude is Everything and the British Deaf Association has worked hard since the first annual event in 2002 to make the not-naturally accessible Trafalgar Square venue easy to navigate.

2009 will see the third annual **Beyond Boundaries Live** (www.beyond boundarieslive.co.uk) event – an interactive festival billed as the UK's most exciting event for disabled people that takes place in Farnborough in Hampshire. In essence a consumer show to encourage you to spend, Beyond Boundaries Live actually offers a fun and hands-on day out. 2009 promises an off-road test track, a celebrity chef cook-off, a ski slope and a rock climbing wall.

Armada. In the Wooden Walls gallery, adjacent to the entrance, a tour led by a guide in costume explains how these wooden warships were built, as described by the 1758 diary entries of a young apprentice boy. There is a museum with an exhibition tracing the dockyard's involvement in slavery, and at the quarter-mile-long Ropery, another guide in period dress explains how rope has been made here for four centuries. There is a wheelchair-accessible Victorian warship, and, if you can manage a ladder, you're free to explore a World War II destroyer, and a Cold War nuclear submarine.

For a 400-year-old dockyard on a sprawling eighty-acre (third of a square kilometre) riverbank site, the museum is remarkably accessible. Just look out for tramlines and cobbles. Both the Wooden Walls gallery and the Ropery have lifts, and there are currently four accessible toilets, all reasonably large. There is a substantial mobility vehicle to take you about, but getting around the warships is really only for those who can climb ladders, although you can get onto the deck of HMS *Gannet* via a ramp. The Big Store and particularly the adjacent National Lifeboat Collection are both easy to access, but beware of trip hazards. There are manual wheelchairs available to borrow, if you need one.

LEEDS CASTLE

Address: Maidstone, Kent ME14 1PL **Website:** www.leeds-castle.com **Telephone:** 01622 765 400 **Hours:** daily 10am–5pm (last entry 3pm), later in summer **Dates:** closed 25 Dec **Entry fees:** [D]£12.50 [H]free [A]£15 [4–15s]£9.50 [C]£12.50

Built for beauty rather than defence, the majestic, if confusingly named Leeds Castle has the grandest of designs and is a perennially popular visit. The castle puts on displays and activities throughout the year, so it's good to know that your ticket gives you unlimited free re-entry for twelve months.

This magnificently sited castle, part of it set on an island in a lake, and the whole thing surrounded by five hundred acres of parkland, has been built up, added to, and improved on for more than a thousand years. The castle's interior is just as impressive as its dramatic external appearance: the main building was sumptuously furnished in the early twentieth century by the last owners. A stone bridge (with stairlift) takes you over the lake to the island, and the second part of the castle. This beautiful building – known as the Gloriette – has been refurbished to give an idea of its appearance in medieval times, complete with the banqueting hall and the bedroom used by Queen Elizabeth I. Other accessible attractions include an oasis of aromatic plants and herbs known as the Culpeper Garden; the world-renowned aviary; and the delightfully eccentric museum of dog collars.

There is plenty of disabled parking near the entrance, where you can also pick up an excellent map and guide to the facilities, and there are lots of restaurants and play areas – although accessibility varies. The woodland garden and kilometre-long duckery walk – well provided with rest areas – are both accessible. Alternatively, you can take the Land Train, accessible to non-powered wheelchairs, which makes various stops around the estate.

SAILABILITY, FRENSHAM PONDS

Address: Pond Lane, Churt, Farnham, Surrey GU10 2QA **Website:** www.sailfrensham.org. uk/sailability **Telephone:** 01252 850089 **Hours:** times vary, contact the club **Dates:** Thurs & Sat, April–Oct (contact the club for specific times and to book a "try sail" session) **Entry fees:** [D] £5 per session

This vibrant sailing club for people with disabilities – the most active in the south of England – has been offering accessible and highly affordable sailing facilities for more than 25 years. Set in beautiful Surrey countryside, Sailability caters for groups and individuals (aged 10 and over) with its fleet of Access and Wayfarer dinghies, a Challenger trimaran and several 2.4m keelboats.

No previous experience is required. Although it caters for all levels of ability and ambition, the club has built a reputation for breeding top-class racers: current members include British and French National Access champions. If you fancy competing with Team GB in the 2012 London Paralympics, here is a good place to start (though you'll need to put in a lot of practice). However, there is no pressure and gentle cruises around the 0.3 square kilometre pond are a weekly feature. While organised sailing such as this is restricted to the summer months, Sailability members race or cruise with the main Frensham Pond Sailing Club – home to more than 350 boats – all year round.

Access is first-class. On-site parking is flat and level and a new pavilion has changing facilities and cover for wheelchairs while their users are out on the water. Hoists are available to transfer the less mobile in and out of the boats. Sailors have access to the main clubhouse which offers sustaining home-made snacks. And the disabled-friendly shower rooms and toilets are excellent. The Access, Challenger and 2.4m boats are designed to be sailed solo, and some of them are fitted with joystick controls. All three classes are also designed not to capsize, although in a stiff breeze, you might be forgiven for thinking that's what's about to happen – thrilling stuff. For another UK Sailability experience, see p.71.

SAMPHIRE HOE

Address: signposted south off the A20, 2km west of Dover.**Website:** www.samphirehoe.com
Telephone: 01304 225688 **Hours:** daily 7am–dusk **Dates:** no closures **Entry fees:** free; pay and display car park: £1 for up to two hours £2, all day, three hours free parking for Blue Badge holders

The 4.9 million cubic metres of rock that came out of the Channel Tunnel had to go somewhere. It was piled in the sea below the cliffs at Dover and the result is a unique, isolated stretch of chalk meadowland – now a nature reserve – called Samphire Hoe. It's a haven for wildlife and human visitors alike.

This brand-new piece of Kent is a magical and ever-changing place: tucked in under the cliffs, it can be a peaceful sun trap and picnic spot on a hot day, but in rough weather the waves can come crashing in. The Hoe is landscaped with small lakes and sown with local wild flowers – look out for granny's toenails (also known as bird's-foot trefoil) – and is home to the rare early spider orchid, which you can see in April and May. Many species of insects and birds have rapidly colonised the area, and if you're quiet, and very lucky, you might see an adder. If you like sea-fishing, then try your luck along the sea wall – you could even win the fish-of-the-month competition. And be sure to check out the sound sculptures, which evoke the history and the beauty of the nature reserve. These installations have been created by local artists, who have combined pictures, sculpture and sound recordings, to tell the stories of the people who used to live here under the cliffs, and to evoke the haunting natural sounds and beauty of the Hoe.

Next to the car park – which has four designated disabled bays – there is a tea kiosk with a RADAR key-accessible toilet. The kiosk has free maps of the Hoe which show all the paths, the many benches, and the wheelchair-accessible route. The full circuit is two kilometres of asphalt and gravel path, changing to concrete back along the sea wall, with an average gradient of 1:15, but sometimes steeper. The other paths are much rougher and quite challenging. The small shingle beach is accessed by steps, and on rough days the sea wall may be closed, indicated by red flags flying.

WISLEY GARDENS

Address: RHS Gardens Wisley, Woking, Surrey GU23 6QB **Website:** www.rhs.org.uk/gardens/wisley **Telephone:** 0845 260 9000 **Hours:** Mon–Fri 10am–6pm; Sat & Sun 9am–6pm (closes 4.30pm Nov–Feb) **Dates:** closed 25 Dec **Entry fees:** [D]£8.50 [H] Free [A]£8.50 [under 6s]free [6-16s]£2 [C]RHS members free

As the flagship garden of the Royal Horticultural Society (RHS), you would expect Wisley to be pretty special, and you would be right. This is a dream-garden destination, with plenty for everyone, experts and novices alike.

What sets Wisley apart from other public gardens are attractions like the Fruit Mound, a spiral-shaped viewpoint, which looks out over Fruit Fields to the Surrey countryside beyond. And there are world-class examples of all gardening styles, from formal to wild, inspirational model gardens to stimulate the senses, and even a maize maze. The newest and most spectacular jewel in Wisley's crown is the Glasshouse, a state-of-the-art climate-controlled greenhouse. Inside, in various climatic zones, amazing plants of all sizes in realistic settings show how horticulture can be theatre as well. The result is breathtaking, as well as educational. You can take a wheelchair below the surface to see how roots grow underground, and even go behind a waterfall.

There are sixty disabled spaces in the car park, and loan wheelchairs available – including electric buggies by arrangement. All Wisley's shops and restaurants have level entry – including the excellent tea shops. This is a hilly site spread over a square kilometre, so inevitably you will come across steps, and some of the paths are rough. There is, however, an extensive wheelchair route which is easy to follow and takes you to all the best attractions. Even this route can be steep, and you might prefer to wait for the mobility vehicle, which runs every twenty minutes. There are five disabled toilets scattered around the site but they are not spacious, particularly the one in the car park, which should only be used as a last resort.

Wisley Gardens

THE HOME COUNTIES & OXFORDSHIRE

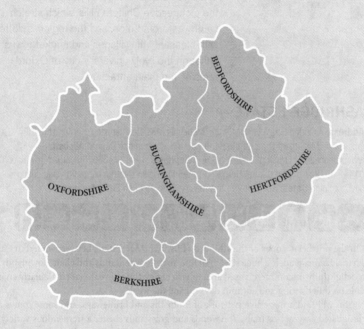

- Ashridge Estate
- Botanical Gardens, University of Oxford
- Christ Church College, Oxford
- Legoland
- The Living Rainforest
- River & Rowing Museum
- The Roald Dahl Museum and Story Centre
- Shuttleworth Collection
- Thames Valley Adventure Playground
- Verulamium Museum
- ZSL Whipsnade Zoo

WHY NOT ALSO TRY ▶▶ ZSL London Zoo

THE HOME COUNTIES & OXFORDSHIRE

Arching around the peripheries of London, the "Home Counties" of England form London's commuter belt. Beyond the suburban sprawl, however, there is plenty to entice. The countryside is at its most appealing amid the picturesque Chiltern Hills, which stretch southwest from Luton, and the region is dotted with pleasant little villages and market towns, although the lively university city of Oxford remains the main attraction.

ASHRIDGE ESTATE

Address: Ashridge Estate Visitor Centre, Moneybury Hill, Berkhamsted, Hertfordshire HP4 1LX (access via Monument Drive off the B4506 from Northchurch to Dagnall) **Website:** www.nationaltrust.org.uk/main/w-ashridge **Telephone:** 01494 755557 (recorded information); 01442 851227 (Visitor Centre) **Hours:** 12pm–5pm (Visitor Centre); car parks open during daylight hours **Dates:** closed from Christmas week to mid-Feb **Entry fees:** free

On the northern slopes of the Chiltern Hills, Ashridge Estate, between Aylesbury and Hemel Hempstead, is a huge stretch of fine, mature woodlands and chalk downland. It's a delightfully uncommercialised area to visit at any time of year, but particularly enjoyable on quiet spring and autumn days during the week.

You will find a maze-like network of footpaths and bridleways, and some routes are designated easy-access trails. The woods and grasslands shelter a tremendous variety of birdlife – including owls, red kites, and all three species of woodpecker – and mammals, including fallow deer. If you visit in the spring, you'll be treated to a carpet of bluebells, illuminating some areas with mauve reflected light, while the beech woods glow orange and red in the autumn. If you can make a bit of a push up to the high point of Ivinghoe Beacon – an Iron-Age hill fort at the end of the Ridgeway trail, one kilometre from the nearest car park – you'll be treated to a superb panorama. Across the estate there are plenty of grassy areas ideal for picnics, where children can safely play; there's a shop and visitor centre at the Bridgewater monument, and there's a tea room with outdoor seating.

The good-sized parking areas at intervals along the drive allow you to get right up to the edge of mature woodland, but the visitor centre car park gets very congested (the three disabled spaces are often full). A further three spaces in a separate area are reserved for visitors using the mobility vehicles that can be reserved through the visitor centre. The disabled toilet (same hours as the visitor centre) is RADAR-key operated and a sign warns that it will not lock from the inside. The main paths and principal car park are hard surfaced, but very uneven in places so most wheelchair-users will need assistance.

BOTANICAL GARDENS, UNIVERSITY OF OXFORD

Address: University of Oxford Botanic Garden, Rose Lane, Oxford, Oxfordshire OX1 4AZ
Website: www.botanic-garden.ox.ac.uk **Telephone:** 01865 286690 **Hours:** daily May–Aug
9am–6pm, Mar–Apr & Sept–Oct 9am–5pm, Nov–Feb 9am–4.30pm **Dates:** closed 25–26 Dec
Entry fees: [D]free [H]free [A]£3 [5–18s]free [C]£2.50

Oxford's botanical garden is a compact oasis, in the heart of the city, where plants are grown for teaching programmes and conservation research. It's a national reference collection with seven thousand different varieties of plant and in fine weather makes a lovely spot for a picnic. You can also use your ticket to visit the Harcourt Arboretum in Nuneham Courtenay, just outside Oxford.

The walled garden is laid out formally, with lawns, borders, trees and a centrepiece fountain. Plants here are grouped in a number of different ways: by country of origin, botanic family or economic use. The area outside the walled garden contains classic features – a water garden, lily pond, rock garden, orchard, vegetable beds and autumn and spring walks. The glasshouses, which can be accessed from the walled garden or by a gravelled riverside walk, hold a wide range of strange and beautiful tropical flora – highly recommended if somewhat tricky to access in a wheelchair.

There's a car park off St Clement's Street about a kilometre away, or you can park, using your Blue Badge, in the disabled bays or on the double yellows lines in Rose Lane, from where there is level access. Look out for uneven cobbles and flagstones at the entrance to the ticket office which has wide glass doors. The garden's gravelled paths are mostly level, but there are no barriers between the riverside walk and the water. The glasshouses are negotiable by wheelchairs but their duckboard walkways are narrow and overhung with plants, while the doors between the various sections are manual and have ramped thresholds. There's a RADAR-operated toilet at the rear of the Conservatory but access for a wheelchair is tight.

CHRIST CHURCH COLLEGE, OXFORD

Address: Christ Church, Oxford, Oxfordshire OX1 1DP **Website:** www.chch.ox.ac.uk
Telephone: 01865 276492 Dedicated access tel: 01865 276150 **Hours:** Mon–Sat 9am–5pm,
Sun 1–5pm **Dates:** closed 25 Dec **Entry fees:** [D]free [H]free [A]£4.90 [5–17s]s£3.90 [C]£ 3.90

In the heart of Oxford is Christ Church, the university's most magnificent college, founded in 1525 and incorporating England's smallest cathedral, which is also the college chapel. It's a highlight of any visit to Oxford.

Christ Church is a working college, with a fascinating history and architecture, including the stunning Cathedral Church; the huge Tom Quad and its enclosing buildings; the cloisters; Sir Christopher Wren's gate house and bell tower which houses the bell known as Great Tom; the Great Hall (which played Hogwarts Hall in the *Harry Potter* films); and the square tower with its beautiful vaulting. A door at the rear of the

Christ Church College, Oxford

cathedral leads you to the cloisters which, like the cathedral, survive from the seventh-century St Frideswide's monastery. Here you can watch a video charting the history of the cathedral and college. Next door, the Chapter House includes a shop and a fine collection of cathedral plate. The college has a picture gallery with a collection of old masters and drawings (extra entry charge). South of the college are the Great Walk and Christ Church Meadow – a tranquil pasture, bordering the rivers Cherwell and Isis, and open to all for walks and picnics.

There are three disabled parking spaces outside the Tom Tower and a disabled toilet off Tom Quad. The easiest entry point is by the main gate in Tom Tower, but some parts of the college are still inaccessible to wheelchair-users. There's a ramp up to the south side of Tom Quad and another into the cathedral by the West Door. A shallow step leads into the Sanctuary and there are steps down into the Latin Chapel. If you have restricted mobility, watch out for uneven flags and cobblestones and uneven stone stairways, some of which have no handrails. You can reach Christ Church Meadow on foot from the college, but wheelchair-users need to leave by the Tom Gate: go 100m to the War Memorial Garden, where you will find ramped access.

LEGOLAND

Address: Winkfield Road, Windsor, Berkshire SL4 4AY **Website:** www.legoland.co.uk (see also www.uglw.co.uk) **Telephone:** 0871 222 2001 **Hours:** daily 10am–5pm, 10am–6pm at weekends, 10am–7pm summer school holidays **Dates:** mid-Mar–early Nov **Entry fees:** [D]£35 [H]free [A]£35 [3–15s]£26 [C]£26; discounts for online sales

Ask any family with a child with special needs where to go on a day out and the answer is almost unanimously Legoland. It's not just that the park is 95 percent accessible to wheelchair users: Legoland has a positive attitude to disability that's reflected not only in the services they offer but also in the can-do attitude of the staff.

Set in 72 acres of attractively landscaped grounds, the park is divided into zones, roughly by age, from Duploland to Adventure Land. Very much a family park, there aren't any of the white-knuckle rides that attract thrill-seeking teenagers. LegoCity is good for kids who can't leave their wheelchairs, with its Orient Expedition safari train ride, with wheelchair-accessible compartments, and Brickadilly's Ferris Wheel which has a gondola that can accommodate a wheelchair. Every visitor can also enjoy Mini-land, the showcase model village built with 35 million Lego bricks, recreating some of the world's most famous landmarks.

Parking is free and very well controlled, with plenty of marshals, and disabled bays closest to the entrance. Once inside, there are no steps, but some paths are quite steep and will require a strong pusher behind a manual wheelchair. For children who have social difficulties with queueing, the theme park operates an exit pass scheme, allowing the guest-plus-three to enter the ride via the exit. You'll need to show an official diagnosis or statement of your child's condition, however, and, on busy days, you may need to queue to get it in the first place, at Guest Services. There is no shortage of accessible toilets, and the on-site catering ranges from hot-dog stands to the Knight's Table Rotisserie.

THE LIVING RAINFOREST

Address: Hampstead Norreys, Berkshire RG18 0TN **Website:** www.livingrainforest.org
Telephone: 01635 202444 **Hours:** daily 10am–5pm **Dates:** closed 24–26 Dec
Entry fees: [D]£6.95 [H]£6.95 [A]£7.95 [5–14s]£5.95 [3–4s]£4.95 [C]£6.95

As you pass through the Living Rainforest's screens you're transported into a hot, damp jungle and the all-encompassing presence of luxuriant flora and beautiful birds and insects. Your ticket is valid for a year so you can go back to see the ever-changing forest – it's always an interesting day out and the weather is guaranteed to be warm (remember to leave your coat in the car).

The Living Rainforest is housed in two giant glasshouses. As you follow the path, foliage brushes your face, and you quickly adjust to the sights, sounds and aromas of an equatorial forest. There's a wide range of creatures to discover, most spectacularly the free-flying and brilliantly coloured butterflies and birds from Amazonia and southeast Asia. Meanwhile, snakes, playful Goeldi's monkeys and the rare West African dwarf crocodile are kept safely behind barriers to protect them from human visitors – and the visitors from them. Look out for insect-eating plants and bird-eating spiders; watch graceful stingrays and the miniature miracle of a butterfly emerging from its chrysalis. Presentations and workshops led by the expert staff give you a genuine understanding of their conservation work and educational motives. The routes are well signposted, and large-print notices describe the exhibits. When you feel in need of energy, the popular café sells very good drinks and snacks.

The accessible car park is laid with compacted gravel and there's a 100-metre-long tarmac path to the entrance. There are wheelchairs available to borrow, and scooters are permitted. The patio is accessible and the play area is on level grass. The toilets are reached through the café. The paths inside the glasshouses have been made of scored concrete – damp, and with appropriately muddy patches in places, but not slippery. Most of the site is level, with the exception of two shallow troughs from which to view eye-level exhibits. There are steps at one end of these, so wheelchair-users may need to reverse out.

RIVER & ROWING MUSEUM

Address: Mill Meadows, Henley on Thames, Oxfordshire RG9 1BF **Website:** www.rrm.co.uk
Telephone: 01491 415600 **Hours:** daily Sept–April 10am–5pm, May–Aug 10am–5.30pm **Dates:** closed 24–25 Dec, 31 Dec & 1 Jan **Entry fees:** [D]£3 [H]free [A]£3.50 [3–16s]£2.50 [C]£3

Set in a picturesque water meadow beside the Thames at Henley, the River & Rowing Museum gives visitors a glimpse into the historic relationships between the town of Henley, the River Thames, and the sport of rowing for which it is renowned. Designed by the award-winning British architect David Chipperfield, this bright, modern, airy museum is a very welcoming place if you have limited mobility.

Henley-on-Thames

The permanent displays introduce the Thames, from source to estuary, review the sport of rowing through the ages, and tell the story of Henley. Visitors can take a virtual tour around the town and then travel through its history, through artefacts, models, boats, video displays and interactive exhibits. The museum hosts a varied programme of special exhibitions and a busy schedule of talks and workshops for children as well as adults. It also houses The Wind in the Willows – a permanent exhibition of delightful dioramas with an audio guide (headphones or loop antenna), which brings Kenneth Grahame's classic story to life (extra charge: same fees as museum).

The museum is a flat and easy ten-minute walk from Henley station and also has its own free car park at the rear. An enjoyable alternative means of getting here is on the combined river and museum trip from Reading to the museum's jetty – there's a new, wheelchair-accessible boat now operating on this service. At the museum itself, ramps run up front and rear to the main foyer, the shop, a pleasant café and a broad sun deck with benches and tables. There's also a disabled toilet on this lower level. There is plenty of room for wheelchairs through most of the site, and staff are happy to assist. The exhibits are on two floors, with a drive-through lift which takes a chair and a couple of helpers. The gallery doors are wide but manual and one-way, though quite easy to open.

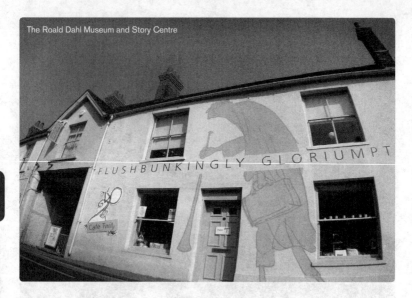

The Roald Dahl Museum and Story Centre

THE ROALD DAHL MUSEUM AND STORY CENTRE

Address: 81-83 High Street, Great Missenden, Buckinghamshire HP16 0AL **Website:** www.
roalddahlmuseum.org **Telephone:** 01494 892192 **Hours:** Tues–Sun, and bank holiday Mondays
10am–5pm **Dates:** closed 22 Dec–1 Jan **Entry fees:** [D]£5.50 [H]free [A]£5.50 [5–18s]£3.95
[C]£3.95

Roald Dahl was determined that all his papers, manuscripts and photographs should
remain together in Britain. The result is a charming, family-friendly museum set up by
his widow, Felicity, which immerses you in Dahl's mischievously subversive and imagi-
native world.

Most of the exhibits are aimed at children aged around 6 to 12 with a creative bent,
though there is enough to keep little ones – and grown-ups for that matter – interested
too. Budding writers and Dahl enthusiasts will get the most out of the museum. Two
galleries, Boy and Solo, tell the story of the author's life, while the Story Centre inspires
young minds to get inventive with plot, character and language. All of this is based
around a large, accessible courtyard with the shop and galleries on one side, the Story
Centre across the end, "Miss Honey's Classroom" and the worryingly named "Children
Eating Room" opposite, and the essential *Café Twit* at the top. The courtyard itself provides an overspill eating area for the café and hosts refreshingly amateurish storytelling
sessions on sunny days.

The museum is in the centre of Great Missenden, and while there's a Blue Badge bay
about 100m down the High Street, the nearest convenient parking is the pay & display
car park 250m away, with a pavement approach to the museum entrance. The whole
museum site is step-free, apart from a single step into *Café Twit*. There is a ramp but the

inside is so small that wheelchair users are probably best off with the courtyard seating if stopping for a delumptious home-made treat. Getting into the disabled toilets can prove tricky if the courtyard gate is open.

SHUTTLEWORTH COLLECTION

Address: Shuttleworth Aerodrome, Old Warden, Biggleswade, Bedfordshire SG18 9EP **Website:** www.shuttleworth.org/shuttleworth_home.asp **Telephone:** 01767 627927 **Hours:** 9.30am–5pm (4pm Nov–Mar; last admission one hour before closing); check special hours on event days **Dates:** closed Christmas week & 1 Jan **Entry fees:** [D]£10 [H]Free [A]£10 [0–16s]Free [C]£9; check special prices on event days

The Shuttleworth Collection is a unique presentation of aircraft, flying machines and flight-related exhibits, showcasing the first hundred years of human flight. It includes a huge range of civilian and military aircraft and also incorporates cars and carriages.

This world-famous collection of more than forty planes, all in flying condition, is housed in eight floodlit hangars. You can trace the history of the aeroplane from Louis Blériot's pioneering early flights (he was the first aviator to cross the Channel in a plane rather than a lighter-than-air balloon) through to the Spitfire of Battle of Britain fame. Air shows are held on event days from May to October, when you can see those magnificent Edwardian flying machines take to the skies. For keen aerophiles, one of the highlights of a visit is the chance to see aircraft restoration in progress in the workshop. Also on the Shuttleworth site are the Regency-style ornamental Swiss Garden, the Bird of Prey Centre and the expansive Jubilee Play Centre which will delight children of all ages and abilities (different entry charges and opening hours apply to each attraction).

The brown tourist signs for Shuttleworth are misleading as the entrance is in Hill Lane about a mile east of the village of Old Warden. The parking area near the entrance is level. Access to the shop (with the ticket desk) and the light, airy restaurant, is easy. Further on, however, there are varying surfaces, including some trip hazards due to gullies and hangar door rails, and a few awkward doors. Trickiest are the steep ramps between hangars which may prove too much if you're a manual wheelchair-user, unless you have a strong helper, and may be difficult if you're a walker with impaired mobility.

Spitfire from the Shuttleworth Collection

THAMES VALLEY ADVENTURE PLAYGROUND

Address: Bath Road, Taplow, Maidenhead, Berkshire SL6 0PR **Website:** www.tvap.co.uk
Telephone: 01628 628599 **Hours:** Tues–Thurs & Sat 10am-3.30pm, Fri 10am–5pm (over 16s
only); Sun & Mon closed **Dates:** closed 24–26 Dec (call to check) **Entry fees:** [D]£6 per child,
based on voluntary contribution [H]free (advance booking essential)

It's not flash nor fancy and the paint is peeling off a little, but this place doesn't feel run-
down, just well-loved. And it's really not hard to see why the children and their families
who come to the Thames Valley Adventure Playground (TVAP) love it. This is a playground where children of all abilities can play together: whatever your child's disability,
even if confined to a wheelchair, they could have a go on pretty much everything.

Roundabouts? No problem – just wheel right onboard and make sure the gate shuts
behind your son or daughter so their chair doesn't fly off. Swing? They've got one that

The sandpit at Thames Valley Adventure Playground

will take a wheelchair, or a swinging bed if you prefer. Surely not the zipwire. . . Yes, there is even a zipwire with a secure bucket seat and a wooden fort with a wheelchair walkway up to the top. Indoors, you'll find a soft-play room, craft area, sensory room, music room and a large area with toys and dressing-up clothes. A new extension over the lake, due to open in 2009, features a glass-floor view of the water and fish beneath.

For most of the week, TVAP is open exclusively for children with special needs and their families (Fridays are exclusively reserved for special-needs adults). As you would expect, everything is completely accessible. There is lots of parking outside, though none designated as disabled (it doesn't need to be). The toilets are equipped with hoists, a large changing bed, grab rails, and various seats. Staff are all trained to deal with all kinds of disabilities and they're a very friendly bunch too. There is no catering on site but plenty of space, indoors and out, to eat picnics.

VERULAMIUM MUSEUM

Address: St Michaels Street, St Albans, Hertfordshire AL3 4SW **Website:** www. stalbansmuseums.org.uk **Telephone:** 01727 751810 (group bookings 01727 751820) **Hours:** Mon–Sat 10am–5.30pm, Sun 2–5.30pm (last admission 5pm) **Dates:** closed Christmas & New Year (call ahead for details) **Entry fees:** [D]£2 [H]£3 [A]£3 [child]£2 [C]£2 (admission is free for local residents)

Verulamium, founded by the Romans, was the site of Britain's first Christian martyr-dom, when a Roman soldier called Alban was executed for sheltering a Christian priest in 209 AD. Today, the extraordinary story of the city of St Albans and its Roman origins is brilliantly portrayed in the museum, which is set in an enormous area of parkland – an attraction in its own right. Home to some of the finest Roman mosaics and frescoes in northern Europe, the museum displays everyday life in Roman Britain in a highly accessible manner.

You'll find recreated Roman rooms, hands-on discovery areas, video presentations and touch-screen databases. Look into the kitchen of a Roman housewife and learn about the food she prepared; see the lead coffin of a wealthy citizen and hear an actor tell his story; visit the reconstructed carpenter's workshop and absorb the sounds of the workshop and the bustling street. The excellence of the museum continues in the attractive shop, which sells a well-judged selection of high-quality souvenirs and books. Near the museum, the neighbouring building (free entry) showcases a typically magnificent town house in its display of Britain's earliest central heating system, the underfloor, hot-air hypocaust, clad in a mosaic floor.

There is a bit of a slope up from the disabled spaces in the car park to the step-free entrance. A manual wheelchair is available from the shop if required and they can provide a powered mobility scooter if you want to cross the park to the hypocaust. Accessible toilets are downstairs (there's an excellent lift hidden behind the reception desk). Most displays are at a good level for wheelchair users, but some of the older cabinets are a little high. There are good, even surfaces throughout the museum and ample space to get around. Groups can book handling sessions for the visually impaired. Although there's nowhere to get a snack at the museum itself, you'll find a café in the park.

ZSL WHIPSNADE ZOO

Address: Whipsnade, Dunstable, Bedfordshire LU6 2LF **Web:** www.zsl.org/zsl-whipsnade-zoo
Tel: 01582 872171 **Hours:** 10am–6pm (closes 4pm Oct–Feb; last admission one hour before closing time) **Dates:** closed 25 Dec **Entry:** [D]£13.90 [H]Free [A]£15.40 [3–15s]£11.90 [C]£13.90; car entry, allowing you to drive through the park £14 (free to Blue Badge holders)

The Zoological Society of London's Whipsnade Zoo is one of Europe's largest wildlife conservation parks, home to more than 2500, mostly endangered, animals. Occupying six hundred acres of countryside on the edge of the Chiltern Downs, this is very different from the traditional city zoo and a really enjoyable and worthwhile day out.

Whipsnade has big open paddocks that allow a relatively natural habit for many large species, including camels, bison and rhino, though the big cats are securely penned. The Children's Farm allows close contact and the whole family can join the charming lemurs in their enclosure. Wallabies, mara (long-legged relatives of the guinea pig), muntjac deer and peacocks wander freely through the park. The "Passage through Asia" route – allowing you to drive through a section where all the animals are unenclosed – is a particular highlight, though watch out for yak and camel jams ahead.

Blue Badge parking is free, but you may want to be set down by the gates as there are steep slopes from the car park. Taking your car in is the best option as you can get to much of the park and see many of the larger mammals from your car – and there's parking throughout. A train (wheelchair-accessible) and a bus (not) are also available. If you're walking or using a wheelchair, you'll find access is step-free almost everywhere, but some paths are steep and even rutted, and the Woodland Bird Walk has a bark-litter floor. To see it all does require covering long distances and gradients, so either a powered wheelchair or a fit pusher are probably essential. There are good disabled toilets around the park, but those nearest the entrance are surprisingly difficult to access.

WHY NOT ALSO TRY...

ZSL London Zoo

Address: Outer Circle, Regents Park, London NW1 4RY **Website:** www.zsl.org/zsl-london-zoo **Telephone:** 020 7722 3333 **Hours:** Mar–Oct 10am–6pm, Nov–Feb 10am–4pm (last admission one hour before closing) **Dates:** closed 25 Dec **Entry fees:** [D]£14 [H]Free [A]£15.50 [under 3s]Free [3–15s]£12.50 [C]£14

Based on the northern edge of Regents Park, Whipsnade's sister ZSL site, London Zoo, is the world's oldest scientific zoo. Highlights of this animal kingdom include the recently opened Gorilla Kingdom and perennial favourites the penguins, giraffes and majestic Sumatran tigers. If "up close and personal" is more your thing, then the Clore Rainforest Lookout, a tropical biome full of freely roaming South American monkeys, shouldn't be missed. For a site with many listed buildings, the zoo has done a great job to ensure that all the main attractions (except the aquarium - ask at the Information Kiosk to arrange rear entry level access) are directly accessible, and there are six disabled parking bays right opposite the entrance.

EAST ANGLIA & THE EAST MIDLANDS

- Anglesey Abbey Gardens
- Black Cat Equestrian Centre, Sutton-on-Sea
- Blicking Hall, Gardens and Park
- Brixworth Country Park
- Bure Valley Railway
- Clumber Park Adapted Cycling
- Dunwich Heath Coastal Centre and Beach
- Foxton Locks and the Canal Museum
- Lincoln Cathedral
- The National Horseracing Museum
- National Space Centre
- Prickwillow Engine Museum
- Sailability, Rutland
- Sainsbury Centre for Visual Arts
- Sheringham Park
- Sherwood Forest Country Park
- Silverstone Race Days and Driving Experience
- Theatre Royal, Bury St Edmunds
- Wicken Fen Nature Reserve

FOOD & DRINK ▶▶ Lincoln
FOOD & DRINK ▶▶ Norwich

EAST ANGLIA & THE EAST MIDLANDS

Renowned for its wide skies and flat landscapes, East Anglia's scenery – from the once inhospitable fenlands to bucolic river valleys and unspoilt stretches of coast – is undoubtedly its main draw. The East Midlands, by comparison, can initially seem a little short of star sights, but don't be fooled. There is plenty to explore here too, with the area's industrial history playing a key role in many of its attractions.

ANGLESEY ABBEY GARDENS

Address: Lode, Cambridge, Cambridgeshire CB25 9EJ **Website:** www.angleseyabbey.org
Telephone: 01223 810080 **Hours:** winter 10.30am–4.30pm; summer 10.30am–5.30pm
(hours vary) **Dates:** closed Mon & most Tues; check website **Entry fees:** summer [D]£8.40
[H]free [A]£8.40 [5-16s]£4.20 [C]£4.20; winter, and arrivals not by car, half-price

The perfect setting for a summer family picnic, featuring gardens full of hidden surprises, the estate of Anglesey Abbey – a Jacobean mansion on the site of the original, thirteenth-century priory – makes for a fine day out. The grounds are particularly appealing to keen gardeners.

The 98 acre grounds are well laid out, with meandering paths leading you to numerous themed gardens and hidden treasures, including more than a hundred sculptures dotted throughout the formal and landscaped gardens, and a working watermill – the Lode Mill – dating from the eighteenth century. However, if you want to go off the beaten track there are also wide expanses of lawn and meadows of wild flowers to explore. The Abbey's January and February snowdrop display is famous; in the spring it mounts an impressive display of more than four thousand hyacinths; and in the late summer the dahlia feast is something to behold. Unfortunately, the house itself remains barely accessible, and if you are a wheelchair-user or you struggle with stairs, your tour will be limited to two rooms on the ground floor. The on-screen virtual tour is scant compensation.

Anglesey Abbey has fourteen disabled parking bays, all on tarmac and the furthest no more than 50 metres from the house. A new visitor centre has recently opened and the restaurant, shop and garden centre are all fully accessible. If you require them, adapted picnic tables and cutlery are available. There are nine powered buggies and one five-seater vehicle with driver. The main drive to the Abbey is tarmac-surfaced and the other paths, although loose gravelled, are still easy to push a wheelchair over.

BLACK CAT EQUESTRIAN CENTRE, SUTTON-ON-SEA

Address: Huttoft Road, Sutton-on-Sea, Lincolnshire LN12 2QY **Website:** www.blackcat equestriancentre.co.uk/index.htm **Telephone:** 01507 442631 **Hours:** daily 10am–4pm (7pm in summer) **Dates:** closed 25–26 Dec (call to check) **Entry fees:** riding lessons £10 per half hour, £17 per hour; carriage-driving lessons £26 per hour

This large riding centre has a wide range of facilities, including two outdoor schools, an indoor school, a show-jumping course, a cross-country course and harness driving. It also has the advantage of being in Sutton-on-Sea, one of Lincolnshire's prettier coastal resorts, just south along the coast from Mablethorpe. A visit can easily be combined with a trip to the seaside.

A family-run business, the Black Cat Equestrian Centre is carefully designed to suit people of all ages and abilities at every level of experience – from the nervous and apprehensive to the confident and self-assured. They usually have around twenty horses at the centre, so if you book ahead, you'll find a mount to suit your abilities and style. And because of the centre's connection with Lincoln College's Reach-Out course for people with learning difficulties, Black Cat are experienced at providing literally hands-on equine encounters for people of every ability.

The staff are helpful, experienced and happily allow extra time for assisting visitors with disabilities. But contacting them prior to visiting is a good idea, as the exact nature of your disability will determine whether you are able to ride or learn carriage-driving. People with learning disabilities, sensory impairments and mobility difficulties are regular users, though if you're a wheelchair-user and can't stand independently you may find it difficult to use the specialist horse-mounting block. Car park and path surfaces are mostly uneven, so extra care is needed, and there's a shallow step into both the otherwise accessible toilet and reception area.

BLICKLING HALL, GARDENS AND PARK

Address: Blickling, Norwich, Norfolk NR11 8NF **Website:** www.nationaltrust.org.uk/blickling **Telephone:** 01263 738030 **Hours:** variable, check for details **Dates:** seasonal, check for details **Entry fees:** [D]£9.10 [H]free [A]£9.10 [under 16s]£4.50

Set in beautiful gardens and surrounded by historic parkland with woods and lakeside walks, this splendid Jacobean house, dating from the 1620s, is one of the finest in Britain. Even the library, with more than twelve thousand books, is one of the most significant private collections in the country.

Your first view of Blickling commands attention as your eyes are drawn down the main drive, tunnelled between two hundred-metre-long, four-metre-wide yew hedges, towards the elegant Jacobean facade. Elaborate plasterwork is a feature, especially in the immense Long Gallery which houses the library. The rooms have all the fine furnishings and fabulous views of the surrounding lake and gardens that you'd expect. The splendour of the house is matched by the extensive gardens with vibrant floral borders in summer and rich colours in the autumn. The parkland offers some lovely walks, seasonally graced by daffodils and rhododendrons. Three scooters are available and there's a three-kilometre circular route, suitable for wheelchairs. The restaurant specialises in produce from the estate, including apples and game. And local crabs are used for their Norfolk crab cakes, a seasonal speciality.

The nine Blue Badge parking spaces aren't clearly marked and parking can be casual. The courtyard here has plant sales, one of three accessible toilets (the others being in the more distant main car park and at the visitor centre), and the entrance to the secondhand bookshop which is just accessible, if tight, for wheelchairs. The 100m route to the house includes a steep, paved ramp. As you enter, the restaurant and shop are both fully accessible. Beyond the shop is the visitor centre, with hearing loop. The lift makes most of the house accessible and wheelchairs are available for use inside. The visually impaired are aided by a large print or Braille guide and a tactile collection.

Blicking Hall

BRIXWORTH COUNTRY PARK

Address: Northampton Road, Brixworth, Northamptonshire NN6 9DG **Website:** www.northamptonshire.gov.uk/leisure/countryside/cparks **Telephone:** 01604 883920 **Hours:** daily 9am–5pm car park and toilets; 10am–4.30pm shop (4pm in winter). **Dates:** closed 25 Dec; shop closed 25–31 Dec. **Entry fees:** free

Set in the heart of beautiful rural Northamptonshire, Brixworth Country Park is a national showpiece for an accessible countryside. This small yet perfectly formed park offers great possibilities if you want to picnic, walk, push or cycle in woodland, meadow and reservoir surroundings.

As well as the sensory garden, children's play and activity areas and the shop and café, the park offers three short circular routes of five hundred metres, one and two kilometres, which seem to immerse you fully in the outdoors while still being accessible. You can stroll quietly through the woods and meadows, or pause to watch from the accessible viewing hide, where you may catch a glimpse of wildlife – including foxes, squirrels, waterfowl and woodland birds. The walking routes also give access to an eleven-kilometre circuit around the reservoir if you'd like more of a walking or cycling challenge. They have bikes to hire on site. The park makes a great destination for a leisurely half-day trip and a relaxing amble through the great outdoors.

Disabled parking is free of charge and situated just in front of the visitor centre and shop at the start of the walking trails. Wide doorways are evident throughout the buildings and all the doors are easily opened or equipped with push buttons. There's a well-kept disabled toilet next to the shop. The café is spacious with movable chairs and tables. Walking routes are clearly signed and colour-coded and the paths are hard-surfaced, with some undulations but no steep gradients, so that a regular wheelchair user should be able to manage independently or with a little assistance. Although the park has no hand-bikes to hire, it offers two trampers (very sturdy power chairs), manual wheelchairs and two types of passive seating to be attached to bikes.

BURE VALLEY RAILWAY

Address: Aylsham Station, Norwich Road, Aylsham, Norfolk NR11 6BW **Website:** www.bvrw.co.uk **Telephone:** 01263 733858 **Hours:** Aylsham Station open daily **Dates:** Seasonal timetable operates, including Santa specials. No service in Jan (call or check website for timetable) **Entry fees:** free entry to station, including shop and restaurant. Return train ticket [D]£10.50 [H]£10.50 [A]£10.50 [C]£9.50

This narrow-gauge (38cm) railway, built in 1990 and mainly operated by steam locomotives, runs for fourteen kilometres through the picturesque Norfolk countryside between the market town of Aylsham and the Broads capital of Wroxham, with three intermediate halts at Brampton, Buxton and Coltishall. If you thrill to the smell of soot and the rhythm of the rails, then this is the outing for you.

The track's narrow gauge does make for a slightly bumpy ride and the purpose-built carriages require a flexible spine and the ability to duck your head on entering. Once you're seated, however, the carriages are very comfortable. The scenery on the 45-minute journey is varied and offers a good sample of the Norfolk countryside as you pass through farmland and water meadows, skirt woodland and even get views of water-mills. The special boat train combines the nostalgic steam loco trip with a cruise on the Broads (£16 all-in). At Wroxham station, a fifteen-minute walk or push is required to link with the fully accessible boat. Staff are happy to arrange a taxi link but you'll need to book that in advance.

All the facilities at Aylsham (including the workshops) and at Wroxham are level -access and have very helpful staff, and it can be fruitful to call ahead to make enquiries and reservations. The train's specially designed wheelchair coaches can accommodate four manual chairs (though fewer powerchairs or scooters) plus seating for friends and family. Access is via double doors with detachable ramps. When a full service is in operation each train has two of these coaches. If you start your journey at Aylsham you enter the station via a paved ramp from the large car park, which contains three adjacent Blue Badge bays. Manoeuvrability in the booking office/shop does require a little skill but no such problem exists in the *Whistlestop* café, which has sufficient space and flexible modern fittings, and offers snacks and meals from easily readable menus.

CLUMBER PARK ADAPTED CYCLING

Address: Worksop, Nottinghamshire S80 3AZ **Website:** www.nationaltrust.org.uk/main/w-clumberpark **Telephone:** 01909 544917 **Hours:** park always open (for restaurant, shop, exhibition and chapel hours see website) **Dates:** no closure dates (but call to check Christmas dates) **Entry fees:** free, cars £4.80 (including Blue Badge holders); cycle hire £6 (2hrs), £12 (one day); adapted cycle, wheelchair and mobility scooter hire free

Although large, with 21 kilometres of pathways, Clumber is a disabled-friendly park, incorporating interesting historical information, quality amenities, some stunning views and a unique variety of deciduous trees. One of the most popular tourist targets in the region, the park is well-known for its handsome woodland walks and fine, Gothic revival chapel.

Owned and operated by the National Trust, Clumber comprises 4000 acres of park and woodland south of Worksop in northern Nottinghamshire. It was once the country seat of the dukes of Newcastle and it was here in the 1770s that they constructed a grand mansion overlooking their own personal lake. The house was dismantled in 1938, when the duke sold the estate, but many of the outbuildings – including stables and barns – have survived. The adapted hire kit comprises manual wheelchairs, tandems, trikes, buggies for children and a Trandem – an adapted bike/wheelchair/hand-cycle combination. The Trandem requires a disabled person to have a reasonably fit companion to tour the extensive woodland and parkland paths.

The disabled parking bays are 160 metres from the main facilities. A useful access leaflet details the distance and variable path surfaces of three accessible routes, the longest of which is 6.5 kilometres, the shortest having resting seats and smooth flat paths. The shop, kitchen garden, conservation centre and tea rooms, serving tasty refreshments, all have flat or ramped access with spacious, light interiors suitable for wheelchair users. The chapel has a ramped entrance, limited space and low lighting. Accessible toilets are located near the main visitor area, and there's a RADAR-key-operated WC behind the conservation centre.

DUNWICH HEATH COASTAL CENTRE AND BEACH

Address: Dunwich, Saxmundham, Suffolk IP17 3DJ **Website:** www.nationaltrust.org.uk/main/
w-dunwichheathandminsmerebeach **Telephone:** 01728 648501 **Hours:** dawn–dusk **Dates:**
dates vary, check website **Entry fees:** free (£4 parking for non-National Trust members)

Dunwich Heath is an area of outstanding natural beauty with tracts of heather and gorse, woods, sandy cliffs, unspoilt beaches and lots of local wildlife. While certainly appealing to natural history enthusiasts, this lowland heath is a wonderfully remote-feeling area to blow away the cobwebs, and many people visit regularly.

Dunwich Heath

There are three designated paths taking you over the heath – the 4km gorse walk, the 2km heather walk and the 1.8km birch walk. All three walks provide magnificent displays of gorse and heather in the spring and summer, but, as suggested by their names, they take you over different parts of the heath, so you need to decide which walk you want to do depending on what you want to see. If you walk down the path to Minsmere Beach, you may glimpse a sand martin returning to its nest in the cliffs. There is also a sea-watch hut with lookout points where you may, if you're lucky, spot seals and harbour porpoises, as well as many seabirds. Ashore, the wildlife-viewing is less uncertain, with the area home to many different species, from glow-worms to red deer.

The car park has eight Blue Badge bays, two within twenty metres of the visitor centre and six with views across the beach and no more than fifty metres away. There's a single mobility scooter and one three-seater buggy with driver, available for disabled or elderly visitors. These vehicles can only be used on designated routes (staff at the visitor centre will give you the details). The heath's paths are laid with the sort of gravel you can push a wheelchair over, although the path down to the sea has seven shallow steps and requires assistance. The beach itself is shingle, so quite difficult to access. Guide dogs are limited to parts of it only.

FOXTON LOCKS AND THE CANAL MUSEUM

Address: Middle Lock, Gumley Road, Foxton, Market Harborough, Leicestershire LE16 7RA
Website: www.foxtonlocks.com **Telephone:** 0116 279 2657 **Hours:** summer, daily 10am–5pm, winter Sat–Wed 10am–4pm subject to staff availability (call to check) **Dates:** closed at Christmas (call to check) **Entry fees:** [D]£2 [H]£2.50 [A]£2.50 [0–16s] free [C]£2

You might think Foxton Canal Museum is strictly for enthusiasts – the sort of place that's not to be missed if nineteenth-century canal engineering puts a glint in your eye. In fact, most people find it a fascinating and entertaining place, and a visit is worth the effort even if it's not entirely ideal for people with limited mobility.

The museum is in the old boiler house of a construction known as the Foxton Inclined Plane or Foxton Barge Lift, built in the early 1900s to deal with regular traffic jams of barges trying to get through a series of locks up a 23-metre rise in canal level. The small museum, housed in the old boiler room, tells the story well and is staffed by a full-time keeper supported by volunteers, who happily share their expertise and enthusiasm. When you see the massive slope where the lift stood, you'll appreciate the scale of the engineering. You can make the visit into more of a day out by strolling around the paths and facilities near the locks and visiting the nearby pub, *Foxton Locks Inn* (0116 279 1515), which serves up snacks and meals.

Neither of the car parks is very near the museum – call ahead to get directions to a Blue Badge parking space closer to the museum – and this isn't the most accessible of visits: take care with vulnerable adults and children. Wheelchair-users will need strong assistance to get to some areas of the site, including the museum, though once inside, the museum is level throughout. Beware also of the locks and ponds, most of them un-fenced and often holding deep water. Accessible toilets are in the car park near *Foxton Locks Inn* and across the canal from the museum, via an accessible bridge. Despite the slopes, there are plenty of level, grassed areas, enabling you to watch as boats use the locks, which makes any difficulties with access worth the effort.

LINCOLN CATHEDRAL

Address: Lincoln, Lincolnshire LN2 1PX **Website:** www.lincolncathedral.com **Telephone:** 01522 561600 **Hours:** daily, summer Mon–Fri 7.15am–8pm, Sat & Sun 7.15am–6pm; winter Mon–Sat 7.15am–6pm, Sun 7.15am–5pm **Dates:** occasional closures for special services; call or check website **Entry fees:** [D]£4 [H]free [A]£4 [5–15s]£1 [C]£3

This beautiful church, right in the heart of the historic city centre, dominates Lincoln's sky-line. While the cathedral's architecture and interior are imposing, it is also a place of peace and spirituality and a must-do visit if you're in the area.

The entrance is through the west door into the nave with its vast vaulted ceilings and massive pillars. Down the left side, a series of beautiful and tactile wooden sculptures de-pict the stations of the Crucifixion. Beyond them, the north-south transept is illuminated by a unique pair of rose windows – the Bishop's Eye and the Dean's Eye. You then come

Lincoln Cathedral interior

Perfect for a quick bite to eat at lunch, and well-regarded in the local area, **Cafe Zoot** (5 Bailgate; 01522 536663; www.cafezoot.co.uk) ticks all the basic boxes for accessibility with ground-floor eating and toilets available. Close to the cathedral in the bustling Bailgate area, the restaurant not only has a cosmopolitan menu but regularly offers deals as reasonable as two meals for only £9.99.

to the oldest part of the building and the heart of the cathedral, St Hugh's Choir, with its beautiful oak carvings. Behind the High Altar is the aptly named Angel Choir, the well-camouflaged home of the celebrated and much searched-for Lincoln Imp. Through the northeast transept is the Cloister, a tranquil setting for quiet reflection, which provides access to the nine-sided Chapter House and a fine library designed by Sir Christopher Wren. There are interesting and informative free guided tours at intervals throughout the day.

Many of the roads around the Cathedral and the surrounding area are narrow and cobbled, with limited access to vehicles. Although disabled parking is permitted for up to three hours in the restricted areas, it can be tricky at busy times. The ground floor of the cathedral is wheelchair-accessible, with the exception of the three side chapels dedicated to the Armed Forces. Just inside the entrance, there's a touch model of the Cathedral, including a site layout, with a foot-operated audio guide, and, in the northeast transept, a touch exhibition with Braille descriptions. The café, although quite small, provides snacks and lunches and the furniture is movable. There is only one disabled toilet in the cathedral, but a new toilet block is coming soon.

THE NATIONAL HORSERACING MUSEUM

Address: 99 High Street, Newmarket, Suffolk CB8 8JH **Website:** www.nhrm.co.uk **Telephone:** 01638 667333 **Hours:** 11am–4.30pm (last admission 4pm); opens 10am on Newmarket race days **Dates:** Mar–Nov, check for closures **Entry fees:** [D]£5.50 [H]£5.50 [A]£5.50 [C]£4.50

Situated in the capital of English racing, this museum is surprisingly interesting to non-buffs, and it offers a feast of memorabilia to anyone with a strong interest in horse-racing.

The museum covers all aspects of racing, from its early royal origins to modern-day heroes, both human and animal. Even if you're not a student of the turf you're likely to be touched by the exploits of jockeys like Gordon Richards, Lester Piggott or Frankie Dettori and by horses as famous as Desert Orchid or Red Rum. On a more physical level you can learn how to feed a racehorse and even ride one on the horse simulator. From the Practical Gallery a lift takes you to the upper floor, featuring an exhibition of racing-related art, with originals by Stubbs and Munnings. In addition, there's always a special exhibition: in 2009 it's the history of Tattersalls, the world's oldest bloodstock auctioneers. You can also sign up for one of several equine tours: the two-hour "Classic" (£23) visits a training yard and the gallops. The tour minibus is not wheelchair-accessible, however, and getting aboard involves three steps. You can stay inside and view the various venues but the minibus stops frequently and the tour is designed as an on-and-off journey around the working facilities of the racecourse.

Apart from one kerbside Blue Badge bay outside the main entrance, Blue Badge parking is situated in All Saints car park, about 400 metres from the main ramped entrance. The museum is fully accessible, with ramps allowing access to galleries and a lift to the upper floor. Accessible toilets are inside the main toilets, although getting into the gents might present a problem for large powered chairs (volunteer staff are happy to arrange exclusive use of the ladies). The restaurant is fully accessible, with a paved, grassed and gravelled area outside.

NATIONAL SPACE CENTRE

Address: Exploration Drive, Leicester, Leicestershire LE4 5NS **Website:** www.spacecentre. co.uk **Telephone:** 0870 607 7223 Dedicated access tel: 0116 261 0261 **Hours:** Tues–Sun 10am–5pm (last entry 3.30pm) **Dates:** closed Mon and occasional other days (call to check) plus 25–26 Dec & 1 Jan **Entry fees:** [D]£10 [H]Free [A]£12 [5–16s]£10 [C]£10

National Space Centre

As you approach the National Space Centre, you can't miss its famous rocket tower. With its conveniently central location, this is the UK's largest planetarium and exhibition of space exploration. Whether or not you consider yourself a fan of space matters, it's visually and mentally highly stimulating: you could easily spend the day here. But if you are an enthusiast who fancies their next day-trip a little further afield, you can visit Tranquility Base to test your suitability for a career as an astronaut.

Another highlight of the visit is the arresting thirty-minute film show in the Space Theatre, included in your ticket price, which combines the UK's biggest planetarium with a futuristic cinema experience as films are projected onto the huge, domed ceiling. Around the rest of the site, six spacious galleries tell various stories: of the origins of the universe; of unmanned space probes; and of space travel. There are plenty of genuine space artefacts, including satellites, rockets, food packs and even a toilet from a space station, and a good range of hands-on activities keeps visitors of all ages engaged. Beneath the gigantic rockets is *Boosters*, which serves a small range of fairly priced drinks, sandwiches and snacks, and in Cargo Bay you can shop for toys and souvenirs, ranging from predictable tat to educational items – which could add considerably to the cost of your day.

There are plenty of disabled parking spaces near the entrance, though there's quite a long exposed transfer down a significant slope to the entrance itself. Automatic doors open onto the spacious main lobby. A lift takes you to the upper level and a larger lift is available on request. From there the rocket tower lifts take you to all levels. Displays are easily accessible and spacious, though a few of the interactive features are out of reach to wheelchair-users and the flight deck simulator is up a short flight of steps. The Space Theatre has step-free access and spaces for wheelchairs where companions can sit alongside. There are disabled toilets off the main lobby and at the back of the ground-floor galleries.

PRICKWILLOW ENGINE MUSEUM

Address: Main Street, Prickwillow, Ely, Cambridgeshire CB7 4UN
Website: www.prickwillow-engine-museum.co.uk **Telephone:** 01353 688360

" *Noisy, greasy, oily diesel engines based in an early nineteenth-century pump house may sound like an attraction best left to the nerds but if you have any interest at all in Britain's industrial heritage you should visit, or you will miss out on a hidden gem.*

This bright, airy museum presents a history of the draining of the unique landscape that is the fens. The original building has been recently extended which has helped to make the visitor facilities accessible. Photographs, historic maps, agricultural implements and artefacts are laid out around six large diesel pumping engines. The engines are often demonstrated on events days (phone ahead for details). Parking is easy, a hearing loop is available and the site is run by helpful volunteers.

The museum has a picturesque setting by the bridge over the River Lark at the eastern edge of Prickwillow village, just a few miles from Ely and Newmarket. Travelling on the roads in the area can be like a roller-coaster ride, with humps and bumps in the land where drainage has caused it to sink, but the location is ideal for picnics and walks. For those lucky enough to be visiting the area by boat there are moorings available. "

Reader Review from John Scott

SAILABILITY, RUTLAND

Address: Rutland Sailing Club, Gibbet Lane, Edith Weston, Oakham, Rutland LE15 8HJ
Website: www.rutland-sailability.org **Telephone:** 01572 755927 (advance booking essential)
Dedicated access tel: 0116 271 9170 (Alan Naylor) **Hours:** Thurs 9.30am–3.15pm, Sat
9am–12pm **Dates:** only Thurs & Sat, Apr–Oct (weather permitting) **Entry fees:** first visit free,
second visit £5, third visit club membership required (£40 per year)

Sailing is freedom: there's nothing that quite compares with the splashes on the hull and the breeze on your face as you skim across the surface of the water using nothing but the harnessed power of the wind under your control. This exhilarating sport can be enjoyed largely regardless of any disability.

Sailability (a registered charity; www.sailability.org) exists to help you gain the confidence to fulfil your sailing potential. At Rutland Sailing Club, they have 23 boats, ranging from small, one-person, single-sail craft through two-person twin-sail boats to multi-hulled craft for six people. Rutland Sailability claim never to have had to turn anyone away due to their disability, and indeed their professionalism, expertise and facilities are impressive, enabling most disabled people to be sailing independently (with an instructor) within minutes of being on the water. The lake here is a good size and invariably has a breeze, even on a seemingly still day. Sailability's volunteers are friendly, experienced sailors as well as being knowledgeable about the sailing adaptations available for disabled people.

Parking is no problem and they have an electric cart to transfer you from car to jetty if required. The jetty has four hoists and there's plenty of specialist sailing kit to allow anyone, even if with very little mobility, to sail completely independently. Their accessible changing rooms, with multiple wet rooms, shower chairs and ceiling hoists, put numerous other disabled changing rooms to shame. There's a decent café and bar in the clubhouse, which has a gentle ramp to the first floor, low, movable seating and tables, and a large deck overlooking the lake. They also offer on-site adapted residential accommodation. For another UK Sailability experience, see p.44.

SAINSBURY CENTRE FOR VISUAL ARTS

Address: University of East Anglia, Norwich, Norfolk NR4 7TJ **Website:** www.scva.ac.uk
Telephone: 01603 593199 **Hours:** Tues–Sun 10am–5pm, Wed 10am–8pm; closed Mon
Dates: closed 24 Dec–1 Jan & bank holiday Mondays **Entry fees:** free except for special
exhibitions

The Sainsbury Centre for Visual Arts houses an impressive collection of international work, including pieces by Francis Bacon and Henry Moore, and mounts special exhibitions which change every few months. The centre, which opened in 1978 to house the Robert and Lisa Sainsbury Collection, forms part of the University of East Anglia and the building was designed by Norman Foster.

In the shadow of the Cathedral spire, **The Refectory** (Norwich Cathedral, The Close, NR1 4DH; 01603 218322; www.cathedral.org.uk) is an award-winning restaurant, and a great place to relax with a morning coffee. The newly refurbished **Theatre Royal Norwich** has three new fully accessible bars and a restaurant (Theatre Royal Restaurant, Theatre Street, NR2 1RL; 01603 598577; www.theatreroyalnorwich.co.uk) serving locally sourced produce. You don't have to have tickets to a performance, but bear in mind that closing time is at the end of the last show's interval and at 6pm on non-show days. **Ivory's Restaurant and Cafe Bar** (The Assembly House, Theatre Street, NR2 1RQ; 01608 627526; www.assemblyhousenorwich.co.uk) serves a traditional Sunday lunch or evening meal in elegant and welcoming surroundings, and is named after Sir Thomas Ivory who designed the building in 1754. Expect to pay around £14 for two courses.

At the heart of the Sainsbury Collection is the Living Area, housing the permanent display, which mixes works from across the world – and across the millennia. As well as Bacon and Moore, the exhibits cover five thousand years of output, including pieces from other modern Europeans such as Alberto Giacometti, Jacob Epstein and Pablo Picasso, as well as ancient art (a ceramic hippo from Egypt's twelfth dynasty, a powerfully worked Greek figurine dating from 2400 BC), among the 1300 pieces. The building itself, a vision of high-tech, was extended underground in 1991 to house the Lisa Sainsbury collection of modern pottery, including works by Lucie Rie, Hans Coper and Bernard Leach. The site was expanded again in 2006 and looks set to acquire regular new levels and wings into the future: Sir Robert Sainsbury has described the building as "the best thing in the collection."

Access to the centre is via the main entrance to the university; then you follow the signs to the centre. There are four Blue Badge parking spaces immediately outside the main entrance and level access into the building. The galleries are fully accessible via ramped access but wheelchair-users may need assistance. A manual wheelchair is available on request. You can get snacks and meals at the *Gallery Café* and *Garden Restaurant*. Building work is being undertaken in 2009: check with the centre for visitor and access details while this is ongoing.

SHERINGHAM PARK

Address: Wood Farm, Sheringham Park, Upper Sheringham, Norfolk NR26 8TL **Website:** www.nationaltrust.org.uk/main/w-sheringhampark **Telephone:** 01263 820550 **Hours:** dawn–dusk, with seasonal variations **Dates:** closed 25–26 Dec **Entry fees:** free (£4 parking for non-National Trust members)

If you're looking for somewhere for a leisurely Sunday afternoon stroll, then Sheringham Park is an ideal place to visit. With its beautiful sea views and extensive woodland this is the perfect place to recharge your batteries.

Sheringham Park was purchased by the National Trust in 1986 and is considered an outstanding example of the work of the eighteenth-century landscape designer Humphry Repton. There are various paths which you can take on foot but only one, laid with concrete, that is wheelchair-accessible. If you borrow an NT scooter you have to agree to stick to this path. It takes you through woodland and then brings you past Sheringham Hall which is a private residence but from where there are some marvellous coastal views. It's not a circular walk and you have to turn round and retrace your route back the way you came, but this isn't really a problem: you'll be bowled over by the displays of specimen trees and, in May and June, azaleas and rhododendrons in bloom. The walk takes about one and a half hours at a moderate pace. After some bracing country air there's no better way to finish your outing than with a good cup of tea from the courtyard kiosk.

On arrival at Sheringham, NT members can park in the Blue Badge bays free of charge, though non-members need to pay. The visitor centre is fifty metres away (if you want to borrow one of their mobility scooters they may ask you to take a short driving test). Catering is provided in an open courtyard, so bring a warm coat in the winter. A RADAR key is needed to access the disabled loo but overall disabled facilities are excellent.

Sheringham Park

SHERWOOD FOREST COUNTRY PARK

Address: Edwinstowe, Mansfield, Nottinghamshire NG21 9HN **Website:** www.nottinghamshire.gov.uk/home/leisure/countryparks **Telephone:** 01623 823202 **Hours:** daily summer 10am–5pm, winter 10am–4.30pm **Dates:** closed 25 Dec **Entry fees:** free

Most of Sherwood Forest, once a vast royal woodland of oak, birch and bracken covering all of northern Nottinghamshire, was cleared in the eighteenth century – and nowadays it's difficult to imagine the protection it provided for generations of outlaws, most famously Robin Hood. These days, the country park, at the heart of Sherwood Forest National Nature Reserve, is a wonderful survivor in a transformed landscape.

The park comprises a little less than 450 acres of surviving woodland, including the Major Oak, the creaky tree where Maid Marion and Robin are supposed to have "plighted their troth". A family attraction, particularly suited to 5 to 12s, the Country Park offers forest walks and various samples of medieval-style Robin Hood-related entertainment: accessible activities include archery, a fairground and jousting. Of the three colour-coded walks through the forest, the 1.6km blue walk that passes the Major Oak is fully accessible for wheelchair-users. The path, which has gentle slopes, is surfaced and has picnic tables and benches en route. The red and green routes are longer, not fully surfaced, have some steep slopes and tend to get muddy in places during wet weather.

Parking is easy and all the buildings at the visitor centre have flat or ramped access, though some buildings are small, with only standard-width doorways. There are disabled toilets here. Wheelchairs are available on free loan but there's only one electric one, so call ahead to book. The *Forest Table* restaurant is good value, with wheelchair-accessible tables. The nearby craft centre has a spacious café and access (sometimes rather tight) to all craft workshops.

Sherwood Forest Country Park

SILVERSTONE RACE DAYS AND DRIVING EXPERIENCE

Address: Silverstone circuit, Northamptonshire NN12 8TN **Website:** www.silverstone.
co.uk **Telephone:** 0870 458 8200 Dedicated access tel: race days 0870 458 8232; driving
experience 0870 458 8299 **Hours:** 8am–6pm; but varies depending on event **Dates:** closed
25 Dec & 1 Jan **Entry fees:** race days from [D]£10 [H]free [A]£10 [5–15s] free [C]£10; driving
experience from £99

Watching a race or driving yourself, the whole experience of being at the home of British motor-racing is unbeatable. Whether you're in a car or watching from trackside, the
throaty roar of straining engines, the scent of fuel mixed with scorched rubber, and the
exhilaration of speed – felt in your gut or vicariously – all make the hairs on the back of
your neck stand up.

Silverstone's place in the history of motor-racing is assured: since 1948, the driving
legends and manufacturers who have done battle around this five-kilometre circuit are
essentially motor-racing's roll of honour. Numerous race days take place at Silverstone
throughout the year, with the biggest being the British Formula One Grand Prix. Ramped
viewing platforms and disabled RADAR-key toilets (keys available to buy on site) are situated all around the course. With the exception of race days, it's also possible to transfer
between the platforms during your visit. If you want try the driving experience, several
cars are available, though note that if you wish to drive yourself and require hand controls,
the exclusive option is the Ferrari 360 F1 Modena – although few budding racers will be
unhappy about that. Alternatively, you can elect to be driven around the circuit by a professional instructor or arrange to take your own car onto the track.

The Silverstone staff are well trained to deal with disability-related needs, though calling
in advance is recommended. The organisation has taken on suggestions from previous disabled users and all visitors are treated individually and sensitively. For some people doing
the driving experience, getting into the vehicle is tricky, but with prior notice Silverstone
will do their best to allow you to experience the track as a passenger or driver, whatever
your disability and even, with an instructor, if you're blind.

THEATRE ROYAL, BURY ST EDMUNDS

Address: 6 Westgate Street, Bury St Edmunds, Suffolk IP33 1QR **Website:** www.theatreroyal.
org **Telephone:** 01284 769505 **Hours:** box office Mon–Sat 10am–6pm; open door, dependent
on performances, Tues & Thurs 2–4pm (guided tour 2pm), Sat & Sun 10.30am–1pm (guided
tour 11am) **Dates:** no closures **Entry fees:** performance prices vary, [D]£2 reduction at some
performances [H]free; open door, free; guided tours £6

The Theatre Royal is the only surviving example of a Regency playhouse in the country.
Opened in 1819, it has recently been restored and is thoroughly worth a visit. In fact, it's
worth arriving half an hour early to appreciate it in full.

In the care of the National Trust, the Theatre Royal is one of only eight Grade I-listed theatres in the country. The refurbishment has restored the entrances to the pit, the Georgian forestage and the dress circle boxes – the latter approached on level access from the foyer, and containing the only four wheelchair-accessible seats in the house. Entering your box, you're instantly absorbed by the original, Neoclassical design and the elegant curve of the two rows of boxes. The colour scheme, from the dark earth-hued floor to the stone tones of the dress circle and up to the painted sky on the ceiling – together with the kind of perspective scenery which would have been used two centuries ago – all serve to create a perfect, all-round illusion that is intimate and proportioned on a human scale, while constantly impressive. If your body also needs nourishing, you'll be catered for in the accessible *Greene Room* – the new foyer bar-restaurant that serves tasty meals, including vegetarian options, from two hours before the performance.

Theatre Royal box office staff and stewards are all knowledgeable and fully aware of the access issues facing disabled patrons. There is access from two kerbside Blue Badge spaces, with two more, available for evening performances, at the Greene King Brewery Museum, opposite. Dropping off at the front, then parking in the Greene King staff car park (200 m from the back of the theatre) is the best option (note there's no wheelchair access from this car park). Inside the theatre, the pit, reserved in Georgian times for the hoi polloi, is not wheelchair-accessible, and only accessible to walking-impaired customers by 25 broad, shallow steps with a handrail on both sides. The upper circle and gallery are inaccessible.

WICKEN FEN NATURE RESERVE

Address: Wicken Fen, Lode Lane, Wicken, Ely, Cambridgeshire, CB7 5XP **Website:** www.wicken.org.uk **Telephone:** 01353 720274 **Hours:** 10am–5pm (4.30pm Nov–Jan) **Dates:** closed 25 Dec **Entry fees:** [D]£4.75 [H]free [A]£4.75 [5-16s]£2.65 [C]£2.40

Wicken Fen is one of Britain's oldest nature reserves and one of the most important wetlands in Europe. It's home to more than seven thousand species of wildlife including otters and rare butterflies. The reserve has a raised boardwalk which makes it an ideal place for disabled visitors to explore the fens.

Wicken Fen is a remnant of the once extensive Cambridgeshire fenlands and has been managed for centuries by sedge-cutting and peat-digging, producing this unique habitat. It is now one of England's most diverse wetland sites and a nationally important habitat for molluscs, with 88 species of slugs, snails and bivalve shellfish recorded here. It's a great bird-watching area, too (bitterns and marsh harriers being frequent visitors), and if you're quiet and visit the more out-of-the-way areas, you may see frogs, toads, newts and even a grass snake. You can take the leisurely 1.2km walk along the boardwalk or a more challenging 3.2km walk on either the nature trail or the adventurers' trail. All three routes have hides along the way. Borrow a pair of binoculars on arrival to ensure you have a good chance of seeing some of the more timid wildlife as well as the birdlife. Konik ponies (originally from Poland) and Highland cattle can also be seen grazing in the reserve.

Wicken Fen has two disabled parking spaces outside the visitors centre. There are two manual wheelchairs to borrow. The boardwalk is completely flat and very easy to walk on but it can get a little slippery in wet weather. The hides are also fully accessible, with movable benches, so it is possible to get up really close to the windows.

THE WEST MIDLANDS & THE PEAK DISTRICT

- Alton Towers
- Cadbury World, Birmingham
- Calke Abbey
- Chatsworth House
- Clent Hills all-ability trails
- Crich Tramway Village
- Cromford Canal
- Croome Park
- Hoo Farm
- Ironbridge Gorge Museums
- Pedalabikeaway, Forest of Dean
- RAF Museum, Cosford
- Royal Shakespeare Company, Stratford-upon-Avon
- Shugborough Estate
- ThinkTank, Birmingham
- Warwick Castle
- Worcester Porcelain Museum

WHY NOT ALSO TRY ▶▶
Shakespeare's Globe

THE WEST MIDLANDS & THE PEAK DISTRICT

Birthplace of the Bard, Cadbury's chocolate and the industrial revolution, the West Midlands offers a range of attractions to suit all visitors. Although parts of the region are undeniably bustling and built-up, this is a mostly quiet area, characterised by rolling countryside, stately homes and castles and Britain's first national park, the awe-inspiring Peak District, which offers every outdoor activity imaginable, from the sedate to the strenuous.

ALTON TOWERS

Address: Alton, Staffordshire, ST10 4DP **Website:** www.altontowers.com **Telephone:** 0870 5 20 4060 **Hours:** daily 10am–5pm (later openings in holidays) **Dates:** mid-Mar–Oct **Entry fees:** [D]£18 [H]£18 [A]£36 [4–11S]£27 [C]£36 (discounts available online)

Thrills, speed and exhilaration: Alton Towers dispenses these essential fixes from a wide range of white-knuckle rides contrived to excite the most hardened adrenaline junkie. Covering around five hundred acres of land including landscaped gardens and a water park, it's a magical place for kids, but if the high-speed rides are not your thing then walking in the grounds or soaking in the resort spa are an appealing alternative.

On arrival, a disabled visitor accompanied by up to two carers can obtain priority passes, which allow you to enter the rides through the exits as opposed to queueing for long periods – a great way of easing your day and making the most of your time. Access to some rides is challenging and the level of enjoyment you'll get from Alton Towers depends to some extent on your own abilities: *Oblivion* and *Nemesis* are relatively easy to get onto (and both these rides also have some extra-large seats if required), whereas the *Flume* and *Congo River Rapids* are a little trickier and might need more consideration. How much you enjoy the theme park also depends on just how scared and gut-shaken you want to be: rides such as *Rita-Queen of Speed*, *Runaway Mine Train* and the infamous *Air* will have your stomach performing somersaults.

Disabled parking is available for Blue Badge holders in the express parking area, close to the main entrance. Guest Services is located just inside the park entrance and they'll provide all the access information you need and are always happy to answer queries. You can borrow manual wheelchairs from them. All the park's toilets are wheelchair-accessible.

CADBURY WORLD, BIRMINGHAM

Address: Linden Rd, Bournville, Birmingham B30 2LU **Website:** www.cadburyworld.co.uk
Telephone: 0845 450 3599 **Hours:** vary throughout the year (check website) **Dates:** daily
Mar–Oct, variable closures Nov–Feb (check website for details) **Entry fees:** [D]£13 [H]free
[A]£13 [4-15s]£9.95 [C]£10

Visiting Cadbury's chocolate factory in the heart of Bournville, where they boast the
biggest chocolate shop in the world, is the stuff of childhood dreams. Although Cadbury World is essentially for children and provides the closest they'll get in real life to
Willy Wonka's chocolate factory, there's plenty to see and do for the adults.

For a commercial operation, largely conceived to encourage you to consume more
chocolate, the tour combines amusements, heritage and education in a surprisingly appetising way. Divided into fourteen zones, from the *Aztec Forest* (chocolate's origins),
via *The Cadbury Story* (Quaker work ethics and workforce welfare) to *Essence* (create
your own confectionery), you're going to learn a lot about chocolate here – though not,
apparently, much about cacao plantations or the cocoa trade. You'll leave with detailed
insights into how chocolate is made, how Cadbury came to be and the Quaker beliefs
that made Bournville what it is today. And you'll also get plenty of free chocolate.

Queues can sometimes be a problem in school holidays but priority queues for
wheelchair-users or others requiring assistance are usually set up. Facilities are largely
inclusive and the whole place is accessible for all, with just two exceptions: the staircase
to the factory packaging facility and the exclusively fixed seating in the picnic area outside. If you're bringing your assistance dog, note that it won't be allowed in production
areas, though they will provide a dog-sitter while you visit those parts of the site.

> " The Cadbury World exhibition tells you the story of how John Cadbury
> invented his famous chocolates. It takes about an hour to get around,
> and it is a fabulous journey with lots of different sights and sounds. Apart from
> a small area of the packaging plant, the attraction is fully accessible to those
> in wheelchairs, with lifts throughout and accessible toilets. You can take a ride
> through a magical land called Cadabra, where one of the Beanmobiles has been
> adapted for wheelchair access.
>
> In the World's Biggest Cadbury Shop there are bargains and souvenirs to buy
> and the Cadbury Café is a pleasant place to relax. I think Essence is the best
> thing about Cadbury World. It tells the story of how Dairy Milk was first thought
> up, and as you are leaving the area you enter a room where you can invent your
> own cup of chocolate mixture, using sweets and liquid chocolate. Cadbury
> World is great for chocolate addicts and anyone who is a child at heart. "
>
> *Reader Review from Katie Fraser*

CALKE ABBEY

Address: Ticknall, Derby, Derbyshire DE73 7LE **Website:** www.nationaltrust.org.uk/calke
Telephone: 01332 863 822 **Hours:** House Sat–Wed 12.30–5pm, closed Thurs & Fri; park daily
dawn–dusk (check website for details) **Dates:** Mar–Oct (check website for details) **Entry fees:**
[D]£8.50 [H]free [A]£8.50 [5–15s]£4.20 [C]8.50

If you want to visit a grand country house with breathtaking views and a real range of
interesting diversions for kids as well as adults, you won't do much better than Calke
Abbey, which was built on the site of an old abbey and dates from 1704.

On arrival you're immediately struck by the faded grandeur of your surroundings.
Tucked in the heart of the Derbyshire countryside, this magnificent Baroque mansion
was donated to the National Trust in the 1980s by its owners who were struggling to
maintain it (they'd only added electricity twenty years earlier). Apart from arresting
any further decline in the condition of the house, the Trust has preserved much of its
appearance as it was then, partly to exhibit the decline of the stately home in the twentieth-century. Crammed in the house is a treasure trove of fine art, extraordinary satirical
cartoons, some ostentatious furniture, an extensive collection of stuffed animals and a
wide variety of other oddities. Outside, look out for the old ice house in the garden.

Sufficient disabled parking is located next to the main reception which also has wheelchairs available. If you need assistance, a special mobility cart can take you to any part of
the grounds. Inside, the evocative surrounds of the ground floor are fairly easily accessible, but the upper floor is more difficult to get to. With no lift, you'll need to be able to
navigate a large oak staircase to get up there. Although a shame if you can't access the
upper rooms, it doesn't make a visit futile. However, do ask staff to provide you with
the virtual tour, if only to see the magnificent silk bed. If your mobility does permit
the climb, there is a manual wheelchair available at the top of the stairs. If you fancy
eating the great, locally produced food in the restaurant it might be best to plan a visit
at a quieter time.

CHARLECOTE PARK

Address: Warwick, Warwickshire CV35 9ER **Website:** www.nationaltrust.org.uk/main/w-
charlecotepark **Telephone:** 01789 470277 **Hours:** Fri–Tues, park & gardens from 10.30am,
house from noon (closed Wed & Thurs) **Dates:** park & gardens throughout the year, house
Mar–Oct and 6–21 Dec (check website for details) **Entry fees:** [D]£7.45 [H]free [A]£7.45
[5–15s]£3.70 [C]£7.45

Charlecote Park is a remarkable, seven-hundred-year old estate with a superbly main-
tained Tudor mansion and exquisite gardens. A few miles east of Stratford (Shakespeare
is said to have been caught poaching in the park), it is surrounded by a landscaped deer
park and well-planted gardens and grounds.

Inside the house, the décor is preserved in all the heavy, Elizabethan-style Victorian refurbishment of the mid-nineteenth century. It contains a vast collection of portrait paintings and antiques, all still owned by the Lucy family, for whom Charlecote has been the family home since the fourteenth century. You can participate in traditional Tudor games on Capability Brown's formal lawns, and there are acres of space to take a picnic or go for a country walk. On days when the house is open, the main tours start at 11am and last for an hour, when it opens to non-guided visitors. Throughout the year, tours of the outbuildings, costume talks, deer safaris, family trails and other park activities keep visitors busy and entertained.

On arrival, disabled parking is available in the grounds, with a 200m transfer (which can be arranged for you). There are three disabled toilets. Paths and doorways are wide and smooth enough for manual and electric wheelchairs alike, with ramped access to everywhere but the second floor of the house (no lift). Large print and Braille guides are available for those with impaired vision. Great care has been taken to make as much of the property as possible accessible to all, including the tractor safari, which has ramped access to the passenger carriage. Paths in the grounds, though, are mostly of gravel and not all easy for unassisted manual wheelchairs. The shop, and the restaurant with its pleasant patio, are reasonably accessible.

CHATSWORTH HOUSE

Address: Bakewell, Derbyshire DE45 1PP **Website:** www.chatsworth.org **Telephone:** 01246 565300 **Hours:** park open daily; house daily 11am–5.30pm; garden 11am–6pm (last admissions one hour earlier) **Dates:** closed 24 Dec–mid-Mar **Entry fees:** [D]£12.50 [H]free [A]£12.50 [5–15s]£6.50 [C]£10.50

Chatsworth House, on the edge of the Peak District in Derbyshire, is a vast, extraordinarily handsome mansion, dating back to the seventeenth century. It's deservedly popular and a highly recommended day out – though ideally out of the major visiting periods, to give yourself some breathing space.

Owned by the Duke and Duchess of Devonshire, the house has been updated and

Chatsworth House and grounds

> *The Chatsworth website advises people with disabilities to contact Kirstie before booking tickets. We are so glad we followed that advice, because we had an amazing day out. We think that every attraction should have a Kirstie. From the moment we arrived until we made our weary way home, the day was magical.*
>
> *When we arrived the gateman was expecting us. He introduced us to one of the house guides who gave us a personal tour of the ground floor before delivering us to another guide who took us in a lift to the top floor. The gateman had earlier helped us with restaurant reservations for lunch, so we could avoid long queues. Anyone in a wheelchair will understand how difficult dining out can be, and how much it was appreciated that careful thought had been put into seating us at a fully accessible table at the edge of the room.*
>
> *After lunch we explored the garden, which has well-marked accessible routes for wheelchair users.*
>
> Reader Review from Pamela Crampton

expanded over the centuries, but the current incarnation remains a harmonious whole. The interior includes showpiece exhibits like the four-poster bed in which George II died and the Great Dining Room, set as it was for the visit of George V and Queen Mary in 1933. An enduring highlight is the magnificent collection of paintings, including works by Tintoretto, Van Dyck and even Rembrandt – his *Portrait of an Old Man* hangs in the chapel. The house is surrounded by magnificent grounds, with a wide range of attractions, from a grotto and artificial waterfall through to a nursery and assorted greenhouses. The excellent online access guide includes a clear map indicating the location of benches, gradients, accessible toilets and other details.

Disabled parking is close to the entrance to the house and there are accessible toilets nearby, as well as in the restaurant and at the farmyard. An adapted golf buggy can take visitors from the lodge up the hill to the shops and refreshments, while a wheelchair-accessible trailer offers rides to the woods and lakes behind the house. Access to the house is a little trickier, though the north wing can be accessed by a ramp at the Orangery shop. If you can't do stairs, you can arrange a full-access visit in advance. All the refreshment venues and shops have flat access and, with the exception of the garden shop, have plenty of space. The main children's attraction, the farmyard and adventure playground, has a lift and ramp access.

CLENT HILLS ALL-ABILITY TRAILS

Address: Nimmings Wood car park, between Hagley and Bromsgrove, Worcestershire **Website:** www.nationaltrust.org.uk/main/w-clenthills **Telephone:** 01562 712825 Dedicated access tel: 07747 693514 **Hours:** café daily 10am–4pm **Dates:** trails open throughout the year **Entry fees:** free, paid car park at Nimmings Wood (no discounts)

The Clent Hills provide a fine chance to escape from Birmingham and other regional cities. They roll across nearly four hundred acres of woodland and grassland and, at up

THE WEST MIDLANDS & THE PEAK DISTRICT

to 300m altitude, provide superb panoramic views in every direction, from the Black Country and Birmingham to the Welsh Borders.

Nimmings Wood car park is not the easiest place to find, but once you've navigated the small country lanes, tight bends and steep hills to get to the car park, it becomes clear why the Clent Hills are such a draw. The views of the surrounding area are truly spectacular from the car park, and after a twenty-minute stroll up the accessible trail, the rewards are even better. Up here, too, you'll find the Standing Stones, a faux-megalithic circle created as a folly. The woodland is rich in wildlife, with buzzards a regular sight above the tree canopy. As well as the accessible trail, there are miles of paths to navigate if you're able to explore further. The hills are much loved locally, and provide a regular outdoor escape for many Brummies – everyone will tell you a trip up here isn't complete without a bacon butty from the café by the car park.

You may want to call ahead to get clear directions to Nimmings Wood car park. The accessible trail itself runs about 800m up the hill and back down again and you should be prepared for very hard going after rain. The path may by "accessible", but it's rough, and isn't always suitable for an unassisted manual wheelchair. More warnings: the car park's accessible toilets are relatively small and awkward to negotiate for wheelchair-users and the café counter is up a step.

CRICH TRAMWAY VILLAGE

Address: Town End Crich, Matlock, Derbyshire DE4 5DP **Website:** www.tramway.co.uk **Telephone:** 01773 854321 **Hours:** daily 10am–5.30pm (with variations; see website) **Dates:** closed Nov–mid-Feb **Entry fees:** [D]£10 [H]free [A]£10 [3–15s]£5 [C]£9 (12 months free repeat admission)

No visit to the Derbyshire countryside is complete without taking in the sights and sounds of the national tramway museum; this is a hugely enjoyable day for children, vehicle-buffs and non-devotees alike. Moreover, Crich has gone to great lengths to be accessible to people with restricted mobility.

Supported by visitor fees and donations, the Tramway Museum Society (a registered charity) has preserved Crich village as a living museum of vintage vehicles and of tram-era life. They've amassed an extensive collection of trams from around the UK and all over the world to provide fascinating insights into the role played by trams in the transport network. You can see the restoration work the museum is undertaking on several vehicles. During the early 1990s the museum bought an old Berlin tram, which has now been adapted with a lift to allow access to wheelchair-users (if you're exceptionally keen, and have sufficient mobility, you can even sign up for a driving-experience day and learn to pilot a tram). Once you've had a stroll around the village and got your fill of trams, you could try to find a table in the tea rooms, or perhaps withdraw to the *Red Lion* for a pint.

Parking is reasonable and the museum has built a wheel-way path across its cobbles for the benefit of wheelchair-users. Wheelchairs can be borrowed for a small deposit and the friendly staff are always on hand to address any questions. Lifts have been fitted over the workshop so that you can access the viewing gallery.

CROMFORD CANAL, DERBYSHIRE

Address: Cromford Wharf, Matlock DE4 4LS **Website:** www.derbyshire-peakdistrict.co.uk/cromfordcanal.htm **Telephone:** 01629 823204 **Hours:** no closures **Dates:** no closures **Entry fees:** free

Picturesque and enchanting are the words that most aptly describe the Cromford canal, as it flows through the Derbyshire countryside. The gentle stroll along the towpath is the perfect, low-key outdoor trip.

The canal, completed in 1794, provided a link with the Erewash canal and nearby Derby and Nottingham. At its terminus in Cromford, the canal is close to Cromford Mill – the world's first hydro-powered spinning mill – which provided the mill with a necessary transport link. Close by is Leawood Pumphouse, with its fine old beam engine that used to maintain the water level in the canal. It's been restored and is usually fired up on busy days in the summer, to the delight of enthusiasts. You can walk the nine kilometres from Cromford to Ambergate, of which the first three kilometres, as far as High Peak Junction, are suitable for wheelchairs. Natural history enthusiasts will enjoy the diversity of wildlife in the area, renowned for its butterflies and dragonflies; the southern, less accessible stretch, between Whatstandwell and Ambergate, runs through a Site of Special Scientific Interest managed by Derbyshire Wildlife Trust.

Sufficient disabled parking can be found at Cromford Wharf, which also has an accessible RADAR-key toilet. The well-compacted towpath can be navigated reasonably well, whether you're on foot or in a wheelchair. At the wharf there's an accessible tea room where you can read up about the canal and its history before setting off. Although you need to take care on some stretches of the path, most of it is very easy to get along and there are benches at intervals if you need to take a breather.

Cromford Canal

CROOME PARK

Address: Croome D'Abitot, Worcestershire WR8 9DW **Website:** www.nationaltrust.org.
uk/main/w-croomepark **Telephone:** 01905 371006 **Hours:** Apr–Aug daily 10am–5.30pm; Mar,
Sept, Oct Wed–Sun 10am–5.30pm; Nov–Jan Sat & Sun 10am–4pm (open from 26 Dec–1 Jan
10am–5.30pm) **Dates:** closed 22–25 Dec and 2 Jan **Entry fees:** [D]£4.35 [H]free [A]£4.35
[5–15s]£2.15 [C]£4.35

Work started on Croome Park in 1751, but even though it has been in place for so long,
it has perhaps not previously received the full recognition it deserves. With much work
being put into the grounds, however, it is now being seen for the superb example of Capability Brown's landscaping that it is. The fine Worcestershire countryside all around
only adds to the appeal, and Croome Court, the house – also designed by Capability
Brown – is likely to open to the public soon.

Croome is famous as Brown's first design triumph, before his career took off and he
transformed many country estates. The property in its entirety covers around 650 acres,
but the "pleasure ground" area, taking in all the sights, is a very manageable, two-hour
walk. Along the route, you'll encounter an array of architectural, sculptural and natural
delights, including the Church of St Mary Magdalene (a Brown design), the Temple
Greenhouse (Robert Adam) and a stunning lake at the bottom of the property (Brown
again). Recent restoration work has seen a 1940s theme emerge, with the visitor centre
now in the old RAF buildings. There's a World War II-style English canteen, too, serving superb, locally sourced meals, cakes and drinks.

A great amount of thought and effort has been put into making Croome as accessible
as possible while keeping its original feel. The reception building, canteen and toilets
all have wide entrances, and most of the paths around the estate are smooth enough for
self-propelling manual wheelchair-users. There is a steep hill on the way down to the
lake, however, and the ramps over the lakes offer little ground clearance and can be a
pain to negotiate for some wheelchairs. The staff are extremely friendly and knowledgeable, however, happily helping to find alternative routes around the grounds.

HOO FARM

Address: Preston-on-the-Weald Moors, Telford, Shropshire TF6 6DJ **Website:** www.hoofarm.
com **Telephone:** 01952 677917 **Hours:** Tues–Sun, Mar–Sept 10am–6pm, Sept–Nov 10am–
5pm, closed Mon **Dates:** closed Dec–Feb (special openings for Halloween and Christmas, check
website for details) **Entry fees:** [D] £5.25 [H] £5.25 [A] £5.75 [2-14s]£5.25 [C] £5.50

Hoo Farm is one of an enterprising band of farms up and down the country that have
turned land over to the creation of farm-themed family attractions. The formula is
pretty simple – play areas and activities to keep everyone busy, and lots of animals.
And it works.

You can easily spend a whole day on Hoo Farm. As well as the standard pigs, sheep, goats, cows and ducks to visit, and the obligatory rabbits and guinea pigs to pet, it is home to a surprising variety of wildlife, including foxes, owls and deer – and unexpected exotic creatures, such as meerkats and peacocks. If you want to see all the animals, you may need to drag your kids away from the play areas, sandpits and bouncy farm. There is a timetable of events throughout the day – including animal-feeding, pony rides (extra fees), and the like. The highlight has to be the sheep steeplechase, where visitors bet on their favourite woolly wonder, then cheer as they jump helter-skelter over fences, topped by woollen "riders" bobbing entertainingly on their backs.

There is disabled parking with three bays right next to the entrance. If you need one, you can hire a manual wheelchair. Access around the site is level, though wheelchair-users may require assistance on the gravel paths, and the wooded areas can get muddy in wet weather. Hand-washing facilities are at an appropriate height. The tearooms (open school holidays and weekends) are accessible but cramped so you might prefer to bring your own picnic. Lastly, there are wheelchair-accessible toilets just inside the entrance.

IRONBRIDGE GORGE MUSEUMS

Address: various locations around Ironbridge Gorge **Website:** www.ironbridge.org.uk **Telephone:** 01952 884391 **Hours:** daily 10am–5pm **Dates:** closed 25–26 Dec and 1 Jan (some museums closed Nov–Mar) **Entry fees:** unlimited 12-month entry to all museums [D]half-price [H]half-price [A]£14.95 [C]£9.95–£12.95 [5–18s]£9.95; individual museum prices from £1.95 to £10.50 – see website for details

This part of the Severn Gorge, south of Telford, was where the Industrial Revolution began after Abraham Darby I perfected the art of using coke to smelt iron. It is most famous as the site of the first cast-iron bridge, opened in 1781. The heavy industries that filled the gorge with furnaces and smoke may have long since disappeared, but the region still offers a chance to enter a bygone age. Awarded UNESCO World Heritage status in 1986, the Ironbridge Gorge is today home to ten museums celebrating the area's unique industrial past. To really do it justice you need a couple of days to explore, but a day-trip will allow you to take in the highlights.

Any visit to the area has to start with the Iron Bridge itself. This impressive and graceful structure is easily recognised as the symbol of the Industrial Revolution. The Toll House on the south side of the river provides an overview of the history of the bridge but does not have the best access. For the bigger picture, head to the Museum of the Gorge, along the main road in the village. The audiovisual displays here explain the area's significance in world history and why it was designated a World Heritage Site. Car parks at both the bridge and Museum of the Gorge are pay & display, but free for Blue Badge holders. The Iron Bridge can be crossed by wheelchair-users but has a steep, 1 in 8 slope to its crest. The exhibition area of the Museum of the Gorge is level and fully accessible.

Nearby Coalbrookdale was at the heart of industry – this is where you'll find Darby's original Old Furnace as well as the impressive Museum of Iron and the area's newest attraction, *Enginuity*, both housed in former buildings of the mighty Coalbrookdale ironworks. The Museum of Iron interprets the importance of the early iron industry, while the interactive *Enginuity* exhibit allows children to get stuck in and explore the workings of modern-day objects. Both museums are fully accessible to wheelchair-users and are well worth a visit.

At Blists Hill Victorian Town you can enjoy a slice of life as it was a century ago, with authentically recreated stores, workshops and characters in period dress. Not all the buildings are easily accessed – ask for the excellent Physical Access Guide at reception for full details. There's a steep incline part way through the town which is unsuitable for unaccompanied wheelchair-users. However, period transport – either horse-drawn or Model T Ford bus – is often available, and free for disabled visitors. Otherwise, it's possible to return to the main entrance, go by car to the staff car park, and enter the Lower Town from there. This must be arranged in advance through the entrance staff.

Down the hill, the Coalport China Museum houses examples of the finest work of the former factory. There is also a Social History gallery and a very good "learning through play" area for kids. Over the river, the Jackfield Tile Museum showcases decorative tiles in a surprisingly engaging fashion with various sets, including an underground station, a butcher's shop and a pub. New lifts were installed at the museums in 2007, making them both now fully accessible. Both also provide hands-on opportunities, with pre-booked workshops and drop-ins during school holidays. The ceramic workshops at Coalport include adapted potter's wheels, suitable for wheelchair-users to have a go on.

Once you're in the Ironbridge Gorge, you're likely to require a car to get between the museums, even those close to each other. The obstacles include uneven surfaces, lack of pavements and steps everywhere. There are disabled parking bays at all the museums, though there's little suitable parking elsewhere if the car parks are full. All the main museums have disabled toilets. You can find accessible cafés at Blists Hill, Jackfield and the Museum of Iron. The fully accessible *Coalport Youth Hostel*, next to the China Museum, also has an accessible café, serving home-made food. It's open at weekends and during school holidays, 10am–4pm.

PEDALABIKEAWAY, FOREST OF DEAN

Address: Cannop Valley, near Coleford, Gloucestershire GL16 7EH **Website:** www. pedalabikeaway.co.uk **Telephone:** 01594 860026 Dedicated access tel: 01989 770357 **Hours:** Apr–Oct 9am–6pm, Nov–Mar 9am–5pm **Dates:** closed Mon (except Jul–Aug and all school holidays) **Entry fees:** [H]free; other prices dependent on bike choice, see website for details

In the middle of the picturesque Forest of Dean, the Pedalabikeaway centre offers a range of bikes to hire and caters for visitors with disabilities. Their family cycling trail is a popular route – anyone with a bike can do it – with more challenging side routes to try out.

Pedalabikeaway offers the opportunity to try different cycles, from tandems (good for people with hearing or sight impairments who have a steering companion at the front) to trikes. The main, twenty-kilometre circular cycle trail (allow a couple of hours) winds through the forest scenery, with picnic areas scattered around the paths and clearings. The trails are a mix of smooth forest floor and steeper, undulating-to-hilly trails for the tougher enthusiasts. Trails take riders though the changing deciduous and conifer woodland with autumn an especially nice time of year to visit as the fallen leaves make for a slightly softer ride. Other cyclists along the trail tend to be few and far between, making this a perfect getaway in very pretty surroundings.

On arrival there are plenty of Blue Badge parking bays available, all very near to the bike-hire shop and reception (which has a step at the entrance and also houses the café). You should call ahead to book if you want to hire an accessible bike as numbers are limited. The disabled toilet is a good size and clean, but it doubles as the ladies changing room. The biggest obstacle to access is the occasionally rather rough condition of the trail, which is also moderately hilly – front steerers on sight-impaired tandems and rear pushers on wheelchair-tandem bikes will find it hard going, especially in damp conditions. Before you set off, be sure to get the map, and have a chat to the helpful staff about suitable routes.

RAF MUSEUM, COSFORD

Address: RAF Museum, Cosford, Shropshire TF11 8UP **Website:** www.rafmuseum.org.uk
Telephone: 020 8205 2266 Dedicated access tel: 01902 376200 **Hours:** Visitor Centre
10am–5pm; Test Flight 10am–5.30pm; War Planes 10am–5.30 pm; Cold War 10am–6pm;
Hangar One 10am–6pm; Fun 'n' Flight Interactive Mon–Fri 10am–4pm, Sat & Sun 11am–4pm
Dates: closed 24–26 Dec and early Jan (check website for details) **Entry fees:** free

If you like aviation or aircraft, a visit to the Royal Airforce Museum at Cosford should be right at the top of your list, but even non-aviation buffs are likely to leave with a clearer sense of the reality of active service.

Over seventy aircraft are housed in four buildings with the exhibits laid out to be easily accessible to the ambulant, semi-ambulant or full-time wheelchair users. With aircraft on display ranging from the experimental to those used in active service, it's easy to imagine what it must have been like to be on board during action. Even captured enemy aircraft are on display, providing an interesting comparison with the British planes on show. There are also engines, missiles and military vehicles and numerous interactive displays to keep the kids occupied. After a good look around, there's a coffee shop and visitor centre with the usual opportunities to take away a memento of your day. This is the sister site to the RAF Museum in Hendon, north London.

Cosford requires a fair amount of transferring between the buildings. Access to the visitor centre from the conveniently located disabled parking spaces is along a downhill tarmac path. Pedestrian entry is through a rotating door but there's a separate entrance for wheelchair-users. The four museum buildings (each has accessible toilets) are level-access and spacious, although in one of them the pedestrian walkways could be better indicated for visually impaired visitors. The one split-level building housing the Cold War exhibition has a lift giving access to a very effective viewing gallery. The overall site has a slight gradient and some visitors may find the return trip to the car park quite steep.

RAF Museum, Cosford

ROYAL SHAKESPEARE COMPANY, STRATFORD-UPON-AVON

Address: The Courtyard Theatre, Southern Lane, Stratford-upon-Avon, Warwickshire CV37 6BB
Website: www.rsc.org.uk **Telephone:** 0844 800 1114 Dedicated access tel: 01789 403436
Hours: vary, check website for details **Dates:** vary, check website for details **Entry fees:** [D]£14
[H]£14 [A]varies between £5-£42; check website for details

The Royal Shakespeare Company is one of the most prominent publicly funded theatre companies in the UK, aiming to keep Shakespeare's work at the forefront of British theatre. RSC productions are extremely popular and you should book disabled seats as far ahead as possible.

The Courtyard theatre is a 1000-seater temporary structure making way for the new Royal Shakespeare Theatre across the road. The new theatre is set to be complete in 2010 but until then the Courtyard is an impressive and beautifully designed stand-in, blending industrial-style theatre space with traditional notes. The atmosphere of the theatre is one of energy and informality, reflected in all the productions, with their envelopment of the audience in the action on stage. As well as Shakespeare, the RSC puts on a variety of plays by contemporary writers – a total of some eight to ten productions each year, with recent appearances by the likes of David Tennant and Sir Ian McKellen.

The theatre has disabled parking, with further Blue Badge bays directly outside. Arriving late before the performance can be a problem, however, with the road cluttered up with cars and coaches. Once you're inside, every aspect of your RSC experience is likely to be straightforward and enjoyable, from the low-level reception desk to the wide corridors throughout the building and the excellent visibility from the disabled seats. The disabled toilets, located on every level, are clean and spacious, and the bars are low-level, close to the disabled seating, and don't seem to get too crowded.

Shakespeare's Globe, London

Address: 21 New Globe Walk, Bankside, London, ES1 9DT
Website: www.shakespearesglobe.org **Telephone:** 020 7902 1400
Dedicated access tel: 020 7902 1409 **Hours:** varies (check website for details)
Dates: varies (check website for details) **Entry fees:** ticket prices vary

If the RSC is up your street, a visit to the Globe Theatre in London is a must. A completely authentic copy of Shakespeare's theatre, the Globe is connected to an ultra-modern complex so as to be totally accessible. It's stunningly situated on the South Bank too, with breathtaking views of many of the iconic buildings of twenty-first-century London. The very brave can watch in the pit (standing only) where you may be moved around by actors, scenery or fellow viewers, or rained on, as the play unfolds. Wheelchair-users or those with limited mobility can book a seat in one of the "Gentleman's Rooms", where you can look down on the stage and the rabble in comfort. You will be escorted there through fascinating backstage areas, possibly getting the chance to speak to the odd actor, and accompanied out at the end.

SHUGBOROUGH ESTATE

Address: Shugborough, Milford, Stafford, Staffordshire ST17 0XB **Website:** www.shugborough.org.uk **Telephone:** 01889 881388 **Hours:** open daily from 20 March 2009 (check website for details) **Dates:** for 2009 closure dates, check website in advance **Entry fees:** [D]£9.50 [H]free [A]£12 [5–16s]£7 [C]£9.50

The expansive Shugborough Estate in Staffordshire is a historic farm estate, restored as far as visitor comfort will allow to eighteenth-century conditions, with costumed workers, the food in the café and the cheese-making methods all traditional.

Shugborough could be cheesy in tone, too, but the staff's evident enthusiasm (the character guides are based on historical staff from the estate) and the genuinely illuminating way they bring history to life keeps it all fresh and enjoyable. The day is structured around various scheduled events, each one offering you the chance to participate: give a helping hand with the cheese-making in the servants' quarters; try your hand at milking a cow; see how the flour mill operated; and watch the ironmonger at work in the forge. You'll have the opportunity to see what it was like to live as a servant, and outside there are plenty of farm animals to keep the children entertained. For a drink or snack, visit the *Lady Walk Tearoom* with its historically inspired menu, including game pie and steak and ale pie. For a gobstopper or a stick of licorice, call at Mrs Fagan's Sweet Shop.

On arrival, disabled parking is available next to the reception. The estate is big, and there's an accessible shuttle and land train service to transfer to the house. Alternatively, the walk is relatively smooth and takes in some lovely countryside. Many of the estate buildings are listed, which inevitably means that some are inaccessible to wheelchair-users – including the mill and the manor house. Some provision has been made to overcome this, with a stair-climber available at the manor house for example (though unaided transfer is needed to use it). Ramps are placed where possible and alternative routes are indicated by the helpful staff. There are two disabled toilets, though at opposite ends of the estate.

THINKTANK, BIRMINGHAM

Address: Millennium Point, Curzon Street, Birmingham B4 7XG **Website:** www.thinktank.ac **Telephone:** 0121 202 2222 **Hours:** daily 10am–5pm **Dates:** closed 24–26 Dec **Entry fees:** [D]£7.25 [H]free [A]£9.25 [3–15s]£7.25 [C]£7.25

ThinkTank, the rebranded Birmingham Science Museum, dates from 2001. Covering the sweep of past, present and future science and technology, it has ten zones, bursting with interactive displays and activities, spread over four floors: ThinkBack, ThinkHere, ThinkNow and ThinkAhead. Allow at least a half day, and longer if possible.

Although often awash with young children, there is plenty to engage big kids and adults as well, with many of the zones and interactive displays being aimed at older

Warwick Castle

guests, and events run specifically for adult education such as "My friend MEG, the mind reader", a neuroscience presentation. ThinkTank's coverage is diverse, and ranges from the steam machinery of the Industrial Revolution that created Birmingham, down in ThinkBack on level 0, to explorations of the workings of the human body in Things about Me in ThinkNow, on level 2. Multimedia shows at the in-house planetarium in ThinkAhead, on level 3 (additional modest payment), are utterly compelling. Think-Tank's education programme is also multi-level, with a schools programme, lectures and family activities and events.

On arrival, there is plenty of Blue Badge parking near the entrance. ThinkTank, created in partnership with the visual-impairment specialists at Queen Alexandra College, is a beacon of great design, with every element crafted to ensure accessibility. The displays, for example, are unusually low-level, enabling wheelchair-users to see into the glass cabinets. In addition there's plenty of free space around the exhibits, and captions and text on the walls are generally low-level and large. The accessible toilets are spacious and clean and the café has a low counter for easy access.

WARWICK CASTLE

Address: Warwick, Warwickshire CV34 4QU **Website:** www.warwick-castle.co.uk **Telephone:** 0870 442 2000 **Hours:** daily 10am–6pm **Dates:** closed 25 Dec **Entry fees:** [D]£17.95 [H]free [A]£17.95 [4–16s]£10.95 [C]£12.95

The great mass of Warwick Castle still keeps an eye on the town of Warwick as it did hundreds of years ago. Built in 1068 by William the Conqueror, fortified in the fourteenth century and restored in the nineteenth century to the magnificent sandstone hulk you see today, the castle is a perennially popular and lively attraction.

Owned by the same entertainment operators who manage Alton Towers and Madame Tussaud's, Warwick Castle tries to be more than a historical site – indeed some visitors think it's anything but. With its period-costumed character guides hamming it up and lashings of additional entertainment, it may not be David Starkey or Simon Schama, but it's still a lot of fun, and the voices of minstrels and jesters and the clash of battling knights all add to a slightly frenetic and robustly commercial, theme-park atmosphere that kids in particular love. Whenever you visit, there'll be a lot going on, both inside the castle itself and beyond the walls, in the relatively peaceful grounds where lawns and woods sweep down to the river. If you go to River Island though, the jousting and merriment is likely to be in full swing: you may even get to watch the firing of the trebuchet – the world's largest siege machine. Do try to see *Kingmaker 1471* – the multimedia show – which gives some insight into the lives of those for whom the castle was home.

There's accessible parking on-site (£3) and Blue Badge bays in Warwick town centre. The castle has some tricky access issues, particularly if you have reduced mobility, and steps and narrow corridors prevent access to some areas, especially to wheelchair-users. However the grounds have hard paths and most gradients aren't steep. For those with visual impairments a touch tour can be arranged in advance. The castle has some manual wheelchairs available for loan and there's plenty of seating and good handrails on some of the difficult steps.

WORCESTER PORCELAIN MUSEUM

Address: Severn Street, Worcester, Worcestershire WR1 2NE **Website:** www.worcesterporcelain museum.org.uk **Telephone:** 01905 746000 **Hours:** Mon–Sat 9am–5.30pm, Sun 11am–5pm **Dates:** closed Easter Sunday and 25–26 Dec **Entry fees:** [D]£4.25 [H]free [A]£5.00 [5–15s]free with paint-a-plate, from £4 [C]4.25

Tucked away in the heart of Worcester, this museum and visitor centre both showcases a traditional English craft, and provides a retail heaven for the bargain-hunting house-proud.

Visitors to the Porcelain Museum learn a great deal about the history of porcelain – the super-heated version of pottery that turns much of the clay to a kind of glass and give it its shiny, brittle translucence. It's a lot more interesting than it might sound. An expert introduction recounts the history of porcelain and the founding of the Royal Worcester factory in the 1750s. Cabinets display intricately detailed pieces made for Lord Nelson, Queen Victoria and other notables. The centre runs paint-a-plate activity sessions (£4 for a plate, or £8 for a model), principally intended for children, though artistically inclined adults are welcome to join in (unfortunately the studio has stairs-only access). If you want to take some professionally finished porcelain home as well as your painted efforts, a visit to the adjacent Bestware shop or seconds and clearance shop should probably be on your agenda – though beware of buying plates that don't lie flat on the table.

Once you've navigated the narrow one-way streets in the city centre, you'll find two disabled parking bays near the museum. Access to the museum is by a large glass double door that provides level-access entry to the shop which is unfortunately difficult to negotiate for wheelchair-users. The tour encompasses level, spacious areas and access to the upper floor by lift. There's a small change of level on the first floor which can be negotiated by a self-operating platform lift. Stairs at the end of the tour require you to retrace your route if you can't manage them. The café, which has movable furniture, is recommended for good coffee and cakes.

THE SOUTHWEST

- Abbotsbury Swannery
- Avebury Stone Circle
- Blue Pool
- Buckfast Abbey
- The Camel Trail, Padstow
- Crow Beach
- Corinium Museum
- Donkey Sanctuary
- The Eden Project
- Helicopter to the Isles of Scilly
- Looe Beach Wheelchair
- Monkey World Ape Rescue Centre
- Mount Edgcumbe House and Country Park
- Paignton Zoo
- Sherborne Castles and Grounds
- South Devon Railway, Buckfast Butterflies & Dartmoor Otter Sanctuary and Rare Breeds Farm
- SS Great Britain
- Steam Museum of the Great Western Railway
- Stourhead
- Tate St Ives and Barbara Hepworth Museum
- Thermae Bath Spa

FOOD & DRINK ▸▸ Sherborne
FOOD & DRINK ▸▸ Swindon

THE SOUTHWEST

The past is perhaps at its most tangible in England's southwest, where ancient Neolithic sites and charming historic houses pepper the predominantly rural landscape. This handsome region is not one for instantly striking visitors with dramatic scenery and imposing vistas – it settles instead on beguiling them with its genteel towns, bucolic landscapes and crumbling coastline, gently but effectively coaxing them to return time and time again.

ABBOTSBURY SWANNERY

Address: New Barn Road, Abbotsbury, Dorset, DT3 4JG **Website:** www.abbotsbury-tourism. co.uk/swannery.htm **Telephone:** 01305 871858 **Hours:** daily 10am–5pm or 6pm (call to confirm); last admission 1 hour before closing **Dates:** closed 2 Nov–20 Mar **Entry fees:** [D]£8.50 [H]free [A]£9 [5–15s]£6 [C]£8.50

The ballerina Anna Pavlova studied swans at Abbotsbury Swannery in the 1920s for her legendary role in *Swan Lake*. If you come in May or June you're likely to see fluffy cygnets all over the site. But there are plenty of swans all year round, together with a multitude of other birdlife – don't forget your binoculars. And even if birds aren't your thing, it's easy to while away a very pleasant day here.

Low fences throughout mean it's easy to get up close and personal to the birdlife. Along the trails there's plenty of information about birds, wildlife and the history of the swannery – established in the eleventh century by Benedictine monks to supply their dinner table. You'll also come across various display areas, a duck trap and a hide with a window at wheelchair-user level. If you include a feeding time in your visit – either midday or 4pm – you can get hands-on experience feeding the swans while taking in an enthusiastic talk from the swanherd about the set-up. By the disabled car park is a willow maze, with a grass surface, which should keep you and any children entertained for a while, before you finally succumb to the temptations of the cakes in the café.

Abbotsbury is a twin-centred site where the café and shop are separated from the swannery entrance by 400m, so it pays to organise your visit if you have restricted mobility. Disabled parking next to the shop and café is effectively two bays in an adjacent lay-by. To reach the swannery, disabled drivers need to drive the 400m and park in the car park next to the entrance. There are three wheelchairs on loan on a first-come-first-served basis, so it's advisable to arrive as early as you can. The swannery has two very accessible walks, totalling around 800m in length, helpfully on packed gravel paths that only get a little deep and loose in the picnic area.

Abbotsbury Swannery

AVEBURY STONE CIRCLE

Address: near Marlborough, Wiltshire SN8 1RF **Website:** www.nationaltrust.org.uk/main/w-avebury **Telephone:** 01672 539250 **Hours:** stones no closures (museum and gallery daily 10am–5pm, or 10am–4pm Nov–Jan) **Dates:** stones no closures (museum and gallery closed 24–26 Dec) **Entry fees:** free access to the stones; museum and gallery [D]£4.20 [H]free [A]£4.70 [C]£2.35

Avebury is a small village near Marlborough in Wiltshire, built in the middle of a huge Neolithic (new stone age) henge, or stone circle – part of a complex of ancient settlements dating back five thousand years. As you pass the earthworks and standing stones on the main road running through the village, you sense the site's significance: at the height of its importance it was the Neolithic equivalent of St Peter's in Rome, and today visitors still remark about the atmosphere, which becomes particularly magical at dusk.

The National Trust's museum has an interactive exhibition describing the history of the site and its reconstruction in the 1930s while the adjacent gallery exhibits many of the artefacts found during excavations in the area by the archeologist Alexander Keiller. Although now a UNESCO World Heritage Site, and one of the most important megalithic (giant stone) sites in Europe, many of the stones are missing, taken to be used for building materials over the centuries or periodically destroyed because of their pre-Christian origins. Out among the stones, you are free to wander at will, but be aware that the grass can be long and cattle graze in the area, so it can be messy.

Blue Badge holders can use the car park in the High Street; otherwise there's the pay & display National Trust car park 500m away. The village is flat but there are cobbled areas and some narrow pavements. Parts of the henge itself have level access to the stones, which you're free to get right up to. The Trust museum and gallery and the vegetarian café and toilets are all accessible. The *Red Lion* pub serves great food but their toilets are not wheelchair-accessible and the accessible toilets next door lock up at 6pm.

BLUE POOL

Address: Furzebrook, near Wareham Dorset BH20 5AR **Website:** www.bluepooltearooms.co.uk
Telephone: 01929 551408 **Hours:** grounds open 9.30am, teahouse, museum and shop 10am,
closing times vary seasonally **Dates:** 1 Mar–30 Nov; teahouse, museum and shop mid Mar – end
Oct **Entry fees:** [D]free [H]£5 [A]£5 [5–14s]£2.50 [C]£3.80 (family tickets £12.50)

"It's never blue", says the redoubtable Miss Barnard, the owner of the Blue Pool, "it varies between green and turquoise." Whatever you decide the colour is from one moment
to the next, the clay in suspension in this 12m-deep lake renders the water lifeless and
unfit for aquatic plants or animals – or for that matter people swimming. But despite its
inhospitable conditions, its striking appearance and tranquil surrounds undoubtedly
make it worth a visit, if only to soak up the unique atmosphere.

This lozenge-shaped, 200m-long jewel of the Dorset countryside, nestled in the forest, is utterly peaceful, features some substantial woods and heathland to explore, and
has a wonderful time-warped tea room that, in terms of décor and fittings, has hardly
changed since it opened in 1935. Once you've bought your tickets, and possibly had a
look at the small museum of clay and clay-mining, head off around the fifteen-minute
shoreline path encircling this Site of Special Scientific Interest. Keep your eyes open
for various woodland mammals or, if you can identify them, a Dartford warbler or the
exceedingly rare sand lizard.

There's plenty of parking at the entrance but no specific disabled bays. If the fairly
steep slope to the ticket office looks too much, you can ask for the main gate to be
opened and to drive all the way up to the tea room. Three manual wheelchairs are available for loan. All the buildings have level or ramped access, although this may not be
obvious to the casual observer, and they are very proud of the standard of their toilets.
One of the walks around the pool – the Red Route – is wheelchair-accessible, though
the clay surface can get sticky in wet weather. The tea room serves English comfort food
and is accessed through double doors that need unbolting for wheelchair access.

BUCKFAST ABBEY

Address: Buckfastleigh, Devon TQ11 0EE **Website:** www.buckfast.org.uk **Telephone:** 01364
645500 **Hours:** abbey 6am–9pm; shops 9am–5pm; restaurant 10am-4pm **Dates:** no closures
Entry fees: free

This magnificent abbey with its tranquil gardens by the river Dart is a living monastery
with a thousand-year history. A peaceful sanctuary, the abbey is home to a community
of Benedictine monks who have always welcomed guests, and it attracts visitors from
around the globe.

Buckfast Abbey was founded nearly a thousand years ago and stood for five hundred
years until Henry VIII's dissolution of the monasteries. A community of Benedictine
monks returned in 1882 to rebuild it on its medieval foundations. It was completed in

1938. The monks were gifted stone masons, as evidenced throughout the abbey. Don't miss the bronzes and stained-glass windows, the largest of which, at the rear of the abbey, seems to radiate light even on a dull day. The brothers lead a life of study, prayer and work. Their commercial acumen supports them well: in the abbey gift shop you can buy the famous Buckfast tonic wine, honey from the Buckfast hives, biscuits and jam. The Monastic shop, in a restored eighteenth-century mill, sells gifts made by the Buckfast brothers as well as by monks and nuns from across Europe, while the abbey bookshop is the largest religious bookshop in southwest England. Outside, the physic garden, sensory garden and lavender garden all boast interesting designs and unusual plants and herbs – and are as much for the benefit of the monks' work and leisure as for the pleasure of visitors.

The abbey is less than a kilometre from the A38, and has ample free parking. Most of the grounds, gardens and buildings, including the church, and the restaurant, with its twelfth-century arch, are wheelchair-accessible. Accessible toilets are situated at the entrance to the church and beneath the restaurant. The gift shops are reasonably accessible but can be crowded in high summer.

THE CAMEL TRAIL, PADSTOW

Address: Padstow, Cornwall **Website:** www.padstowcyclehire.com or www.trailbikehire.co.uk
Telephone: Padstow Cycle Hire 01841 533533, Trail Bike Hire 01841 532594 **Hours:** no closure dates for trail (for hire shops, check websites) **Dates:** no closure dates for trail (for hire shops, check websites) **Entry fees:** trail free, hire rates vary

Starting from the beautiful setting of Padstow Harbour, the Camel Trail follows a disused railway line along the Camel Estuary. Along the way there's plenty of contrasting scenery and lots of places to stop for a well-earned pasty or pint.

Very popular with cyclists, the trail is a relatively level path with a compacted surface which you can follow to Wadebridge (8km), or more ambitiously Bodmin (18km), or even all the way to the end of the trail in Wenfordbridge, a total of thirty kilometres. Travel as far as Wadebridge and you're on the estuary, with sandbanks, muddy creeks and rocky shores. In winter you can expect to see wigeon, long-tailed duck and goldeneye, as well as divers, grebe and waders. Spring and autumn bring many migrant birds, while in summer the estuary hosts heron, little egret, cormorant, oystercatcher and several species of gull. If you're lucky you may also spot seals at play in the water. Beyond Wadebridge the route is increasingly wooded, before it emerges on the fringes of Bodmin Moor.

Designated parking spaces (£1 per hour) can be found in Padstow at the car park by Rick Stein's fish and chip restaurant – a great place to reward yourself – and disabled toilets are opposite the tourist information centre on the North Quay. The two cycle-hire centres at the start of the trail can offer wheelchairs, bikes with trailers and even, with advance booking, a wheelchair tandem – a rickshaw-like contraption with the wheelchair-user riding up front in comfort, while a companion pedals behind. They also have maps and details of the trail.

CROW BEACH

Address: near Braunton, Devon

❝ *What can be more refreshing than arriving home laden with fresh Devonshire fare, without so much as a penny spent? A beach can be home to a world of free organic fare, ready and waiting to be foraged. We arrived at Crow Beach near Braunton, a beautiful estuary beach looped around a north Devon headland, armed to the hilt with our rakes and buckets; we were in search of cockles.*

This quintessentially British coastal attraction is great for a cheap and fun day out. If you visit as we did on a summer's morning, when the tide is out, your bucket will soon be brimming with the freshest and tastiest cockles imaginable.

If you are arriving in Braunton from Barnstaple, take the first left by the pedestrian crossing, just past the surf shop. Then turn right as you pass the surfing factory toward Velator Quay, and then take the small toll road directly to Crow Beach car park. Disabled access has been considered, with a wooden platform snaking through the sand dunes from the car park, all the way to the beach. ❞

Reader Review from Hamish Smith

CORINIUM MUSEUM

Address: Park Street, Cirencester, Gloucestershire, GL7 2BX **Website:** www.cirencester.co.uk/coriniummuseum **Telephone:** 01285 655611 **Hours:** Mon-Sat 10am–5pm, Sun 2pm–5pm **Dates:** closed 25 Dec (call ahead to check details) **Entry fees:** [D]£3.95 [H]free [A]£3.95 [5–16s]£2 [C]£2.50–£3.10

Crammed with beautiful old buildings, elegant Cirencester is a classic example of a Cotswolds market town, with a wealth of history. The Corinium museum tracks the story of the city from prehistoric times through the nineteenth century, and pays special attention to the town's Roman heritage, reflecting its once significant role as the second largest Roman town, then known as Corinium.

There is a great amount of evidence of the Roman's occupation of the town on show at the museum. The jewellery on display is stunning and there are of course many magnificent mosaics to take in – most being best viewed from the first-floor gallery. The displays are well lit and there are plenty of touch-screen information points as well as hands-on puzzles and games to help hold children's interest. Don't miss the small but charming Roman garden. In 1985, many rare artefacts and over two hundred bodies were unearthed during the discovery of a Saxon cemetery in nearby Lechdale. Following that find, the Saxon gallery at the museum holds the eerily fascinating and painstakingly pieced together figures of a Saxon man and his child, along with the reconstructed grave of a wealthy 'princess' who had been buried with hundreds of expensive possessions. In Medieval times Cirencester was a thriving wool town and home to one of the largest Augustine abbeys in the country. That treasure was sadly destroyed during the dissolution of the monasteries, but thankfully there are some sculptures and carvings left behind to give an idea of its grandeur in the Medieval gallery.

There are only a couple of disabled parking spaces outside the museum, but there are other car parks in the vicinity with disabled spaces. The whole museum, refurbished in recent years, is surprisingly modern and is accessible to wheelchair-users. There is a lift to the first-floor galleries and a ramp down to the Saxon and Medieval galleries, but access to the Roman Garden is tight. An audio presentation on the upper level has a loop system, Braille notices are placed around the museum, large print guides are available as well as audiovisual guides and you'll come across two large print information lecterns too.

THE DONKEY SANCTUARY

Address: Sidmouth, Devon EX10 0NU **Website:** drupal.thedonkeysanctuary.org.uk [omit www.] **Telephone:** 01395 578222 **Hours:** daily 9am–dusk **Dates:** no closures **Entry fees:** free, though donations are welcomed

Founded in 1969, the Donkey Sanctuary at Slade Farm House, Sidmouth, is a charity providing a peaceful home for more than four hundred rescued and unwanted donkeys on nearly a square kilometre of land. You can meet the donkeys and enjoy the outstanding views from the trails.

Start at the visitor centre, where you can pick up a map showing the various trails. Staff can advise on the suitability of the trails depending on your abilities and the weather, but the best ones for wheelchair-users are usually A, C, F and G, which mix paved, hardcore and grass surfaces and moderate slopes. Trail A, the 45-minute central walk, goes down to the main yard and barn, where you'll find the older donkeys. Further on, you'll encounter donkeys with special needs, the hospital and recuperation paddocks, and donkeys for adoption. There are plenty of seats, resting areas, indoor and outdoor picnic areas and a restaurant. Feeding donkeys is discouraged but bins are provided for you to leave suitable treats such as carrots. Trail C features the curiously unkempt-looking Poitou breed, from France, and a maze. This is fun for children: you buy a sealed maze map from the visitor centre for £1 and get your money back if you return the envelope unopened. Most of the trails cross beautiful countryside and Trails F and G have wonderful sea views. As well as donkeys, look out for the mules and the recently acquired Canadian miniature donkeys.

There is plenty of parking for Blue Badge holders less than five minutes from the visitor centre. There's a slight slope down to the centre which can be avoided on your return by using the level path via the adoption paddocks. The sanctuary's maps mark accessible toilets and sheltering points on the various trails. Three manual wheelchairs are available – in summer you should pre-book. Dogs on leads are welcome.

THE SOUTHWEST

THE EDEN PROJECT

Address: Bodelva, St Austell, Cornwall PL24 2SG **Website:** www.edenproject.com **Telephone:** 01726 811911 Dedicated access tel: 01726 818895 **Hours:** summer daily 10am–6pm (last admission 4.30pm), winter daily 10am–4.30pm (later on Fri and weekends) **Dates:** closed 24–26 Dec (check website for maintenance closures) **Entry fees:** [D]£15 [H]free [A]£15 [5–15s]£5 [C]£7–£10 (discounts for those arriving on foot or by bicycle)

The Eden Project's awe-inspiring scale only becomes apparent once you've passed the entrance, at the lip of this cavernous former clay mine. Standing in the landscaped grounds below are the vast, geodesic biomes – colossal, eco-friendly glasshouses – imaginatively and entertainingly showcasing the world's plant-life in all its diversity. Eden is a feel-good, botanical theme park, a registered charity that's low on tat and high on changing the world, and by any standards one of the UK's best family attractions.

The Mediterranean Biome features the sights and scents of warm temperate zones – the Med, the Cape in South Africa and northern California – with herb and vegetable gardens, fruit trees and a vineyard. The Rainforest Biome takes you on a trek through the jungles of Malaysia, West Africa and South America, where huge trees tower overhead, with exhibits on fair trade and deforestation. Don't miss the coffee, bananas and mangoes growing here, or the accessible interactive activities. The rainforest can get extremely warm and humid, but there are plenty of seats to rest on, and there's an air-conditioned refuge in the middle, where you can chill out if the heat gets too much.

Eden has excellent access: on arrival, marshals direct you to parking spaces. Apple 2 car park, closest to the entrance and visitor centre, has Blue Badge parking and manual wheelchairs to borrow. Low-floored park-and-ride buses shuttle between the car parks and there are also buggies to transport people with mobility difficulties. There's excellent food at numerous accessible restaurants and cafés, where the bulk of the produce is local and organic. Toilets are also plentiful and accessible. There are slopes throughout the site, but these are mostly manageable and most of the few steps and steep gradients have alternative routes. For powered wheelchair- and scooter-users most of Eden is a breeze, while solo manual wheelchair-users can get help from one of Eden's trained volunteers.

The Eden Project

HELICOPTER TO THE ISLES OF SCILLY

Address: British International Heliport, Penzance, Cornwall TR18 3AP **Website:** www.
islesofscillyhelicopter.com **Telephone:** 01736 363871 **Hours:** Mon–Sat several flights each day,
no service on Sun **Dates:** flights throughout the year **Fees:** scenic flights with immediate return,
all passengers £66 (£46 if booked on day of flight, subject to availability); return fares, depending
on length of stay and season [A]from £90–£170 [2–11s]from £65–£105; no disabled or helper
discounts; assistance dogs £63 return

The longest established scheduled helicopter service in the world, from Penzance to the
Isles of Scilly, carries tourists to their holidays and offers scenic flights, as well as serving as
a lifeline for the islands' inhabitants.

The flight itself takes just twenty minutes to either St Mary's or Tresco, some 45
kilometres southwest of Lands End. You soar at remarkably low altitude along the Cornish
coastline, with fabulous views of the castle-like monastery of St Michael's Mount, before
heading out over the sea, swooping over fishing boats and wave-battered rocks. To get the
best view, choose one of the single seats on the left-hand side; or, if you can manage the
walk, there are two seats at the rear with curved windows, giving even better panoramas
of the stunning scenery. Heading back, you take in Lands End, the famous Minack Cliff
Theatre carved into the granite overlooking Porthcurno cove, and dozens of other beaches,
coves and villages. It's a hugely enjoyable, rather self-indulgent way to spend an hour or
two: if you can, try to give yourself a few days on the islands themselves, with their gardens
and idyllic beaches, and leave a little holiday money in Tresco or St Mary's.

The heliport building, just five minutes from the train station, from where there's a
regular shuttle bus (£2), is fully accessible, with a small café and accessible toilet. There
is a pay car park (£7 per day). There are five fairly steep steps up to the helicopter: if you
can manage these, your wheelchair can be taken with you to the door; if you have no
mobility you're transferred into a narrow wheelchair, hoisted into the helicopter, and then
transferred into your seat on board the aircraft.

LOOE BEACH WHEELCHAIR

Address: East Looe Town Trust, the Guildhall, Fore Street, East Looe, Cornwall PL13 1AA
Website: www.looetowncouncil.gov.uk/tourism.htm **Telephone:** East Looe Town Trust 01503
263709 (mornings only); tourist office 01503 262072 **Hours:** 8am–5pm **Dates:** Apr–Sept
Fees: £5 per day (no advance bookings)

Looe is a quaint historic seaside town off the main A38 between Liskeard and Plymouth,
dating back to 1645. Many of its shops and restaurants are in listed buildings and face
each other across lanes only two metres wide but some premises have been wheelchair-
adapted. The sandy beach (which is cleaned daily) is a bucket-and-spade seaside resort,
offering very safe swimming and popular with holidaymakers of all ages.

In 2007 the East Looe Town Trust obtained an all-terrain wheelchair for use on the
beach. The chair is sturdy and comfortable and has large, ball-like wheels. It can't be
self-propelled so you need a helper to assist you – and staff are not available to help
to lift or transfer people from their own wheelchairs into the beach wheelchair. The
transfer is straightforward enough, however, and once you're in, your assistant will find
manoeuvring the wheelchair easy enough – even across soft sand and down to the sea if
you want to dip your toes or try something more adventurous. Turning the wheelchair
is tricky at first, but easier with practice, and the experience of using a wheelchair on
the beach is great fun.

Looe has two car parks but only limited spaces near the beach. The chair is available
from the beach workshop close to the lifeboat station. Wheelchair-accessible toilets are
close by. Unfortunately, you're not allowed to take the wheelchair into town and the fact
that there is only one means you should turn up early to have a good chance of hiring
it, especially on a sunny summer's day.

MONKEY WORLD APE RESCUE CENTRE

Address: near Wool, Dorset BH20 6HH **Website:** www.monkeyworld.org **Telephone:** 01929
462537 (information line 0800 456600) **Hours:** 10am–5pm (Jul & Aug to 6pm) **Dates:** closed
25 Dec **Entry fees:** [D]£7.25 [H]free [A]£10.50 [3-15s]£7.25 [C]£7.25–£8.75

Neither a zoo nor originally a tourist attraction, Monkey World was set up in 1987 as
a sanctuary dedicated to rescuing apes and monkeys that had been abused by their
owners. The centre houses more than 240 primates and is an internationally respected
conservation and captive-breeding centre. It's also a lot of fun to visit.

If you can overcome the many steep slopes, Monkey World makes for an inspirational
day out. The dedication of the staff, the results they achieve and the affection they have
for their charges are plain to see. For sight-impaired visitors, three life-sized sculptures
of orang-utan, chimpanzee and marmoset heads are available to feel. Regular daily talks
on eight of the species in the centre are given by the primate-care staff: printed versions
of these are available on request. The centre was originally founded to care for chimps,

and their four chimp groups are still the main attraction, along with three groups of delightful orang-utans, five species of superbly arboreal gibbons and seven species of monkeys, marmosets and lemurs.

Parking at the centre is somewhat freestyle but at least a dozen spaces are reserved for disabled drivers. More than twenty motorised scooters are available to borrow (£10 refundable deposit with ID) and it's definitely worth booking one in advance. The various collections in the 260-hectare site are linked by steep winding paths and the signage is still not all it could be, so it is easy to get lost. However, the particularly steep and narrow Woodland Walk is the only part of the centre that is inaccessible to wheelchair users. One of three child play areas features wheelchair-accessible swings.

Orang-utan at Monkey World

MOUNT EDGCUMBE HOUSE AND COUNTRY PARK

Address: Cremyll, Torpoint, Cornwall PL10 1HZ **Website:** www.mountedgcumbe.gov.uk
Telephone: 01752 822236 **Hours:** house open Sun–Thurs 11am–4.30pm **Dates:** house open last weekend of Mar to end Sept; park open all year **Entry fees:** house and garden [D]£4 [H]free [A]£5 [5–15s]2.50 [C]£4

Mount Edgcumbe House is a magnificent Tudor mansion, set in a country park spreading across nearly nine hundred acres of fine countryside and spectacular coastline facing Plymouth across the Sound. While the park's topography makes full access tricky for wheelchair-users, there is more than enough for a whole day in what you can get to.

Built in 1547, Mount Edgcumbe House barely survived a bombing raid in 1941 and the gutted interior was restored in eighteenth-century style between 1958 and 1964. The house is beautifully furnished and includes sixteenth-century tapestries, eighteenth-century Chinese and Plymouth porcelain and various other family possessions, such as the 1871 accessible carriage of the Countess of Edgcumbe. From upstairs, there are some wonderful views, and you'll find a dressing room where children can dress dolls with Victorian dresses and get a picture taken of themselves in period costumes. In good weather, you'll want to spend much of your time in the gardens, which include the fancy Earl's Garden behind the house, and a series of formal gardens in different styles, including English, French, Italian, plus the Jubilee gardens and a New Zealand garden, which features a geyser and native plants and trees.

There's disabled parking and accessible toilets by the house, and wheelchair-users access the house from the rear. Note that the lift to the upper floor can't accommodate large chairs, but a narrow wheelchair is available. From the house, you can join the Edgcumbe's multi-use trail, which is easiest for wheelchair-users where it goes through the largely level Deer Park. Elsewhere on the estate, some of the moderate inclines (in the Earl's garden for example) may prove difficult for manual wheelchair users without strong assistants. If you want to see the formal gardens down towards the jetty at Cremyll, you're best advised to take the Edgcumbe Eco-Bus or drive down there, seeing them at the end of your visit – there's another car park at the Cremyll gates.

PAIGNTON ZOO

Address: Totnes Road, Paignton, Devon TQ4 7EU **Website:** www.paigntonzoo.org.uk
Telephone: 01803 697500 **Hours:** daily 10am–5.30pm **Dates:** closed 25 Dec **Entry fees:** [D]£11.90 [H]free [A]£11.90 [3–15s]£8.40 [C]£9.80

Paignton Zoo blends education and conservation work in its displays of animals and plants in recreations of their natural habitats. It's a slightly hilly site, parts of which can be difficult for people with limited mobility, but with more than three thousand creatures, there is a lot to see, and you can happily spend a day here.

When deciding where to go, stick to the yellow trail if you want the most wheelchair-friendly route. It takes you from the main entrance to close-up views of flamingos and parrots, and then to a pair of lakes with islands populated by monkeys and gibbons. The yellow route also brings you to the animal encounter area – close impressions of giant tortoises, red pandas, peacocks, porcupines, meerkats and kangaroos – and to the impressive Reptile Tropics and the new crocodile swamp. A path winds through the swamp giving you face time with crocodiles above and below the water. Keep a look out, too, for the world's biggest snake, the reticulated python, usually curled up in one of the trees. The orange route is also reasonable, and takes you to the African Savannah, with giraffes and elephants and the baby black rhino and its parents. The pink route, however, is more difficult and includes steps, though fortunately it only accesses a small part of the zoo.

Whilst far from being one hundred percent accessible, the zoo has begun to consider the needs of wheelchair-users when upgrading habitats and aims to make all new exhibits accessible. There are two free car parks; the main one is on a slight incline while the overflow car park is more level but you do have to cross a busy road. You could also take the *Jungle Express* road train around the lakes, but you will need to be able to transfer onto a seat. The shops located in the main entrance are fully accessible, as are the various snack bars and the *Island Restaurant*, which cooks with locally sourced produce.

SHERBORNE CASTLES AND GROUNDS

New Castle Address: New Road, Sherborne, Dorset DT9 5NR **Website:** www.sherbornecastle.
com **Telephone**: 01935 812 072 **Hours:** Tues–Thurs, Sat & Sun, Bank Holiday Mondays
11am–4.30pm (Sat: castle interior 2–4.30pm only) **Dates:** Mar–Oct **Entry fees:** castle and
gardens [D]£9 [H]free [A]£9 [0–15s]free [C]£8.50 (castle only: half price) **Old Castle Address:**
off the B3145, Sherborne, Dorset DT9 3SA **Website:** www.english-heritage.org.uk **Telephone**:
01935 812730 **Hours:** daily Apr–Jun 10am–5pm; Jul–Aug 10am–6pm; Sep 10am–5pm; Oct
10am–4pm **Dates:** closed Nov–Mar **Entry fees:** [D]£2.50 [H]£2.50 [A]£2.50 [C]£2

Perched on a low hill, the "new" Sherborne Castle has an impressive lakeside setting
and its State Rooms reflect a variety of decorative styles – Tudor, Jacobean, Georgian
and Victorian. Used as a Red Cross hospital in World War I and as the D-Day landing
HQ in World War II, the castle also has some interesting historical connections.

Sir Walter Raleigh originally tried to modernise the twelfth-century Old Castle (the
ruins across the lake), but instead decided to build a new home on the site of the hunting
lodge in the Deer Park which eventually became the "new" Castle. Details of paintings,
furniture and ornaments can be found on information sheets in each room, via a Braille
guidebook, or by asking the very helpful guides. After a dose of history, you can enjoy a
bite to eat in the café before burning off the calories by taking a very pleasant walk in the
grounds, pausing to feed the ducks. If you can take more than one castle in a day, it's very
much worth visiting the ruins of the Old Castle too, only a well-signposted short drive
around the 800m lakeshore road. The grounds around the ruins, although grassy, tend to
be compact and so can be pretty much freely explored. On a sunny day, it's a serene spot to
relax with a picnic, but be sure to position yourself so you can take in the enchanting views
over the lake to the "new" castle.

Sherborne Old Castle grounds

Often overlooked on the tourist map, Sherborne is perhaps one of the most attractive towns in Britain. After a visit to the two castles, there is more on offer a short drive away in the genteel town centre, which is a great place to while away an afternoon. Top of your visit list should be the magnificent Sherborne Abbey, worth a look not least for its striking ceiling. After a heritage trail that long, you'll be in need of refreshments. There are many quaint cafés in the town, but none so charming as **Oliver's** (19 Cheap Street, Sherborne, Dorset, DT9 3PU; 01935 815005) which serves filling down-to-earth snacks and a comforting range of home-made cakes and desserts. It's a gem of place, but with much of its appeal lying in the nooks and crannies of its antique interior, access is less than perfect. To get the most from a visit, avoid busy times and have a companion with you to order at the counter. Use the Somerfield car park just behind the café, and enter via the side entrance. This helpfully avoids access via the slightly steep Cheap Street as well as the steps inside from the counter to the main seating area. If the sun is shining, there are tables outside, or instead you could pop in before a visit to the castles and stock up on takeway treats for a picnic.

At the "new" castle, there's no marked disabled parking in the grassy car park, which is likely to be problematic on a busy day. Wheelchair access to the castle is via a ramped side entrance. Inside, if you can't manage stairs, however, access is limited to the ground floor as there's no lift. Outside, the courtyard next to the café and shop is cobbled, with a mat around the edge to make it a bit less bumpy. The paved paths around the grounds vary in steepness but there's usually a gentle option. The car park at the Old Castle is a short distance from the ticket office, but it is possible to be dropped off closer to the entrance. You enter the castle itself via a sloping timber bridge, but after that all areas are level except steps to the chapel area of the ruins, and there are benches around to perch on.

SOUTH DEVON RAILWAY, BUCKFAST BUTTERFLIES & DARTMOOR OTTER SANCTUARY AND RARE BREEDS FARM

Addresses: South Devon Railway Trust, The Station, Dartbridge Road, Buckfastleigh TQ11 0DZ; Buckfast Butterflies & Dartmoor Otter Sanctuary, The Station, Buckfastleigh TQ11 0DZ; Rare Breeds Farm, Mayhems Cottage, Littlehempston, Totnes TQ9 6LW **Websites:** www.southdevonrailway.org; www.ottersandbutterflies.co.uk; www.totnesrarebreeds.co.uk **Telephones:** South Devon Railway 0845 3451420; Buckfast Butterflies and Dartmoor Otter Sanctuary 01364 642916; Rare Breeds Farm 01803 840387 **Railway hours:** During peak season, train departs: Buckfastleigh 10.45am, 12.15pm, 2.15pm and 3.45pm; Totnes 11.30am, 1pm, 3pm, 4.30pm (journey time 30mins). **Buckfast Butterflies and Dartmoor Otter Sanctuary hours:** 10am–5.30pm (or dusk if earlier); 11am–3pm Nov (otters only) **Rare Breed Farm hours:** 9.30am–5pm **Dates:** mid-Mar–Oct, plus some other dates (check websites) **Entry fees:** combined [D]£18.30 [H]Free [A]£18.30 [5–14]£12.30 [C]£16.30 (separate fares/entry fees also available: check websites)

Although you can do these activities on their own, a good-value combined ticket covers the steam train ride as well as entry to Buckfast Butterflies & Dartmoor Otter Sanctuary (next to Buckfastleigh station) and the Rare Breeds Farm at Littlehempston station at the other end of the line, just outside Totnes (the farm is only accessible by the steam train service). The ticket also includes the Vintage Bus service to Buckfast Abbey (see p.98), though this bus is not wheelchair-accessible. Altogether, this is a highly enjoyable day out that needs a little organisation if you're in a group. The train and Buckfast Butterflies & Dartmoor Otter Sanctuary are both feasible in poor weather, too.

At the South Devon Railway station at Buckfastleigh you'll find a railway museum, workshop, miniature railway and play area, all free. The steam train has a wheelchair-accessible coach, but no direct access to the buffet car. Staff are very helpful and will get refreshments for you. The train chugs for half an hour along the picturesque Dart valley, terminating at Littlehempston, just north of Totnes, on the left bank of the river. A footpath leads over the Dart and into Totnes town centre, about one kilometre away.

Totnes Rare Breeds Farm is adjacent to the South Devon Railway station at Littlehempston, outside Totnes. The farm offers a level site, reasonable surfaces for wheelchairs and ample opportunities to feed and pet many of the mostly domestic animals, including pygmy goats, pot-bellied pigs, goats, poultry and seaweed-eating sheep. The hospital houses rescued hedgehogs. It's a fascinating place which does excellent work in conservation and bio-diversity. The garden café is accessible, and the staff friendly, offering meals and snacks sourced from local producers.

Buckfast Butterflies & Dartmoor Otter Sanctuary is right next to the South Devon Railway station car park at Buckfastleigh. Entrance is through the shop into a large and very humid greenhouse. Flowering plants and dishes of fruit draw a large variety of tropical butterflies – some the size of small birds and beautifully patterned. The paths of compacted gravel are easily negotiated in a wheelchair and there are several benches where you can rest, observe and plan your next photo.

Access to the otters is from the end of the butterfly house via gravel paths that can be tricky in a wheelchair. The otter sanctuary maintains three species of these playful, semi-aquatic mammals, in separate areas. Where high walls make wheelchair-viewing difficult, staff will take you into a restricted section. The underwater viewing area is easily accessible and shows off these sleek animals at their best, especially during feeding (daily at 11.30am, 2pm and 4pm).

SS GREAT BRITAIN

Address: Great Western Dockyard, Bristol BS1 6TY **Website:** www.ssgreatbritain.org
Telephone: 0117 926 0680 **Hours:** Apr–Oct 10am–5.30pm, Nov–Mar 10am–4.30pm **Dates:** closed 24–25 Dec **Entry fees:** [D]£10.95 [H]free [A]£10.95 [5–16s]£5.65 [C]£5.65–£8.25; 12-month free return visit

When you step aboard Brunel's SS *Great Britain*, launched in 1843, you enter the era of Victorian ingenuity and self-confidence. The visit is a slickly presented, behind-the-scenes immersion in the story of the first ocean liner, the biggest passenger ship of her time, and it makes for an enjoyable and fascinating few hours.

The *Great Britain,* for decades a rusting hulk in the Falklands, has been lovingly restored to some of her former glory in the Bristol dry dock where she was built. Walk through the interactive dockside museum and then go on board to wander round the ship. With a choice of free audio and BSL guides you can find out what life was like for Victorian passengers and crew, from the elegance of the first-class cabins to the cramped and noisy steerage accommodation. Then, if you descend under the rather beautiful glass "sea", you can view the magnificent hull, which is now protected by a state-of-the-art system to control the moisture that was corroding the metal. You can finish your visit in the dockside shop and café, which has some good views of the floating harbour.

There are disabled parking spaces about 90m from the entrance. Every effort has been made to make the site wheelchair-accessible, with ramps and wide doorways, but this is a Victorian ship and dockyard and there are some sloped areas, uneven paths and tight corners. Two narrow, manual wheelchairs are available. Wheelchair-accessible lifts are located in the museum, on board ship and to take you below the glass sea. In wet weather, the wooden deck can be slippery, and in some of the areas below deck the planking is uneven. You'll find disabled toilets on the ship itself and in the museum and café.

STEAM MUSEUM OF THE GREAT WESTERN RAILWAY

Address: Kemble Drive, Swindon, Wiltshire SN2 2TA **Website:** www.steam-museum.org.uk
Telephone: 01793 466646 Dedicated access tel: 01793 466637 **Hours:** daily 10am–5pm
Dates: closed 25–26 Dec & 1 Jan **Entry fees:** [D]£6.20 [H]free [A]£6.20 [5–16s]£4.10
[C]£4.10

Steam, the Museum of the Great Western Railway, gives visitors the chance to experience the sights and sounds of Swindon's GWR Works where so many of the best steam locos in the world were built. It holds massive appeal for the large number of locomotive enthusiasts, but works as an enjoyable outing for most visitors.

Steam is set in the middle of the former Swindon Railway Works, and it takes you into the world of the principal engineer, Isambard Kingdom Brunel, and those who built and drove the engines and travelled on the Great Western Railway. It was a service that became a benchmark for public transport in the middle of the nineteenth century and the GWR Works, at its peak, turned out more than one hundred new locos each year. As well as the big engines and the usual memorabilia and exhibits, the museum is populated by the figures of former railway workers – a few of the more than ten thousand people employed by the Works in the early 1900s. The evocative Works area of the museum gives a sense of day-to-day life for those employees, and the famous locomotive 'Caerphilly Castle' is displayed in all its gleaming glory – a fine example of the achievements of those staff. There is a small café, but if you want something different, just across the car park is the Outlet shopping centre with easy access and a food hall.

This is a very accessible museum: the video displays have captions and subtitles, and if you need help the museum staff are happy to assist. The gravelled car park is right outside the main entrance and auto doors lead into a large foyer, where you'll find the museum shop and café and access to the toilets. Wide doors lead into the museum itself, where all the exhibits are level, or accessible via ramps. There's a lift to a viewpoint over the museum and then an upper level with a view over the adjacent main line.

In the heart of Swindon, **Ashoka** (6-7 Bridge Street, Swindon, SN1 1BU; 01793 511011; www.ashokarestaurant.co.uk) is a friendly Indian restaurant, serving good portions of tasty, traditional dishes, often with great value deals on offer at lunchtime. There is no dedicated car park, but there are public car parks with disabled spaces and on-street Blue Badge parking nearby. There is a single shallow step at the entrance, but staff are always on hand and happy to help if you need it. Light, airy and modern Italian restaurant **Bottelino's** (The Pattern Store, Penzance Drive, Swindon, SN2 2BA; 01793 887 710; www.bottelinos. net) is based in a welcoming building right by Swindon Designer Outlet, and is a comfortable choice for a relaxing bite to eat and a glass of wine after a day of shopping. The restaurant has its own car park with disabled spaces and there is ramped access. The restaurant has its own deli on site, and serves portions so generous they are always happy to provide customers with take-home containers.

STOURHEAD

Address: Stourton, Warminster, Wiltshire BA12 6QD **Website:** www.nationaltrust.org.uk/main/ w-stourhead **Telephone:** 01747 841152 **Hours:** garden daily 9am–7pm; house Fri–Tues 11.30am–4.30pm **Dates:** garden open all year; house 15 Mar–2 Nov **Entry fees:** [D]£10.50 [H]free [A]£10.50 [5–17s]£5.20 [C]£10.50

Stourhead grounds

Stourhead, a Palladian mansion owned by the Hoare family since 1717, has a superb garden with replica Roman and Venetian buildings and an extraordinary folly. The house contains a superb collection of painting and furniture and, together with the gardens, was given to the National Trust in 1946.

In 1902, fire destroyed a large part of the house, but most of the furniture and paintings were saved. Indeed, the original eighteenth-century collection of paintings and furniture is so extensive that nothing substantial has been added. Today, the highlights continue to be the Regency library, the collection of Chippendale furniture and the remarkable four-metre-high Pope's Cabinet made for Pope Sixtus V in 1590 and recently restored. Outside, the grounds are a feast of colour for most of the year and deliberately designed to offer breathtaking views around the lakeside setting. The gardens – a consummate example of the eighteenth-century passion for landscape gardening – were created in 1740 by Henry Hoare II, earning him the moniker Henry the Magnificent. There's a two-kilometre walk round the lake, a three-kilometre path to the fifty-metre-high Alfred Tower folly (no wheelchair access to the top) and a five- kilometre circular route that takes in the deer park and an Iron Age fort.

From the disabled bays in the car park, there's a 400m path to the house entrance. There are thirteen concrete steps into the house with no firm hand hold (if you need to use the stair climber, call to book it a day in advance). Once you're inside, all the public rooms are on one floor and accessible. There are several way-marked cycle tracks and footpaths around the wider estate which are accessible to walkers and scooters, with surfaces varying from gravel to grass and compacted woodland soil: some parts are undulating and others get muddy in wet weather.

TATE ST IVES AND BARBARA HEPWORTH MUSEUM

Address: Porthmeor Beach, St Ives, Cornwall TR26 1TG **Website:** www.tate.org.uk **Telephone:** 01736 796226 **Hours:** Mar–Oct daily 10am–5.20pm, Tues–Sun Nov–Feb 10am–4.20pm **Dates:** closed 24–26 Dec (also check website) **Entry fees:** both sites [D]£4.50 [H]free [A]£8.75 [under 18s]free [C]£4.50

Opened in 1993 in a striking modernist building, Tate St Ives showcases contemporary art, often focusing on the Cornish art scene that flourished through the middle of the twentieth century. If you love art, you'll want to go out of your way to visit; and even if you're not a natural art-lover, you should visit if you're in the area, as it just might change your mind.

Tate St Ives is directly above the beach, giving its atmosphere a delightful quality, particularly in summer when it chimes with seaside noise. Inside the bright, spacious galleries, you'll find modernist pieces that were created in the immediate vicinity of St Ives itself, or around west Cornwall. Special exhibitions change three times a year. As well as exhibiting local artists, Tate St Ives runs an Artist Residency programme, supporting new talent by providing bursaries and studio space in the town and exhibiting the resulting works. The gallery runs a daily programme of events including free talks and activities, usually with an audio loop and occasionally with a BSL interpreter.

Access is good on the whole, with a ramp and a lift to every floor and they have recently installed disabled toilets. The wheelchair route between Tate St Ives and the Barbara Hepworth Museum and Sculpture Garden (which Tate also manages) is up

Tate St Ives

a cobbled street, past numerous gift shops and galleries. At the museum, one ramp takes you into Hepworth's sculpture workshop, and another into the tranquil garden housing her works. If you're bringing a wheelchair, you need to call ahead to let them know (01736 791102).

THERMAE BATH SPA

Address: Thermae Bath Spa, Hot Bath Street, Bath, Somerset BA1 1SJ **Website:** www. thermaebathspa.com **Telephone:** 0844 888 0844 **Hours:** daily 9am–10pm (some facilities vary) **Dates:** closed 25–26 Dec & 1 Jan (call to check) **Entry fees:** 2-hour session in New Royal Bath [D]£11 [H]£11 [A]£22; 2-hour session in Cross Bath [D]6.50 [H]£6.50 [A] £13; (no under-16s; local residents get further discounts)

The state-of-the-art Thermae Bath Spa is a natural, thermal spa complex combining Georgian architecture with modern facilities, using the flow of a million-odd litres a day of mineral-enriched hot water. Soothing and de-stressing, this place is a Bath must-do – a wonderful treat and great value, especially for local residents.

The main focuses are New Royal Bath, designed by Nicholas Grimshaw, with its futuristic use of glass and wonderful views from the rooftop pool, and Cross Bath, across the street. In New Royal Bath, you can indulge in the Minerva bath, with its whirlpool, jet massage and gentle currents, and the open-air rooftop pool – delightful on a cold day, and with magnificent views across the city. New Royal also has aromatherapy steam rooms and waterfall showers. Cross Bath, with its smaller open-air thermal pool, is housed in an adjacent building, constructed over the Cross Spring sacred Celtic site. Here, you can try out a wide range of spa therapies, including body wraps, massages, hot stones, and dry flotation as well as body care treatments and facials.

Thermae has generally good access credentials, as you might expect, though there's no dedicated car park. Getting to the entrance from the Blue Badge bays in nearby streets means going over slabs and cobbles; then an automatic door leads to reception. Lifts provide access to all levels and there's plenty of Braille signage. Two lightweight shower wheelchairs are available to borrow by clients with helpers. There are accessible toilets and showers, but no hoists in the changing rooms. Steps with handrails take you into the water and assistance chairs give access to the baths. The treatment rooms are a good size and some have raise-and-lower beds. Everything you might need – towels, robes, slippers – is available to hire. The café-restaurant is exclusively for the use of patrons. The separate Cross Bath building (across a quiet cobbled street with dropped kerbs) has a disabled changing room and shower facilities and also has assistance-chair access into the bath.

THE NORTHWEST

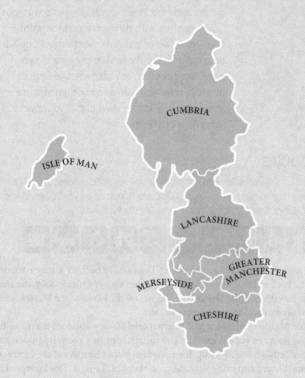

CUMBRIA

ISLE OF MAN

LANCASHIRE

GREATER MANCHESTER

MERSEYSIDE

CHESHIRE

- Albert Docks
- Blackpool Tower
- Blackwell House
- Catton Hall Shooting Ground
- Friar's Crag Walk, Lake District
- Knowsley Safari Park
- Manchester United Stadium Tour and Museum
- Manchester Velodrome
- The Royal Exchange Theatre, Manchester

- RSPB Ribble Discovery Centre, Fairhaven Lake
- Theatre by the Lake, Keswick
- Urbis, Manchester
- Windermere Lake Cruises, Cumbria

WHY NOT ALSO TRY ▶▶ Antony Gormley's Another Place, Crosby Beach

IDEAS ▶▶ Arts

THE NORTHWEST

Once gritty hotbeds of industry, the northern cities of Liverpool and Manchester have truly moved with the times, developing into vigorous urban centres with distinctive cultural identities – and two of the northwest's most popular destinations. For those who prefer a slower pace, the spectacularly scenic Lake District offers respite and, while visitor numbers are always high, finding a dale to call your own still remains a possibilty.

ALBERT DOCKS

Address: Liverpool L3 4BB **Website:** www.liverpoolmuseums.org.uk **Telephone:** 0151 478 4499 **Hours:** varies dependent on venue; check individually **Dates:** closed 25–26 Dec; check venues individually **Entry fees:** varies dependant on venue; check individually

Originally redeveloped in the 1980s, the Albert Docks have become a major tourist attraction. On the back of Liverpool's status as European City of Culture 2008, the area is receiving huge investment. The Docks complex sits on the banks of the Mersey, with views, walks and grassy areas to play and picnic on.

The Merseyside Maritime Museum and International Slavery Museum are magnificent, with several floors of superb exhibits and installations in a converted dockside warehouse, all perfectly accessible to all. The museums place Liverpool at the centre of the world's trading history and bring alive the great status of the port. Tate Liverpool is a nationally important gallery drawing visitors from around the world. The museums and Tate all have excellent cafés and gift shops. Of course you can't visit Liverpool without paying homage to the Beatles, and The Beatles Story doesn't disappoint. Although the basement venue looks awkward at first, it's a surprisingly comfortable and accessible visit. The Docks area has a wide variety of quirky shops (all accessible) and all the usual franchise eateries (and a good number of independents) with menus to suit all pockets. Finally, you could finish the day with a concert at the brand new Arena.

There is designated outside parking and a huge new multi-storey, with lots of accessible spaces. Most staff in the Docks venues try very hard to accommodate the needs of all visitors. The museums are very accessible with plenty of lifts, accessible toilets and hearing loops, and great care taken with signage and information. Tate Liverpool has similar facilities, plus wheelchairs and BSL and Touch Tours. The Beatles Story has lift access and portable ramps. The Arena has excellent wheelchair access and a choice of seats, as you would expect from a new concert venue. Outside, the Docks have a few challenging surfaces, including flagstones and cobbles, but the whole area is criss-crossed with hard paths (with the occasional slight gradient), making all parts accessible.

Antony Gormley's Another Place, Crosby Beach

Address: Mariners Road, Crosby Beach, Liverpool, Merseyside L23 6SX **Web:** www. visitliverpool.com **Tel:** 0151 237 3945 **Hours:** no closures **Dates:** no closures **Entry fees:** free

Crosby Beach provides the perfect spot for a very British bracing walk by the sea- but with a delicious twist. You will be surrounded by one hundred identical, larger than life, cast-iron statues of a human (Gormley himself), set at intervals along the beach. As they stare out to sea, you can't help but be intrigued by this great example of modern sculpture. You'll be particularly impressed if you arrive when the tide is in - seeing scattered, disembodied heads just breaking the waves can be disconcerting! If you can't manage the sand, park at the north end where you will only be yards from the beach, but able to wander along the solid concrete prom. Buy an ice cream or a hot dog and let your imagination run riot.

BLACKPOOL TOWER

Address: Promenade, Blackpool, Lancashire FY1 4BJ **Website:** www.theblackpooltower.co.uk
Telephone: 01253 622242 **Hours:** daily 10am–11pm (some variation with specific venues and events) **Dates:** closed 25–26 Dec **Entry fees:** booked online [D]£14 [H] £14 [A]£14 [5–16s]£11 (some performances included; upgrades available for others; no concessions, disabled or otherwise)

Blackpool Tower and its ancillary attractions are the epitome of the British day at the seaside. It seems to have survived its kitsch reputation and somehow stood the test of time to retain its own ironic appeal. Whatever the weather, you know there's going to be plenty to see and do for the whole family: you pays your money and takes your choice, and you can stay as long as you like.

The tower boasts much more than a trip to the top (using the comfortable lift access) – although this can still take your breath away, especially if you do the Walk of Faith across the glass floor. On a clear day, standing 130m above the earth, you can see straight down to the ground and as far afield as Wales and the Lake District. You can also enjoy the excitement of the traditional circus (depending on your mobility, you can even join a circus skills class) and the truly magnificent Victorian splendour of the tower Ballroom, where the thing is to have high tea while the dancing takes place. Then there are the more modern Jurassic Walk, 3D Cinema, the acclaimed Aquarium or even the new Jungle Jim's Adventureland, with its rope bridges and interactive games.

The tower has no dedicated parking of its own. There is ample parking within two minutes in open car parks or in multi-storey, both with designated spaces, but it can be very busy. The trams are not accessible, but the buses are. The railway station is a ten-minute walk away, while bus and coach stations are closer. Because of its Victorian origins, the tower is not ideal for access in terms of space or illumination, and accessible toilets are only available on levels 1 and 5. All the attractions are accessible, though accessible seating in the circus is limited and booking for it is essential. Throughout the tower, only the ballroom balcony is inaccessible. Wheelchair-users are asked to visit with a helper.

BLACKWELL HOUSE

Address: Bowness-on-Windermere, Cumbria LA23 3JT **Website:** www.blackwell.org.uk
Telephone: 01539 446139 **Hours:** daily 10.30am–5pm (closes 4pm Feb–Mar & Nov–Dec);
Dates: closed 1–17 Jan and 25–26 Dec **Entry fees:** [D]£6 [H]free [A]£6 [5–15s]£3.50

Blackwell, close to the banks of Windermere, was designed by architect MH Baillie Scott for Sir Edward Holt, a Manchester brewing magnate. Completed in 1900 as a prestigious holiday house, it's the archetypal Arts and Crafts home. Combined with its stunning

Blackwell House

location in the centre of the Lake District, it offers a tranquil, civilised step away from the nearby tourist crush.

The charitable Lakeland Arts Trust, which looks after Blackwell, has spent millions restoring the house after the ravages of unsympathetic previous owners, and the benefits are obvious in every room. So much of the extraordinary original interior remains in the house that it has become the focal point of the Arts and Crafts trail in the area. The library holds a specialist collection of books on the movement – call the curator in advance if you want to consult them. There are also changing exhibitions of art, ceramics and crafts throughout the year. The shop has plenty to offer and the award-winning tea room, with its fine lake views, is a must: quirky paintings and drawings are displayed on the walls.

There's parking for about fifty cars, but it's best to arrive early at busy times. Blackwell's spaciousness makes it naturally very accessible. There are lifts to upper floors, and only a few rooms can't be reached by wheelchair due to the occasional short flight of stairs. Staff will show you a book of photographs of these areas so you can acquaint yourself with what has been missed. There are accessible toilets in the house and next to the tea room.

CATTON HALL SHOOTING GROUND

Address: Catton Hall Shooting Ground, Bradley Lane, Frodsham, Cheshire WA6 7EX **Website:** www.cattonhall.co.uk **Telephone:** 01928 788295 **Hours:** call to check **Dates:** closed 25–26 Dec **Entry fees:** clay-pigeon session with instructor £45; quad-trekking £50 (minimum age 18; no concessions, disabled or otherwise)

Shooter at Catton Hall

This is the perfect way to get rid of any pent-up frustrations – shoot them out of the sky. You can book a one-to-one session of clay pigeon shooting with an instructor, or shoot in a small group, and quickly become proficient at picking off the clays. It's surprisingly addictive.

If clay pigeons don't grab you, traditional archery, including longbow or crossbow, air rifle-shooting and falconry are also on offer. They also rent out quad bikes and if you are able to transfer from a wheelchair and have sufficient mobility, you can try some rough and wet cross-country quad-trekking, along a 15km route through Catton Hall estate. Quad bikes have twist-grip controls, so all you need is good enough balance. Whichever sport you choose, be sure to get directions from the website or study a map before setting off, as there are no signs at all in Frodsham, making Catton Hall a little tricky to find.

The site is not ideal, being on a very steep slope, so call ahead if you need level parking, so staff can save a space. Each activity is conducted in a level area so there are no problems there. For the clay-pigeon shooting, all but one of the traps are fully accessible, reached from a solid path with no awkward pushes across wet grass or mud, and there are always people around to assist. Afterwards, you can relax in the huge shooting lodge (one-step entrance but fully accessible inside), or just sit out on the veranda and watch everyone else take their aim.

FRIAR'S CRAG WALK, LAKE DISTRICT

Address: Lake District National Park **Website:** www.lake-district.gov.uk and www.keswick.org/walks.asp **Telephone:** 01768 772645 **Hours:** no closures **Dates:** no closures **Entry fees:** free

Derwent Water in the North Lakes boasts some of the most beautiful scenery in the British Isles. Using the Lake District's excellent *Miles without Stiles* website, you can locate and check dozens of accessible trails in the Lakes, including Friar's Crag alongside Derwent Water, just south of Keswick.

This is a circular route of up to 3.2km, beginning at the Lakeside car park. It takes you past the Theatre by the Lake, and various coffee shops, down to the landing stages where you could take a boat trip or try to identify the various breeds of duck which frequent the area. You then move along the shore to the beautiful Friar's Crag viewpoint, beloved of John Ruskin, where you get a wonderful impression of the extent of the lake and its great depth. The trail leads you around a bay, across a comfortably accessible footbridge and then into beautiful Ings Wood. You then have a choice – completing the loop with a walk over grassland and then through woodland back to the landing stages, or adding a little extra distance by first heading for Broomhill Point (the options are clearly signed and you don't have to retrace your tracks).

The car park at the start of the walk has a dozen Blue Badge spaces and there are RADAR-key toilets in the car park itself, and accessible ones in the Theatre by the Lake and in the coffee shop. There are no facilities of any kind around the walk itself. Trail surfaces are generally smooth but not tarmac so they can become muddy after rain. There are some gradients of up to 1:12 so it's best, if not essential, to be accompanied by a pusher, although the majority of the trail is level and there are no nasty accessibility surprises to negotiate.

KNOWSLEY SAFARI PARK

Address: Prescot, Merseyside L34 4AN **Website:** www.knowsley.com/safari **Telephone:** 0151 430 9009 **Hours:** summer daily 10am–4pm, winter daily 10.30am–3pm **Dates:** closed 25–26 Dec **Entry fees:** [D]£9 [H]free [A]£12 [3–15s]£9 [C]£9

Knowsley Safari Park, in the grounds of historic Knowsley House near Liverpool, is a conservation-led, drive-through wildlife sanctuary with active breeding programmes, where you can come face to face with all manner of exotic animals from emus to elephants. The main safari route is covered in your own vehicle, so there are no access problems there, while a reduced route, passing many of the paddocks, can be followed in a wheelchair or on a mobility scooter.

Once you've entered the park, you can do the drive as many times as you like and are guaranteed close encounters with the impressive wildlife. Some of the rarest highlights include tigers, white rhinos, a pack of highly endangered African wild dogs, beautiful lechwe antelope, shy and exceedingly rare bongo antelope, scimitar-horned oryx, Père David's deer and two-humped Bactrian camels. The park also has less vulnerable species, such as lion, elephant, giraffe and wildebeest. If you drive through Monkey Jungle the encounter with the baboons may be a bit too close for comfort, as they clamber all over the vehicles, occasionally taking a souvenir away with them (there's a car-friendly route which avoids their destructive tendencies). In the pedestrian area, the Bug House has excellent, low displays, the upstairs Sea Lion Show has a ground-level side entrance, and the Giraffe House has easy access and viewing.

Arriving is no problem, with excellent signage and a huge amount of parking, though relatively few designated wide spaces. By the car park are two large, fully-equipped accessible toilets with ramped access, and there are other accessible toilets around the site. In the pedestrian area, there are smooth, wide paths and lots of benches. Even the little land train has a special carriage for wheelchair-users. The shop and restaurant are pretty good too, although restaurant seating is fixed, reducing the number of usable tables, and there's no accessible toilet inside.

MANCHESTER UNITED STADIUM TOUR AND MUSEUM

Address: Old Trafford Stadium, Sir Matt Busby Way, Manchester M16 0RA **Website:** www.manutd.com **Telephone:** 0161 868 8000 **Hours:** daily 9.30am–6pm (last tour 4.30pm; museum closes earlier on match days and outside school holidays) **Dates:** museum and tours all year, call to check for Christmas closures **Entry fees:** stadium tour and museum [D]£12 [H]free [A]£12 [5–15s]£8 [C]£8

The Theatre of Dreams is certainly a dream destination for wheelchair-users. It's accessible throughout and you don't have to be a Man U fanatic to enjoy the museum and stadium tour. If you come for a match, you'll experience state-of-the-art disabled provision, which is just as it should be.

Old Trafford

Tours are simply arranged by phone, with helpful advice available: for example it's best to book a time early in the day, to avoid the bigger groups. Disabled customer-relations are totally professional and the whole experience is very impressive. The tour itself is as comprehensive as you could wish for, and includes the immaculate pitch, the changing rooms, players' tunnel and dug-out, and the museum, with its Trophy Room, Hall of Fame of the club's playing legends, kit displays and interactive history archives. In a way, visiting for a match is even more impressive, in the sense that you're here for the normal business of the stadium rather than making an arranged visit. Facilities for disabled supporters are second to none, with hundreds of wheelchair-plus-companion seats available, including forty with their own sockets for live match commentary.

On arrival, you'll be personally greeted and directed to a choice of disabled parking. The excellent service continues throughout: at every step there are helpful staff, and movement everywhere is smooth and step-free, with ramps or lifts where needed. Individual helpers are available too. The *Red Café* is also totally accessible, and a good place to study your complimentary copy of the *Disabled Supporter's Booklet*.

MANCHESTER VELODROME

Address: Stuart Street, Manchester, M11 4DQ **Website:** www.manchestervelodrome.com
Telephone: 0161 223 2244 **Hours:** 9am–10.30pm, event times vary **Dates:** closed 25–26 Dec
Entry fees: from £9.30 for taster session, plus £9.30 to hire bike; concessions £7.20 plus £7.20

After the cycling triumphs achieved by the TeamGB and ParalympicsGB cyclists in Beijing (including Darren Kenny's four paralympic gold medals), visiting the home of British cycling has become hugely popular. Manchester Velodrome is England's only Olympic-standard indoor track, one of the fastest in the world, and the place where the conquest of world biking was planned and prepared.

Built for the Commonwealth Games in 2002, and part of the Sport City complex, Manchester Velodrome is a huge structure, set on a spacious site, with no design compromises. Spectator seating runs all around the outside of the track; there's a large central space inside the track which can be used for other sports, and it's even possible to fit temporary seating here to watch basketball, for example, while the cyclists practise on the track. The velodrome offers cycling classes for all ages and abilities, and individuals with disabilities can contact the venue and discuss special lessons. If cycling isn't your bag then you may want to visit for the National Badminton Championships, Paralympic Wheelchair Basketball or even the National Cheerleaders' Championships. And with the City of Manchester Stadium (home of Man City), the home track of one of the country's best athletics clubs, Sale Harriers, and the National Squash Centre of Excellence all across the road, you're in sporting heaven.

The Velodrome has huge parking areas with many spaces. There is level or slightly ramped access from outside to the main concourse. Around the track there ar wheelchair and companion spaces with superb views. RADAR-key toilets and catering and retail facilities around the concourse are very accessible. For events in the centre of the track it is even possible to enter the Velodrome via an outside accessible ramped entrance which brings you out at track centre. Alternatively, there's a lift from reception to get you there, though it is small.

THE ROYAL EXCHANGE THEATRE, MANCHESTER

Address: St Ann's Square, Manchester M2 7HD **Website:** www.royalexchangetheatre.co.uk
Telephone: 0161 833 9833 **Hours:** performance times vary; café open from 9.30am **Dates:**
closed 25 Dec **Entry fees:** ticket prices vary; [D]half-price

Situated within Manchester's vast former Cotton Exchange, the futuristic Royal Exchange Theatre demonstrates an electrifying mix of ancient and modern that works on every level. This is an exciting place to visit with every care taken to make your visit a pleasure.

Opened in 1976, most of the steel-and-glass structure of the Royal Exchange Theatre is suspended from four giant columns, erected inside what was once the largest trading hall in the world. Productions in the main theatre are enthralling, with its in-the-round design (the biggest in Britain) meaning every member of the audience feels a connection with the performers. Together with the work of the innovative backstage crew, productions are always memorable. There is also the smaller Studio space, where new and more experimental works are put on for short runs. With pre-performance jazz, Q & A sessions after some performances, and theatre tours, visits here are always accompanied by a sense of energy and enthusiasm. There is a very decent restaurant for lunch or dinner, bars, a shop and continually changing displays, all contained on one huge floor, which makes navigation very easy.

Arriving by car, you'll find twenty or more Blue Badge bays within two minutes of the theatre. Access to the building is by steps or a very comfortable lift. If the lift is out of action, there are several other lifts in the building which can also be used. Staff make every effort to accommodate people with any type of disability. Wheelchair spaces in the main theatre are located on the second row, with excellent unimpeded views and the comfort of not blocking patrons sitting behind. Some performances are BSL-signed and most are audio-described. Studio seats are usually not reserved but an exception will be made if you make a request. There are plenty of accessible toilets.

IDEAS ▶▶ Arts

Disability Cultural Projects (www.disabilityarts.info) continues some of the work of the National Disability Arts Forum, which sadly ended its seventeen years of campaigning for arts inclusion in 2008, following a lack of funding. DCP's work includes a national online access database (www.artsaccessuk.org) and a free weekly newsletter, EtCetera. They also have two functions on the website that are searchable by geographical area – a handy events calendar and a useful directory of links to other organisations involved in disability arts around the UK, from small, local projects to nationwide schemes.

Long-established charity **Artsline** (www.artsline.org.uk), was originally set up to promote access to the arts and entertainment and is still going strong twenty-five years later with a team dedicated to assessing facilities, and an online database of access information for venues from galleries to theatres to cinemas, across London only. They also have a handy link-up with the London Open House event, and have assessed over 130 of the fabulous buildings that open their doors to the public for one weekend every September.

Shape (www.shapearts.org.uk) has been campaigning in London for over thirty years with similar aims. Check out the Shape tickets scheme – for £25 per year membership includes up-to-date listings of all current productions in London including details of assisted performances, a fully accessible online, telephone and postal booking system and regularly reduced ticket prices and waived booking fees. Plus, if you are unable to get to the venue on your own, they have a trained team of volunteer access assistants who can assist you to and from the event at no extra charge.

Viewing hide at RSPB Ribble Discovery Centre

RSPB RIBBLE DISCOVERY CENTRE, FAIRHAVEN LAKE

Address: Fairhaven Lake, Lytham St Annes, Lancashire FY8 1BD **Website:** www.rspb.org.
uk/ourwork/conservation/projects/ribble/doing.asp and www.fairhavenlake.com **Telephone:**
01253 796292 **Hours:** 10am–5pm **Dates:** closed 25–26 Dec **Entry fees:** free; some special
events have a small charge

If you're taking the family to the Blackpool Illuminations then this is the ideal place to
take the kids for a slightly more edifying run-around in the fresh air beforehand. Less
than ten kilometres down the coast from the razzmatazz you'll find yourself in this
oasis of calm on the Fylde Peninsula, between Lytham town and the sea.

The Ribble Discovery Centre at Fairhaven Lake (also known as Ashton Marine Park)
is an education and observation centre on a 600m-long artificial lake, created by enclosing tidal sands and mud banks. The Ribble estuary is an important habitat for many
species of birds, including black-tailed godwits, pink-footed geese, wigeons and golden
plovers. In the spring, redshanks and lapwings nest in the area and at any one time, up
to a quarter of a million migrating birds can be seen here. The centre organises bird
walks and illustrated talks and runs a fully accessible shop, an education room with
interpretation boards and sensory bird-call buttons, and CCTV to view the lake. The
centre is funded by Fylde Council, the RSPB and corporate donations, but it's not an
official reserve and there are no hides, no screens, and no formal research.

The lakeshore is very accessible for people with mobility problems. There's adequate
parking, and a good, hard, level path all around the lake (1.4km; allow 30 minutes;
you can get wheelchair-pushing help from a volunteer if you need it) and they have
a wheelchair-accessible boat for water trips. The education facility tries very hard to
involve people with sensory problems and volunteers are on hand to attend to any specific requests. At various points around the lake are an independent café, RADAR-key
toilets, benches and several parking areas.

THEATRE BY THE LAKE, KESWICK

Address: Lakeside, Keswick, Cumbria CA12 5DJ **Website:** www.theatrebythelake.co.uk
Telephone: 01768 774411 **Hours:** morning until midnight **Dates:** closed 25 Dec **Entry fees:**
[D]reduced price; ticket prices vary depending on seat, stage and production

It may not be what you'd expect to find on the banks of Derwent Water, but Theatre by the Lake, a registered charity funded from the Arts Council Lottery Fund, has succeeded brilliantly in bringing the dramatic arts to a part of the country more commonly associated with bracing walks and cloud-shrouded landscapes. You would be hard pressed to find a more beautiful setting for a theatre anywhere in the country.

Opened in 1999, and since then expanded, the newly extended complex now houses two stages; the large Main House which seats four hundred, and the hundred-seater Studio. Each summer season the company produces a series of works, with an intelligently interlocking programme which enables you to see several different plays in the course of a long weekend. In addition, there's a year-round repertory programme, and the theatre hosts a string of annual festivals, including literature, jazz and film. There's a comfortable café and a good bar, as well as a very reasonably priced and efficiently-staffed restaurant which offers a full pre-theatre menu.

Theatre by the Lake

Reaching the venue is easy: there's a huge car park at the theatre with a dozen or so disabled bays just outside the entrance. The theatre has a wheelchair to transfer you inside if necessary. Inside, seats are taken out for disabled patrons in wheelchairs (by prior arrangement). Access is generally good, with accessible toilets on all floors – though the restaurant's accessible toilet is somewhat tricky to get to. Pre-performance touch tours, captioned performances and audio-described performances are scheduled for certain performances.

Urbis

URBIS

Address: Cathedral Gardens, Manchester M4 3BG **Website:** www.urbis.org.uk **Telephone:** 0161 605 8200 **Hours:** daily 10am–6pm **Dates:** closed 25–26 Dec **Entry fees:** free; guided tour [D]£3, [H]free; entry to some exhibitions by paid admission

If any building represents the confidence and energy of the resurgent Manchester in the aftermath of the 1996 IRA bomb, then Urbis must be it. This huge, glass exhibition centre, with its dramatic triangular profile, sits to the north of the city centre, and strikes a marked contrast with its historical neighbours, Chetham's School of Music and Manchester Cathedral.

Inside, the vast reception area, which reaches to the top floor, gives you an awe-inspiring feel for the scale of the building, as the upper floors seem to recede towards the building's peak. You will find you just want to sit and take it all in. Manchester architect Ian Simpson's building began life as a permanent Museum of the City, celebrating urban culture across the world, but this has been superseded by a diverse series of rolling exhibitions of city life, from *Taxi!* in 2003 to *Urban Gardening* in 2008. There's a well-designed shop, with spacious aisles and low-level displays, and a roomy café with a stupendous glass wall. If you want lunch or dinner, the *Modern*, on the top floor, serves up modern-British fare, based around locally sourced produce, with a stunning, city panorama backdrop.

Urbis aims to be fully accessible and DDA-compliant in everything it does, and staff are certainly alert to the needs of disabled visitors. This is a very comfortable building to navigate – plenty of space, level floors, good lifts and helpful staff – and it has won several national Access awards. Although it has no dedicated parking, there's multi-storey parking with many accessible spaces at the nearby Manchester Arena, and there is easy, public-transport access by bus, metro or train – Victoria railway station is next door.

WINDERMERE LAKE CRUISES, CUMBRIA

Address: Windermere, Cumbria **Website:** www.windermere-lakecruises.co.uk **Telephone:** 015394 43360 **Hours:** schedules vary seasonally; check website and call ahead **Dates:** closed 25 Dec **Entry fees:** prices vary, check website

Windermere is not just England's longest lake, but for many people also its most beautiful. Certainly the rugged majesty of the Lake District scenery is spectacular, and a cruise is the ideal way to appreciate it. You might think boats and piers don't mix with disabled passengers, but these cruises can be a great experience, even for wheelchair-users.

There are numerous choices of journey – starting from Bowness, Waterhead (for Ambleside) and Lakeside – and a wide variety of vessels, offering cruises from less than an hour to three hours. This means a range of permutations is open to you, depending on your disability. When you take the *Swan* from Bowness to Ambleside, for example, you'll find pier access is excellent and a perfectly adequate ramp takes you on deck. There's no wheelchair access to the upper deck or to the downstairs bar and toilets, but there are outside seating areas at both bow and stern, and a wonderfully roomy saloon with fabulous views and a café and shop. And the cruise itself is a delight – an experience you won't forget in a hurry.

Cruising on Windermere

All the relevant waterfront areas are step-free and there's generally plenty of parking, though few designated spaces. Ticket offices are easily reached, with induction loops, and staff are usually helpful and informative. Only a couple of the largest boats are fully wheelchair-accessible, while others have walking access from the pier and some special cruises have commentaries. None of the boats have accessible toilets, but they are available pierside at each destination. It's well worth doing some research prior to your visit: there are timetables and maps on the website but there's little disability information, so call first.

YORKSHIRE & THE NORTHEAST

NORTHUMBERLAND

TYNE & WEAR

COUNTY DURHAM

NORTH YORKSHIRE

EAST RIDING OF YORKSHIRE

WEST YORKSHIRE

SOUTH YORKSHIRE

- Baltic Centre for Contemporary Art
- Cragside
- Dalby Forest
- The Deep
- Derwent Valley Railway Path
- Fountains Abbey and Studley Royal Estate
- High House Farm Brewery
- Imax Cinema, National Media Museum
- Locomotion: The National Railway Museum at Shildon

- Low Barns Nature Reserve
- Magna Science Adventure Centre
- Royal Armouries
- The Sage Gateshead
- Seven Stories, The Centre for Children's Books
- Standedge Tunnel, Huddersfield Canal
- Yorkshire Sculpture Park

WHY NOT ALSO TRY ▶▶ Whitby
WHY NOT ALSO TRY ▶▶ York
WHY NOT ALSO TRY ▶▶ Durham

YORKSHIRE & THE NORTHEAST

Nicknamed "God's own county" for its rolling green hills and serene valleys, Yorkshire is Britain's largest county. The historic city of York is a major tourist draw, while the metropolis of Leeds and the craggy coastline around Whitby are just as diverting. The northeast is full of cultural attractions, from the handsome university city of Durham and the vibrant, youthful Newcastle-upon-Tyne to the majestic fortresses that line the lovely Northumberland coast.

BALTIC CENTRE FOR CONTEMPORARY ART

Address: Gateshead Quays, South Shore Road, Gateshead, NE8 3BA **Website:** www.balticmill.com **Telephone:** 0191 478 1810 **Hours:** daily 10am–6pm (Tues opens 10.30am) **Dates:** closed 25–26 Dec & 1 Jan **Entry fees:** free

BALTIC, a huge "art factory" stunningly located on the banks of the Tyne, and comparable with London's Tate Modern, is housed in the old Baltic Mill – a Hovis flour mill opened in 1950 in the centre of Gateshead. It's right next to the Millennium Bridge and boasts dazzling views of the Newcastle waterfront as well as a constantly rotating programme of progressive exhibitions.

The original postwar shell of the building has been kept and a cutting-edge structure

View from the Baltic Centre for Contemporary Art

fitted inside. The gallery floors are extensive, and exhibitions are on display generally for weeks or months at a time. There is no permanent collection, and the emphasis here is on showcasing innovative and occasionally provocative art, with much space given over to local artists and community projects. Work by more famous names previously housed at BALTIC includes a retrospective of the conceptual work of Yoko Ono and a unique, electronically produced 'visual music' exhibition by Brian Eno of Roxy Music fame.

There is designated parking both alongside the building and nearby. If you can't park alongside, the entrance is reachable by a rough brick ramp, so if you are in a chair, make sure your tyres are fully inflated. The lifts to each floor are huge glass constructions, the shop is bright and easy to get around, the toilets are well designed and the café has plenty of accessible seating with those great views of the river. In practice the staff seem to be well-versed in the centre's accessible features, however, despite BALTIC's strong emphasis on education in general and special requirements in particular, written access information is strangely lacking but regular tours of the exhibitions can include BSL if required. And before you leave, try a visit to the highly rated, independent, rooftop restaurant.

CRAGSIDE

Address: Morpeth, Northumberland NE65 7PX **Website:** www.nationaltrust.org.uk/main/w-cragsidehousegardenandestate **Telephone:** 01669 620333 **Hours:** house open Tues–Sun Mar–Oct 1–5.30pm (4.30pm in autumn); gardens and estate open Wed–Sun Mar–Dec 10.30am–7pm (dusk if earlier); house and grounds open bank holiday Mondays **Dates:** closed 22 Dec–mid-March **Entry fees:** [D]£11 [H]free [A]£11 [5–15s]£5.50 [C]£11

Cragside was the first private house in the world to be lit by hydroelectricity and was the home of the scientific innovator and philanthropist – and arms manufacturer – Sir William, Lord Armstrong. It's an intriguing house to visit, with superb grounds, but access can be tricky (call in advance).

The late nineteenth-century Tudor-style house is chock-full of the evidence of a lifetime of collecting, amassing, spending and inventing. Among the more memorable features are the gargantuan and elaborate fireplace which uses ten tonnes of marble. Armstrong dammed the Debdon Burn below the house and his turbines succeeded in generating enough electricity to power the property's lighting (there are some new interactive exhibits in the Power House). After the room-by-room visit, you can use the virtual computer tour to see any areas that you may not have been able to reach. Refuel with a very good meal in the restaurant before exploring the huge estate. The gardens are stunning (although by no means fully accessible) and feature the largest rock garden in Europe, a tricky rhododendron maze and one of the last surviving colonies of red squirrels in England.

From the car park, it's about 100m gently downhill to the visitor centre. There are accessible toilets here and in the house. Cragside has some rough surfaces and steep gradients, and you won't be surprised to find that the location of the house above the burn means this isn't the easiest site to get around. The house has a ramped entrance, however, and a lift to take you from the ground floor to the six wheelchair-accessible rooms on the first floor. Outside, some gentler, signposted routes include a fully accessible path around a lovely lake.

DALBY FOREST

Address: Dalby Forest Visitor Centre, Low Dalby, Pickering, Yorkshire YO18 7LT **Website:** www.forestry.gov.uk/dalbyforest **Telephone:** 01751 460295 **Hours:** no closures; visitor centre daily 9.30am–4.30pm **Dates:** closed 24–25 Dec **Entry fees:** free (fee for parking)

Being close to Whitby on the rugged North Yorkshire coast, a visit to Dalby Forest can provide a pleasant counterpoint to the seaside. This part of the moors is an area of impenetrable woods, long winding walks, hidden lakes and abundant wildlife – but also smooth paths, picnic areas and a visitor centre.

This heavily forested part of the North York Moors has been developed to make it accessible to the public while retaining its wild heart. In fact most of the coniferous forest was planted in the years after World War I, after the Forestry Commission was founded. You can simply drive through (paying a toll), or you can park in various places to enjoy a walk around a lake, give your kids a chance to let off steam in the excellent play areas, or lose yourself on one of the many well-marked walks. Of the two Dalby Beck walks which begin at the visitor centre, the one marked in red (four kilometres) is fairly level and viable for wheelchair-users as far as Ellerburn Pond (the yellow route isn't practicable). On the way to the pond, you'll find a birdwatching hide and an artificial hibernaculum for over-wintering bats. Parking is at the fully accessible visitor centre near Thornton-le-Dale village (no disabled concessions). The centre has displays on sustainable forest management and graded maps so that you can choose a walk of appropriate length and exertion. On-site is the very nice *Treetops Restaurant*, fully accessible, despite its name.

WHY NOT ALSO TRY...

Whitby

Website: www.discoveryorkshirecoast.com **Telephone:** 01947 602674
With an events calendar packed with everything from Viking invaders to northern soul weekends, this vibrant fishing town is always worth a visit. Most of the attractions are down by the waterside, where there's generally smooth level access. And if you want to make a sandcastle, the sand is solid and can take a wheelchair safely. Historic Whitby Abbey overlooking the town is less easy to get to, with a very long walk across grass from the car park: this is a shame as the atmospheric ruins themselves are pretty accessible and very impressive. Contact the Whitby Disablement Action Group on 01947 602674 for travel info and accommodation tips.

THE DEEP

Address: Hull HU1 4DP **Website:** www.thedeep.co.uk **Telephone:** 01482 381 000 **Hours:** 10am–6pm (last entry 5pm) **Dates:** closed 24–25 Dec **Entry fees:** [D]£8.75 [H]free [A]£8.75 [3–15s]£6.75 [C]£7.25

With its sharply pointed front end, and slick grey aluminium exterior, the landmark building that houses The Deep is distinctly shark-like in appearance – aptly so, because this huge aquarium site houses more than forty sharks and 3500 other fish.

As well as a visitor attraction, The Deep is an educational and conservation charity, equipped with impressively high-tech, interactive displays. You are taken on a descending journey to underground levels, exploring from the early beginnings of sea life to todays oceans, and from the warm waters of the tropics to the icy Antarctic. At every level, the giant tanks contain an array of species, from teeming, coral reef-dwellers of the tropics to the strange creatures of the coldest depths. You can get up close and personal with all the residents, be they beautiful, ugly, timid or downright scary. Kids are kept busy the whole time: watch out for the interactive Magic Pool on your way round, and check the website for news of 3D films and seasonal events. The highlight for visitors of all ages is the breathtaking ride in the world's only underwater lift, back up to the ground floor, through the main tank, home of the sharks.

Access around the whole site is excellent. To start with, arriving is easy – the car park has twelve disabled spaces, right next to a designated disabled entrance. Powered scooters, wheelchairs and walking frames are available free of charge, but it's wise to call ahead to book. If you're on foot, there are seating areas on each level – but be warned that descending between each level involves two ramps, which can be crowded at busy times. *The Observatory* café, with its impressive views over the Humber Bridge and estuary, has space between the tables, and movable furniture. Lastly, on several dates throughout the year, "quiet days" are organised, when the audio system is turned down, the lighting turned up and a BSL-trained member of staff delivers a signed presentation.

DERWENT VALLEY RAILWAY PATH

Address: behind Blaydon Rugby Club, Hexham Road, Swalwell, Gateshead NE16 3AD **Website:** www.durham.gov.uk (search under leisure and culture) **Telephone:** 0191 414 2106 **Hours:** visitor centre daily noon–2pm (weekends closes 5pm) **Dates:** closed 25–26 Dec **Entry fees:** free

The 16 kilometre Derwent Valley Railway Path follows the disused railway line through beautiful, wild countryside, historic parkland and reclaimed industrial sites. Much of the path is level tarmac and, with the stress on easy access and with its nearby road connections, this is a wonderful site to visit for all ages and abilities.

The path is actually a complex of routes rather than a single trail, and offers a wide range of surfaces and views. The most straightforward plan is to follow the river on one of the fully wheelchair-accessible paths on each bank, through the park on the Derwent Walk. You'll pass through woods and meadows, circle lakes and ponds and cross the river. There are fully accessible visitor centres at Swalwell and Thornley Wood, and accessible observation hides overlooking bird-feeding stations, ponds and wetlands. The route encompasses the release zone of the Northern Kite Project where 94 red kites were released between 2004 and 2006, and it's also an area rich in historical sites. Along the railway line trail itself, you'll find the Nine Arches viaduct and Derwenthaugh Park (the site of the Derwenthaugh Coke Works and Crowley's Ironworks), as well as older sites, including the nineteenth-century Axwell Hall, thirteenth-century Hollinside Manor and the Gibside Estate, which dates from 1620.

Starting from the Swalwell visitor centre, with accessible parking, accessible toilet and information point (remember your picnic – there are no food outlets along the trail), you then head off along twelve kilometres of wide, tarmac paths (six kilometres out, a different six kilometres back) with virtually no gradients, with the option of a further network of more challenging footpaths. There is another accessible toilet just past the halfway mark at Thornley Woodlands Centre. If this sounds too tough, or time is limited, shorter circular routes can be taken by crossing the river near Clockburn Lake or returning from the Nine Arches viaduct, just before Thornley. Alternatively, you can pick up the trail at any of six accessible points from lay-bys on A694.

FOUNTAINS ABBEY AND STUDLEY ROYAL ESTATE

Address: Ripon, North Yorkshire HG4 3DY **Website:** www.fountainsabbey.org.uk **Telephone:** 01765 608888 Dedicated access tel: textphone 18001 01765 608888 **Hours:** main buildings open daily March–Oct 10am–5pm, Nov–Feb 10am–4pm; Deer Park daily dawn–dusk (free) **Dates:** closed 25–26 Dec **Entry fees:** main buildings [D]£7.90 [H]free [A]£7.90 [5–15s]£4.20 [C]£7.90

Studley Royal estate, tucked in a wooded valley, is a hidden gem. Most visitors come for the soaring, eight hundred-year-old ruins of Fountains Abbey, Britain's most complete Cistercian foundation, but the estate, laid out in 1720, includes the beautiful, formal Water Gardens, the wide open spaces of the Deer Park, and more than twenty listed buildings, including the Jacobean mansion of Fountains Hall.

The abbey is close to the West Gate and easily visited in an hour or two. But stunning as it is, it makes up only a fraction of the Studley Royal park, whose eight hundred landscaped acres are a joy to visit and, with a picnic, could easily fill a day. At any time of year, wheelchair-exploration is a delight, thanks to smooth, hard paths everywhere, including a recommended wheelchair route from the West Gate, through the abbey and all around the Water Gardens. There are some gradients, but your workout is rewarded with some stunning, often unexpected views. Throughout the year, special events highlight the park's unique features: floodlit walks around the ruins by night together with appropriate music

Fountains Abbey

York

Website: www.york.gov.uk/visiting/disabled.html

Around a one hour drive away from Fountains Abbey, York is one of the great cities of Europe and undoubtedly worth a visit if you are in the area. The city is full of wonderful sights reflecting its central role in British history from Roman times right up to the present. Historical or not, however, this is a busy modern city: parking in the centre even with a Blue Badge is far from easy, so think about using the fully accessible Park and Ride system. The town centre is hilly but not too steep, and most sites are closely grouped and easily reached.

At the magnificent Minster, the largest Gothic Cathedral in Northern Europe, great efforts have been made to give a measure of physical access and to help those with sensory impairments, while areas that can't be reached can be viewed via displays or on video. This architectural masterpiece includes Roman ruins, Saxon remains, wonderful stained glass, brass-rubbing, and a breathtaking roof vista past the gargoyles to the houses beyond.

The Jorvik Viking Centre brings to life the Viking era in York, recreating entire streets wandered by the Vikings, complete with the smells of tenth-century York. Pre-book the accessible capsule to avoid the queues, or you can even book a private evening viewing if your party has several wheelchairs. Outdoors, the Riverside Walk offers miles of flat path, leaving the hustle of the city behind; or more lazily you can enjoy the same sights from one of the many river cruises, starting from the city centre and with good ramped access to the boats. Check the council website above for substantial information on accessibility, parking and toilets as well as details of talking signs.

(shivers and ghosts guaranteed); classical concerts and firework displays using the abbey as a backdrop; open-air Shakespeare; and theatre groups. You can even join a free floodlit drive-through of the estate for disabled drivers.

West Gate car park has about sixty free, disabled spaces and accessible toilets. The abbey itself is accessible with some small ramps – take the usual care on uneven, grassy surfaces – and almost all of the other main buildings boast good access. Only Fountains Hall, in fact, presents a real problem, with lots of unavoidable steps. If you want the accessible facilities at the visitor centre, you'll have to negotiate a very steep hill down to the abbey and formal gardens. Fortunately, a fully accessible mini-bus is laid on to ease this journey – a superb facility. If you only want the abbey and Water Gardens, arrive at the West Gate entrance, where access is relatively flat.

HIGH HOUSE FARM BREWERY

Address: Matfen, Newcastle upon Tyne NE20 0RG **Website:** www.highhousefarmbrewery.co.uk
Telephone: 01661 886192 **Hours:** Thurs–Tues 10.30am–5pm **Dates:** closed Christmas (call
ahead for details) **Entry fees:** includes brewery tour [D]£4.50 [H]free [A]£4.50 [12–17s]£2
[C]£4.50

This award-winning brewery, not far from Hadrian's Wall, was founded in 2003 in converted, listed buildings on the two-hundred-acre High House Farm, by fourth-genera-
tion farmer Steven Urwin. It produces a range of seasonal beers and offers real ale tours,
on which you learn about the beer-making process, and try some samples from a range
that includes the boisterously named ales, *Ferocious Fred* and *Cyril the Magnificent*.

Everything is housed in one complex. Entering from the large car park you are directed up an external staircase, but you can enter independently downstairs, where
there's a platform lift. Upstairs there's a large tearoom and a bar serving High House
ales. Through the bar is the spacious shop, with its bottled ales and local delicacies. This
is also the entrance to the brewery and real ale tour. As you enter the brewery the cut-
away floor allows you to listen to the tour guide while overlooking the brewing equipment below. On the tour, walkers descend the staircase located here, to get a hands-on
experience, but the platform lift is available, so everyone can fully participate. Outside
there's a circular country lane walk, or a farm walk, though it's not recommended for
wheelchair-users because of the uneven surfaces and mud.

This is a surprisingly accessible place to visit. The car park is large and level, but has
loose shale, so wheelchair users need to take care. Once inside, every element can be
accessed. There's a good toilet, a large platform lift, small ramps for occasional changes
in floor levels, solid smooth wooden floors and lots of space. The shell of the building
remains, but the interior has been cleverly modernised.

IMAX CINEMA, NATIONAL MEDIA MUSEUM

Address: Bradford, Yorkshire BD1 1NQ **Website:** www.nationalmediamuseum.org.uk
Telephone: 0870 701 0200 **Hours:** Museum Tues–Sun 10am–6pm **Dates:** closed 25–26 Dec
(call or check website for other closures) **Entry fees:** free entry to the museum, IMAX tickets
[D]£6.95 [H]free [A]£6.95 [under 15] £4.95 [C]£4.95

The National Media Museum is a fabulous, accessible destination, with eight floors of
exhibitions, cinemas, simulators and galleries on photography, film, TV, animation and
science. It's a wonderful day out for children, but few visitors will fail to enjoy it.

Seeing a movie in the blissfully accessible, giant-screen, 3-D IMAX cinema
– the chief attraction – is an absolutely staggering experience with real wow-factor,
leaving you goggle-eyed in your seat, and applauding wildly at the end. Book tickets
in advance. The rest of the museum, with the exception of a couple of simulators, is
equally accessible, with widespread Braille and tactile labels, plus a number of staff who

can sign. Highlights – especially appealing to kids – include the blue-screen interactive studios that allow you to read a TV news bulletin or ride a magic flying carpet. Recent temporary exhibitions have included Here's One We Made Earlier: 50 Years of Blue Peter, and Breaking News: 140 Years of the Press Association.

Thanks to Bradford's busy one-way system and poor signage to the parking, the museum can be tricky to reach, and some of the disabled parking bays are on a slope. Once inside, though, it would be hard to improve upon. At the IMAX Cinema, access is perfect and completely level: a very wide, comfortable back row is fully dedicated to wheelchair-users and their companions, and offers some of the best views in the house. Headphones are provided for those with hearing impairments. The museum café has lots of room, low counters and movable seating throughout.

LOCOMOTION: THE NATIONAL RAILWAY MUSEUM AT SHILDON

Address: Shildon, County Durham DL4 1PQ **Website:** www.locomotion.uk.com **Telephone:** 01388 771448 **Hours:** Mar–Oct Mon–Sun 10am–5pm, Oct–Apr Wed–Sun 10am–4pm **Dates:** closed 22 Dec–2 Jan **Entry fees:** free; entry fees for some events

The very accessible and well thought-out Locomotion, an extension of the National Railway Museum in York, provides a stimulating day out. Railway buffs will be keen to

Durham

Website: www.durhamtourism.co.uk

WHY NOT ALSO TRY...

The magnificent historical centre of Durham is enclosed by a sharp bend in the River Wear. The town centre is fully accessible in the sense that there are no steps, but there are few extensive level areas and some challenging surfaces. Though worth the effort, it's undeniably hard work! The Cathedral in its hilltop position, is not easy to reach on foot. However, it does have a limited amount of Blue Badge parking, or the Cathedral bus (no.40) is a kneeling, wheelchair accessible service connecting the rail station, main car parks and other central points every twenty minutes throughout the day. At the Cathedral itself, staff have worked hard on access, with ramps and signage allowing you a full impression of the history and wonder of the place. A council sponsored access guide for the city is available at www.burrows.co.uk/durhamaccessguide.

YORKSHIRE & THE NORTHEAST

explore Britain's railway heritage in detail, but most visitors are happy simply to wander among these magnificent engines, some of them getting on for two hundred years old.

The museum consists of seven restored buildings and a brand-new structure for the main collection, housing seventy vehicles, all on the site of Britain's first passenger transport line, opened in 1825. At reception, videos and models help you plan your visit and you're then free to wander around the site. You can see the ground floor of the historical cottages, the goods and parcel offices, the station and the coal drops, all of which have interactive info points. As well as the engines, there is restoration work taking place, or you can try your own skills as a railway worker on a locomotive. The Travel Challenges feature presents the impact of transport on the environment. If the edutainment gets too much, there are plenty of picnic areas and space for children to play.

Most buildings are clustered together near the car parks, and are all accessible. There are smooth paved and tarmac pathways between all buildings. The only separate building, housing the main museum collection, is a ten-minute walk on flat tarmac, and a fully wheelchair-accessible bus also makes the journey every few minutes. The collection is displayed on one level, and surrounded by acres of space. Shop, toilets and café are all perfectly accessible. The only thing you may not manage in a wheelchair is a trip on the old steam train, but staff are extremely keen to help where they can.

LOW BARNS NATURE RESERVE

Address: Durham Wildlife Trust, Witton le Wear, Bishop Auckland, County Durham DL14 0AG **Website:** www.durhamwt.co.uk/LowBarnsVisitorCentre.htm **Telephone:** 01388 488728 **Hours:** reserve daily 9am–4.30pm; visitor centre Sat, Sun & bank holidays 10am–4pm (also open on summer holiday weekdays, voluntary help permitting) **Dates:** closed 25–26 Dec **Entry fees:** free (parking at weekends £2)

Low Barns Nature Reserve is set in a secluded location alongside the River Wear in West Durham. Based around two old gravel lakes in a meander of the Wear, and also encompassing woodland, it affords easy access to many types of habitat, and a surprisingly wide range of wildlife: people regularly see roe deer, stoats and even otters.

Essentially this is a circular walk of about two kilometres, starting from the visitor centre around the central Marston Lake, and with the option of a detour to one of the observation hides. There are four hides in all, giving you great views of Marston Lake with its islands and marshes; West Lake with its reed beds and wet pasture grazed by Exmoor ponies; and Alder Wood, which is an ancient wet woodland. There is a visitor centre, butterfly garden, coot pond and observation tower. There's a wonderful boardwalk through the reed beds and also several winter-feeding stations, attracting a huge variety of birds. Look out for brilliant kingfishers and, in summer, even migrant pied flycatchers. In fact, for such a small area there is incredible diversity here.

This is a very accessible site. There is tarmac parking, currently being extended, and an accessible toilet. Paths are level and firm, with few gradients, though they do get muddy and some patches of loose chippings fill puddle areas – electric chairs will have no trouble, but manuals may need a push. Paths to hides are inclined but well surfaced and the boardwalk is flat and wide. All the hides are spacious, with low windows. The only inaccessible feature is the observation tower, but a video link is provided if you can't manage the climb.

MAGNA SCIENCE ADVENTURE CENTRE

Address: Sheffield Road, Templeborough, Rotherham, Yorkshire S60 1DX **Website:** www.visitmagna.co.uk **Telephone:** 01709 720002 **Hours:** daily 10am–5pm (closed some Mondays: call to check) **Dates:** closed 24–27 Dec, 31 Dec & 1 Jan **Entry fees:** [D]£9 [H]free [A]£9 [5–15s]£7 [C]£8 (15% cheaper bought online)

Magna has four huge interactive pavilion structures built inside the shell of what was once one of the biggest steel mills in the world. The thread that runs through the vast centre (500 metres long and twelve storeys high) is the demonstration and celebration of science, and particularly the ear-splitting heavy industry of the north, which is now largely historical. Everything they do at Magna is done on a monumental scale.

The four pavilions represent the four elements, earth, air, fire and water, each one housing themed collections of experiments and demonstrations, mounted informatively and challengingly. You can operate a JCB, blast a rock face, fire a super-soaking hose, shine searchlights and engage in masses of hands-on gadget adoration. Together with a shop, the *Fuel* restaurant, the *Energy* café (all fully accessible) and the extensive play areas Sci-Tek and Aqua-Tek, which also welcome people with disabilities – not to mention the fun to be had from zip wires, abseiling, bungee-jumping and dodgems – there's enough here to occupy most families for a long day. And just to remind you what it's all built upon, at regular intervals they fire up the steel mill's original arc furnace for The Big Melt, in a ground-shaking, post-industrial, multi-media spectacular.

Although the designated parking spaces aren't wide enough to be compliant, once you're inside Magna, the site is superb for those with mobility problems. The incredible scale means it never gets crowded, even when more than a thousand people are here at once. A huge, slightly sloped reception area (with excellent low section) leads to lifts, and the pavilions are connected by long, wide walkways with a perfect metal surface. Make sure your mobility scooter has fully-charged batteries – you could cover miles in a visit – and if you're coming in winter be sure to dress warmly. Note also that visually-impaired visitors may struggle with the low light in much of the building, while hearing-impairment may make the empty, echoing spaces distracting.

Magna Science Adventure Centre

Royal Armouries

ROYAL ARMOURIES

Address: Armouries Drive, Leeds, Yorkshire LS10 1LT **Website:** www.royalarmouries.org
Telephone: 08700 344 344 **Hours:** daily 10am–5pm **Dates:** closed 24–26 Dec **Entry fees:**
free (admission fee for some events)

Light, airy and spacious, this state-of-the-art exhibition space houses an extensive range
of arms and armour from ancient hunting weapons to the present day. More than 8500
exhibits from the national collection, formerly in the Tower of London, are displayed over
five floors in a series of themed galleries. You'll know already if it takes your fancy, but less
enthusiastic visitors usually leave enlightened and impressed too.

The Royal Armouries is not just weapons in cases; there are interactive displays and a
number of audio presentations in each of the galleries as well as film shows and special
events. Daily presentations include horse shows, jousting bouts and falconry, the latter
taking place in the nearby outdoor Tiltyard. One gallery is dedicated to oriental weap-
onry – you won't miss the full body-armoured Mughal elephant. The central part of the
museum is ground floor only – so there's a great view up to the roof. At each level, glass
walkways link the galleries on either side – crossing them is not for the faint-hearted. The
Bistro, located just inside the entrance, offers a good variety of refreshments, especially at
lunchtime, whilst the second-floor café has a more limited choice. There's also a picnic area
on the fourth floor with drinks and snacks machines.

There are six free disabled parking spaces next to the Tiltyard and further (paying) bays
in the nearby multi-storey car park. The entrance is across a level, paved area and, once
you're inside, access between each level is via one of the four lifts, though be warned these
can be extremely busy at peak times. If you need to borrow a manual wheelchair, they have
four to loan. There are accessible toilets throughout. The displays are well lit, although
some of the printed descriptions are hard to read and there's only limited Braille labelling.
In addition to plentiful seating, there's the bonus of portable gallery stools.

THE SAGE GATESHEAD

Address: St. Mary's Square, Gateshead Quays, Gateshead NE8 2JR **Website:** www.thesagegateshead.org **Telephone:** 0191 443 4661 **Hours:** daily 9am–9pm **Dates:** closed 25–26 Dec **Entry fees:** free entry; performance prices vary

Designed by Norman Foster, the remarkable Sage Gateshead sits high above the Tyne, like a great soap bubble of steel and glass. Built to be the northeast's premier concert venue, it hosts music events from classical to rock, from brass to jazz and from folk to soukous.

The now iconic outer shell houses three major spaces. Hall One is a 1700-seater, state-of-the-art concert hall with extraordinarily good acoustics, capable of showcasing the Northern Sinfonia and a solo artist equally well. Hall Two is smaller and more experimental – a ten-sided space with many movable seats where the stage can be reconfigured and even transformed into a dancefloor. The third venue, the Northern Rock Foundation Hall, is a rehearsal and participation space. There's great emphasis on education and experiment and a fizzing energy in everything they do here. Outside the auditoria, a very large public concourse includes a café, bar, chill-out areas and shops: it's a fine, enlivening place to attend a performance, or just to come for a coffee and survey the brilliant view.

There's Blue Badge parking right outside the front door and an abundance of properly designated disabled spaces around the outside. All of them lead to simple, level access to the building. Whether in toilet changing areas (plenty of accessible toilets on every level), loops, venue audibility, ease of movement from one point to another, or low surfaces in retail areas, designers have clearly given the issues careful thought, and put their decisions into workable practice. And it's a very welcoming space indeed, with positive, well-informed staff. If there's one – relatively minor – criticism to be made, it's that the co-ordinated design results in some dark areas and occasionally poor colour contrast for those with visual impairment.

The Sage Gateshead

SEVEN STORIES, THE CENTRE FOR CHILDREN'S BOOKS

Address: Ouseburn Valley, Newcastle Upon Tyne, NE1 2PQ **Website:** www.sevenstories.org.uk **Telephone:** 0845 271 0777 **Hours:** Mon–Sat 10am–5pm, Sun 11am–5pm **Dates:** closed 25–26 Dec **Entry fees:** [D]£4 [H]£4 [A]£5 [4–16s]£4 [C]£4

Housed in a converted warehouse, this very special centre – a registered charity whose trustees include Quentin Blake and Philip Pullman – brings books alive for children in every way possible. Not a conventional bookshop, not a library, this place is quite unique, using every technique possible to provoke children's imaginations and involve them in the wonder of books and reading.

The lowest floor houses the Creation Station, with various activities aimed at school groups. There is a light, airy, fully accessible café on level two, and a gradual slope takes you to the well-designed reception, on level three, with its dropped counter, hearing loop, and plenty of room to sit and catch your breath. There's also a wonderful, colourful bookshop here with displays and activities in abundance. The next two floors are given over to exhibition spaces, currently concentrating on a century of children's fiction, from Toad Hall to Pooh Corner, and mischievous characters in Up to Mischief with Horrid Henry. Level six shows original manuscripts and artwork and the top floor Attic is a magical roof space for storytelling, dressing-up and general fun.

There is no car park and even on-street parking is tricky as the roads are narrow and the area is busy. Try the yellow Quaylink bus, which gets you to within a two-minute walk or push. Once you're here, you'll find the interior of Seven Stories, designed for children, and with DDA in mind, is very accessible. Low levels, space for buggies, bright colours and lots of contrast all work well for children and adults with visual and mobility disabilities. All the passageways are wide and there's a large lift to all levels – though you may have to wait as it's in constant use with buggies, so patience may be needed.

STANDEDGE TUNNEL, HUDDERSFIELD CANAL

Address: Waters Road, Marsden, Huddersfield, Yorkshire HD7 6NQ **Website:** www.standedge.co.uk **Telephone:** 01484 844 298 **Hours:** visitor centre and short boat trips Tues–Sun, from the weekend before Easter to end-Nov 10am-5.30pm (closed Mondays except Bank Holidays); "through trips" 8.30am Weds and Fri all year **Dates:** visitor centre closed Nov–weekend before Easter (no short trips) **Entry fees:** visitor centre free; short boat trips [D]£4 [H]free [A]£4.50 [5–15s]£3.50 [C]£4; "through trips" [D]£10 [H]free [A]£10

At more than five kilometres, the Standedge canal tunnel is the longest waterway tunnel in Britain, and also drills deeper beneath the hills above than any other (194 metres). Fully accessible canal boats make exploratory short voyages into it in season, allowing you to experience a mode of transport that was part of the fabric of the British economy in the nineteenth century.

Living history, kept alive by knowledgeable enthusiasts and locals, is done really well at Standedge (pronounced Stannige): take your place in the glass-roofed boat for a fascinating trip into the Huddersfield Narrow Canal as you enter the torch-lit darkness beneath the Pennines. The tunnel, which opened in 1811, having taken seventeen years to construct, was mostly lined with brick, but was left as bare rock in places. You can still see the footmarks on the tunnel roof where men would "walk" the boat along by lying on the top of the cabin. Look out, too, for the connecting tunnels to the three parallel rail tunnels, only one of which is still in use. The visit takes you 500 metres into the tunnel and back again, and lasts about thirty minutes. Complete your visit with a tour of the fully accessible visitor centre, where you can learn in fascinating detail about the race to connect east and west under the Pennines.

There are four designated Blue Badge spaces at the small visitor centre car park, right by the tunnel entrance. You buy your tickets for short boat trips from the adjacent Tunnel End Cottages, which also has snacks and drinks: the boats are fully wheelchair-accessible. If you want to make a "through trip", all the way to Diggle at the other end, you need to make advance arrangements to travel in the passenger section of an electric tug pulling regular water traffic (boaters cannot motor through, but have to be towed), which takes about three hours. You can contact British Waterways with any questions on 0113 281 6860.

YORKSHIRE SCULPTURE PARK

Address: Bretton Hall, West Bretton, Wakefield WF4 4LG **Website:** www.ysp.co.uk **Telephone:** 01924 832631 **Hours:** open daily April–Oct 10am–6pm, Nov–March 10am–5pm (Longside gallery 11am–4pm & 11am–3pm) **Dates:** closed 25–26 Dec (call to check other closures) **Entry fees:** free (parking £4)

Set in five hundred acres of the eighteenth-century Bretton Estate, the Yorkshire Sculpture Park displays sculpture in the open air, in a woods and grassland setting, rolling down to a large lake. Culturally stimulating and fun – with plenty of room for children to run around – this makes a great day out.

Woodland glades and open spaces provide a landscape context for dozens of contemporary pieces, including works by Barbara Hepworth and huge bronze sculptures by Henry Moore. The Access Sculpture Trail, about 800 metres from the main car park, is a sensory landscape area of the park, developed to be accessible to everyone, and focusing on scent, touch, sound and texture. In addition, there are several indoor galleries around YSP centre – the Bothy, Garden, and new Underground galleries – where you can enjoy sculpture regardless of the weather. There's no direct, hard-surface footpath to the huge Longside gallery, in a converted riding school at the southern end of the park, but if you can manage the distance, you can walk up there along the fence-line (1.1km from the lake in the middle of the park), drive (a couple of kilometres) or take the YSP shuttle bus.

The main entrance and car park are on the north side of the park, outside the village of West Bretton. Free Blue Badge parking bays and accessible toilets are available at all YSP's car parks, and at the Longside gallery exclusive Blue Badge car park at the southern end of the park. YSP covers a large area, and some parts are hilly, so you may want to drive around as much as possible. But many of the paths are easily accessible to wheelchairs and pushchairs, as are all the indoor galleries (for temporary exhibitions) and the visitor centre, shop and café at YSP centre near the main entrance.

Yorkshire Sculpture Park

WALES

SNOWDONIA
NATIONAL PARK

PEMBROKESHIRE
COAST NATIONAL
PARK

BRECON BEACONS
NATIONAL PARK

- Aberglasney Gardens
- Brecon Mountain Railway
- Centre for Alternative Technology
- Conwy RSPB Nature Reserve
- Gigrin Farm
- Llanberis Lake Railway and nearby attractions
- Llangollen Wharf
WHY NOT ALSO TRY ▶▶ National Botanical Gardens of Wales
IDEAS ▶▶ Activity centres and holidays
WHY NOT ALSO TRY ▶▶ Pontcysyllte Aqueduct

WALES

Cross the border into Wales and you'll find an untamed land with a captivatingly different character. Here mountains thrust skywards from the wild and windswept landscape, crossed by spectacularly scenic roads and railways. Though scarred by the impact of a once thriving mining industry and the aftermath of its demise, the region displays a forward-looking spirit, with Cardiff the world's youngest capital, leading the way.

ABERGLASNEY GARDENS

Address: Aberglasney Gardens, Llangathen, Carmarthenshire SA32 8QH. **Website:** www.aberglasney.org **Telephone:** 01558 668998 **Hours:** daily Apr–Sep 10am–6pm, Oct–Mar 10.30am–4pm **Dates:** all year, except 25 Dec **Entry fees:** [D]£7 [H]free [A]£7 [5–15s]£4 [C]£7

Abandoned and neglected for half a century, the house and gardens at Aberglasney have a history which goes back nearly five hundred years. Now, rescued from dereliction, they are gradually being restored to their former glory. For garden-lovers, visiting is a treat of the first order.

Access to the ground floor of this imposing house is level, and here you can see how the interiors have been stripped back to their brickwork, ready for restoration. At the rear of this floor – where most of the walls had practically collapsed – the unique, award-winning "Ninfarium" (a subtropical garden based on the ruin-garden of Ninfa, near Rome) has been created by installing a glass atrium over the tumbledown walls. Outside, level paths take you to the famous Cloister Garden, with its old Jacobean raised terraces. This is a paradise for photographers and gardeners alike, and if you go in autumn you might even catch a glimpse of the naked ladies – a rare leafless lily. There's a top-quality tearoom in the garden, which specialises in home-made food using local produce, and you can sit on the sun terrace and soak in the view of the beautiful pool garden. Just beyond this is a new sunken garden, the geometric design of which perfectly complements Aberglasney's understated grandeur.

The sloping site is set on a damp Welsh hillside. But if you keep to the recommended access route, you'll find it mostly level, firm, and well-drained. There are plenty of seats located around the gardens, but be warned, whilst the low walls might look like tempting perches, they're held together with authentic lime mortar, and are not secure. The Ninfarium has a level route around it; the sun terrace also has level access; and the tearoom is partially accessible, but only on the ground floor and over a 5cm step. You can finish your visit with a trip to the plant shop, and take home a living souvenir.

WALES

National Botanical Gardens of Wales

Address: Llanarthne, Carmarthenshire SA23 8HG **Website:** www.gardenofwales.org. uk **Telephone:** 01558 668 768 **Hours:** 10am–6pm beg Apr–end Oct; 10am–4.30pm beg Nov – end Mar **Dates:** closed 25 Dec **Entry fees:** prices vary depending on season (check website for details)

These lovely gardens within easy reach of the A48, are set in the grounds of Middleton Hall. Remains of the estate, such as the Double Walled Garden, co-exist with the site's twenty-first-century buildings. Highlights include the gigantic, award-winning Great Glasshouse, design by Norman Foster, the largest single-span glasshouse in the world, which houses a vast array of Mediterranean flora, and the lake and pond walks. The site is well-laid out and totally accessible; it's worth allowing yourself plenty of time to see it all. Wheelchairs are available free of charge (book in advance), and there's also a regular shuttle buggy service to take you to most parts of the gardens.

BRECON MOUNTAIN RAILWAY

Address: Pant Station, Pontsticill, Merthyr Tydfil CF48 2UP **Website:** www. breconmountainrailway.co.uk **Telephone:** 01685 722 988 **Hours:** station opens 9.30am, first train 11am, last train times vary; check timetable on website **Dates:** daily Jun–Sep; Tues–Thur, Sat & Sun April–May & Sep–Oct; weekend Christmas Specials only in Dec; closed Jan–Mar; check website for dates **Entry fees:** [D]£9.50 [H]£free [A]£9.50 [2–15s]£4.75 [C]£7.85

There is something magical about a working steam engine: they seem to live and breathe, enchanting both adults and children alike. And the Brecon Mountain Railway is a chance for disabled people to get up close and personal with the real thing.

The train leaves Pant Station for Dol-y-Gaer via six kilometres of the old Brecon to Merthyr Tydfil route, alongside the picturesque Taf Fechan Reservoir, slowing occasionally for sheep on the line. When it reaches Dol-y-Gaer the engine comes back down past the carriages to recouple direct to the guard's van, and makes the return journey going backwards. This brings you face-to-face with the hot engine as it steams and whistles its way back down the line to Pontsticill, where the train stops for a break. You can either get straight back on, or wait a while for another train – but don't miss the last one. There are tables for a picnic here, with views up the valley to Pen-y-Fan (at 885m the highest mountain in the Brecon Beacons) and there's also a children's play area, and a trackside café constructed from three recycled railway carriages. When you do return to Pant Station, have a look in the locomotive workshop, where you can see steam trains being renovated, and even new ones being built from scratch.

Although there are no designated disabled parking spaces in the car park at Pant Station, it is level and mostly asphalt. There is step-free access to the station, café (opens for breakfast at 9.30am), workshop viewpoint and platform, and there's a disabled-access toilet here as well. Access to the guard's van is via a very steep but secure ramp, and this can only be done with assistance from the helpful and enthusiastic staff. Inside the van there are bench seats and space for up to four wheelchairs, and room to turn all but the biggest scooters – they don't have scooters to loan, but a manual loan chair is available. In December, they run very popular Christmas Specials to visit Santa's Grotto.

CENTRE FOR ALTERNATIVE TECHNOLOGY, POWYS

Address: Machynlleth, Powys SY20 9AZ **Website:** www.cat.org.uk **Telephone:** 01654 705950 **Hours:** open daily from 10am–5.30pm or dusk if earlier; cliff railway open mid-Mar–Oct **Dates:** closed 23–28 Dec & 5–11 Jan **Entry fees:** [D]£7.40 [H]free [A]£8.40 [5–15s]£4.20 [C]£5.40; rates are lower in winter

Occupying the site of a disused slate quarry near Machynlleth, with stunning views over the surrounding hills, the Centre for Alternative Technology – Canolfan y Dechnloleg Amgen – is a leading international institute for the development of practical solutions to the world's environmental challenges. It's a charity, supported by huge enthusiasm from staff and volunteers, and it makes for an inspiring and enjoyable visit.

You'll be struck immediately by the vitality and energy of CAT, where visitors meander alongside the resident poultry and ducks, and volunteers and staff lead guided tours and busily tend the display gardens and organic vegetable beds. The trail around the site (audio tours available) allows you to get involved in the interactive displays and explore fully an impressive range of working demonstrations of sustainability in action, covering everything from wind, solar and water power to organic growing via waste and recycling. There are also some fascinating examples of low-energy ecological building, showing each of us how we can reduce our impact on the planet in our everyday lives.

You arrive either on the sixty-metre-high, wheelchair-accessible, wa-

Centre for Alternative Technology

Activity centres and holidays

The **Calvert Trust** (www.calvert-trust.org.uk; Exmoor 01598 763221, Kielder 01434 250232, Lake District 01768 772255) runs accessible outdoor activity holidays at three centres around the UK; at Exmoor, Kielder in Northumberland and the Lake District. Each centre offers a slightly different mix of activities and facilities. Only Exmoor caters for children, while the Kielder site runs supported care breaks. **The Speyside Trust** (www.badaguish.org; 01479 861285), based near the Cairngorms National Park in Scotland, runs fully assisted activity holidays for adults and children with learning and/or physical disabilities, and has four fully equipped accessible lodges that can be hired out. The **Red Ridge Centre** (www.redridgecentre.co.uk; 01938 810821) in Powys, Wales is traditionally hired out to groups for exclusive use but individuals with disabilities can join activity holidays there, and the centre also runs week stays for those who need a carer to accompany them.

ter-powered cliff railway, or from the disabled parking at the top of the site. You can call ahead on 01654 705993 to book a free electric scooter or manual wheelchair. The paths taking you round the site have been widened and levelled as far as possible to improve wheelchair access, though the nature of the CAT site means some are rough, and a couple of them are too steep for wheelchairs, but the centre is packed with things to take in, so you won't miss much. With so much to see, the on-site wholefood restaurant makes for a welcome break. There's a good shop, too, with an excellent range of books and eco-friendly goods, and a very helpful information service at reception.

CONWY RSPB NATURE RESERVE

Address: Llandudno Junction, Conwy LL31 9XZ **Website:** www.rspb.org.uk/reserves/guide/c/conwy/index.asp **Telephone:** 01492 584091 **Hours:** 9.30am–5pm (coffee shop 10am–4.30pm, or 4pm in winter) **Dates:** closed 25 Dec **Entry fees:** members free, non-members [D]£2.50 [H]£2.50 [A]£2.50 [5–15s]£1 [C]£2.50

Conwy RSPB Nature Reserve is the perfect place to get back to nature: you relax instantly and are ready to view the estuary's large range of birds. This is a hidden gem, packed with interest, even for ornithological novices, and remarkably accessible.

At Conwy you'll find an impressive mix of untamed nature – including serious winds off the estuary – and brilliant access for all, which is a very difficult trick to pull off. The boardwalk is superb, taking you straight into the reeds in perfect safety on an absolutely level wooden track. The star species to tick off here are black-tailed godwits, shelducks and, with a bit more difficulty, water rails poking about furtively in the reeds. The main tracks are firm and hard, generally smooth, with only slight gradients, and very well drained so puddles never muddy the issue. The more distant trails are a little more challenging in poor weather, with slightly looser surfaces, but these aren't difficult to avoid. The hides and screens are all adapted for the viewing comfort of wheelchair-users and children.

WALES

The ROUGH GUIDE to Accessible Britain   **149**

Although most RSPB nature reserves would claim to offer what Conwy does, the staff here are enthusiastically trying to improve accessibility at all times and are keen and helpful, without being fussy. The newly built visitor centre contains a welcoming reception area (with low counter and knee recess) and a well laid-out shop with spacious aisles and low displays. There are plans to further improve the car park surface and to provide more than the current three designated spaces, although the car park is huge. They're actively improving the more remote trails, and they post regular updates on the notice board if conditions get challenging. Picnic tables, telescopes, coffee machines and toilets are all accessible and the gates and doors are wide and easily opened.

GIGRIN FARM

Address: Red Kite Feeding Station, South Street, Rhayader, Powys LD6 5BL **Website:** www. gigrin.co.uk **Telephone:** 01597 810243 **Hours:** open daily from 1pm, feeding at 3pm, with seasonal variations **Dates:** closed 25–26 Dec **Entry fees:** [D]£4 [H]£4 [A]£4 [5–15s]£1.50 [C]£4

Gigrin Farm in Powys became the Red Kite Feeding Station in 1993, following a request from the RSPB. The daily feeding of up to four hundred birds is an extraordinary sight and an increasingly popular attraction.

The site is a working farm, so unsurprisingly access isn't perfect, but significant efforts have been made, so if you can manage it, it is worth the effort to see this natural spectacle. Visitors can walk to several kite-viewing hides just before feeding time, and watch as a quarter of a tonne of beef is distributed to the waiting birds which have flown in from the surrounding countryside. What follows is a riot of colour and noise as the kites – resplendent-looking raptors in chestnut, white and black plumage – vie with other birds for the food that has been scattered, and perform natural aerobatics that have become an entertaining feature of the visit. If you're lucky, you may also see

Red Kite

buzzards, and you'll certainly see the splendid peacocks that wander freely around the site. The well-stocked shop is worth visiting, but the separate information and display area is in another timber two-storey building, with a change in levels on the ground floor, which makes access difficult – but this presents no deterrent to seeing the kites being fed.

Gigrin Farm is accessed by a single-track tarmac road. There are no disabled bays, and in fact no formal parking area, and the space available is on a gentle gradient. The main area between the buildings has been tarred and there are no access problems across it or into any of the buildings, all of which are level-access. If you want to see the kites, once you've made staff aware of your disability, you can drive up to the rear of the hides and, using ramped access, view them with other visitors present. A special area in the hides has been designated for visitors with mobility difficulties.

LLANBERIS LAKE RAILWAY AND NEARBY ATTRACTIONS

Address: Snowdonia, Gwynedd, LL55 4TY **Website:** www.lake-railway.co.uk **Telephone:** 01286 870549 **Hours:** Feb–Dec, 3–10 departures per day **Dates:** no services on most Saturdays; no services in Jan; limited service in Feb, Nov, Dec (call or check website) **Entry fees:** [D]£6.50 [H]£6.50 [A]£6.50 [3–15s]£4.50 [C]£6.50 (substantial family discounts)

This steam-train journey, starting out from the foot of Snowdon, is a lovely experience. Based on a simple, effective service that carries you along the north shore of Lake Padarn, it takes in a clear view of Snowdon. Kids adore the trip, but frankly it's fun for just about everybody.

The miniature train – not a toy but once used in the slate mines – pulls several coaches along a track that visits the town of Llanberis, with its typical candy-coloured

Llanberis Lake Railway

houses, and then doubles back to follow the lakeshore northwestwards, before turning round again and returning to its starting point. The sixty-minute round trip includes a stop at a lakeside picnic spot with an excellent children's play area and a wildlife centre and at most stops you can break your journey and pick up a later service. Llanberis itself is the ideal centre for a full day-trip. Apart from being the terminus for the Snowdon Mountain Railway, it boasts the largely accessible National Slate Museum (www.museumwales.ac.uk/en/slate; 01286 870630), the Padarn Country Park where there's accessible parking and toilets (01286 870892), and an opportunity to tour a hydro-electric power station at the visitor centre at First Hydro-Electric Mountain (www.fhc.co.uk/electric_mountain.htm; 01286 870166). The main station at Gilfach Ddu has a large shop and a lovely café to complete your trip.

There are no frills here, but no problems either: there's plenty of parking at Padarn Park station, known as Gilfach Ddu (less than one kilometre from Llanberis town centre and within Padarn Country Park) or in Llanberis itself. The accessible carriage has fold-up benches to accommodate all types of wheelchairs and scooters, and windows offering an unobstructed 360-degree view.

LLANGOLLEN WHARF

Address: Wharf Hill, Llangollen, Denbighshire LL20 8TA **Website:** www.horsedrawnboats. co.uk **Telephone:** 01978 860702 **Hours:** daily, 11am–4pm **Dates:** Easter to October **Entry fees:** horse-drawn [D]£5 [H]free [A]£5 [5–15s]£2.50 [C]£5; motorised aqueduct [D]£10 [H]free [A]£10 [5–15s]£8 [C]£8

If you want a complete break from modern life, what could be nicer than a trip on a horse-drawn canal boat? Peace and quiet, superb Welsh scenery and not even the noise of an engine to disturb the tranquillity. The Horse Drawn Boat Centre offers 45-minute trips along the Llangollen canal, on purpose-built passenger boats, with simple, ramped access for wheelchair-users. Several wheelchairs can be accommodated on each boat, so there's no need to book, and you can choose whether to sit in the open air or under cover. If you want to do the two-hour motor-barge trip across the aqueduct, you'll need to drive to another wharf (or be able to make the bus transfer) and get onto a non-wheelchair-accessible boat. If you can get there, and negotiate four steps onto the boat, the crew will welcome you and make every effort to assist you into position. Besides the boats, the well-maintained canal has excellent, level towpaths, providing the ideal country walk for anyone with limited mobility. There's also the famous and fully accessible tearooms and a well-stocked accessible shop.

Although Llangollen Wharf is superb, getting to it can be challenging. There is next to no signage in the town centre or on main roads, and there's no proper on-site parking for anyone – space for two or three cars on a steep slope, but nothing designated for disabled people. The best option is to dropped off at the wharf and park the car elsewhere. There is a schoolyard nearby which can be used outside school hours, and there's on-street parking and ample parking in the town centre. And the hilly nature of the area can't be avoided; there is no flat way to approach the place. But don't let any of these approach issues put you off – perseverance is amply rewarded.

WALES

Pontcysyllte Aqueduct

Address: Trevor, nr. Llangollen, Denbighshire, **Website:** www. canalboattrust.org.uk **Telephone:** 01691 690322 **Hours:** daily 2pm, 3pm & 4pm in season **Dates:** Easter to October, weekends and bank holidays the rest of the year **Entry fees:** [A]£4.40 [under 16s] free

One of the 'Seven Wonders of the Waterways', this aqueduct is magnificently still held together after 200 years, and suspended 125ft over the River Dee. Unlike the Llangollen Wharf trip, this ride isn't for the faint-hearted. There are two ways across – narrowboat or towpath. Whichever you dare, there's no escaping the excitement of the sheer drops either side.

NATIONAL WATERFRONT MUSEUM, SWANSEA

Address: Oystermouth Road, Maritime Quarter, Swansea SA1 3RD **Website:** www. museumwales.ac.uk/en/swansea **Telephone:** 01792 638950 **Hours:** daily 10am–5pm **Dates:** closed 25–26 Dec & 1 Jan **Entry fees:** free

The National Waterfront Museum uses state-of-the-art interactive technology to celebrate the industry and innovation of Wales, in a way that's accessible and involving. The story is told through the changing lives of the people who made it happen, linking the past to the present, and stressing the international importance of Wales – "the world's first industrial nation," as you'll hear.

The people-friendly building combines the massive brick structure of a 1901 dockside warehouse with a modern new wing of slate and glass. The exhibits are set out in fifteen categories, including energy, people, the day's work, coal and metals, and each area has its own soundscape, evoking the theme. Real lives are featured throughout, from the evocative photos of miners from the local Tower Colliery to the personal accounts of young people working in new industries like IT and design. The achievers category focuses on the careers of famous Welsh women and men, such as Tanni Grey-Thompson, David Lloyd George and Aneurin Bevan. And the connection between culture and history is brought home by examining how lives and work have been linked to Wales's changing industrial heritage. If you plan to visit, be sure to check the website for

WALES

National Waterfront Museum

the packed events schedule: there's a huge variety, from science lectures to interactive "Gener8 days" for budding engineers, a local produce market, and even wine-tasting, and most are free.

The museum makes a big effort to be inclusive. There are five disabled bays right out-side, and plenty more nearby. All entrance ways and interconnecting doors have large pushbutton openers, and there are places to sit, disabled toilets, changing facilities, and a children's play area in the main exhibition. All areas and some displays have interactive touch-screens, complete with audio description and texts in Welsh and English, and real-time BSL interpretation.

RHYL MINIATURE RAILWAY

Address: Marine Lake, Rhyl (10 Cilnant, Mold, Flintshire CH7 1GG) **Website:** www. rhylminiaturerailway.co.uk **Telephone:** 01352 759109 **Hours:** 11am–4pm **Dates:** daily summer holidays; weekends only Easter–Jul & Sep; open bank holidays; check website **Entry fees:** fares [D] £2 [H]free [A]£2 [2–14s]£1 [C]£2; museum free

Here's an attraction to enthral the enthusiast as well as the rest of the family – lovely train trips pulled by steam, electric or diesel locomotives on the seemingly unfeasibly narrow, fifteen-inch (38cm) track for about a mile around the Marine Lake. With all-new station buildings, and a thoughtful concern for accessibility, it's become a very popular outing.

WALES

As it approaches its centenary in 2011, this oldest miniature railway has just completed a very un-miniature rebuild which has aroused great interest among aficionados. When the proposed Marine Lake Environmental Trail starts up from here, there'll be even more interest. Rhyl Railway has a dinky new Central Station, a fine workshop, a museum and a gift shop. Various locomotives are in service, and you can be sure that steam trains – and not some smooth electric substitute – will always be operating on peak days. With an audio-visual presentation, the museum vibrantly chronicles the history of the railway and Rhyl's fairground heritage, and displays locomotives, while the workshop allows you to watch ongoing restoration work.

There is no dedicated parking but there is a municipal car park only 100 metres away, with designated spaces. As the railway building and accessible toilet are virtually new, they're fully DDA-compliant. Where necessary, there are ramps for wheelchair-users and those with mobility difficulties to cross the tracks, and all the approach routes have been checked for compliancy. The whole station site is spacious, and has excellent hard-surfacing. Due to the limited space for wheelchair-access in the carriages, it's best to call beforehand to check availability.

TECHNIQUEST CARDIFF

Address: Stuart Street, Cardiff Bay, Cardiff CF10 5BW. **Website:** www.techniquest.org
Telephone: 029 2047 5475 **Hours:** Mon–Fri 9.30am–4.30pm, weekends & bank holidays
10.30am–5.30pm **Dates:** closed 25–26 Dec **Entry fees:** [D]£4.80 [H]free [A]£6.90 [4–16s]£4.80 [C]£4.80; planetarium £1.20

Committed to making learning fun, accessible and exciting, Techniquest Cardiff is a hands-on interactive science centre for the whole family – and a great place for a day out. You can try your hand at launching a hot air balloon, damming a river, and even observe the smashing to smithereens of a frozen banana. The have-a-go approach is what makes Techniquest so exciting for children and young people.

Techniquest is situated in a recycled Victorian shipyard, full of light and space, and perfect for scientific illumination. On the ground floor, the exhibition is made up of science-based games installations, including explanations of how oil rigs and submarines work, why yachts sail and how rockets fly through space. There's even a colony of leafcutter ants – fascinating to watch. The exhibits are labelled with all the information you need, under helpful headings like Try This and What's Happening? And there are always staff around who are happy to facilitate and explain. The mezzanine is given over to MusicQuest, where you can find out about the science of music and sound, dance on a giant xylophone, and use the whispering dishes to send messages. The centre has its own family-sized lecture theatre, and a planetarium where you can discover how ancient people used the stars to name the days of the week. And if you want to see the frozen bananas, head for Cool Science.

There are eight disabled parking bays at the front entrance to Techniquest, and once inside, there's step-free access to all public areas, places to sit down, and a café. The lecture theatre has very steeply raked seating, but there are seats down at the front, and space for wheelchairs, and there are similar facilities in the planetarium. The accessible toilet is roomy, as is the lift.

WALES MILLENNIUM CENTRE, CARDIFF

Address: Bute Place, Cardiff CF10 5AL. **Website:** www.wmc.org.uk **Telephone:** 08700 40 2000 Dedicated access tel: Minicom: 029 2063 4651, Touch Trust: 029 2063 5660 **Hours:** performance days: weekdays 10am–close, weekends 11am–close; non-performance days: weekdays 10am–6pm, weekends 11am–5pm **Dates:** closed 25 Dec & 1 Jan **Entry fees:** free entry to the centre; performance prices and discounts vary (free entry for helpers)

The award-winning Wales Millennium Centre has a commitment to engaging with the disabled community which is as impressive as the building's iconic design. Theatres can be tricky places for disabled people, but in this case, every effort has been made to make your visit as welcoming and accessible as possible.

Since opening in 2004, the WMC has become a world-renowned venue for the arts, but it is also an inclusive meeting place for the local community. The magnificent Donald Gordon Theatre hosts art events ranging from hip-hop to ballet, opera to musicals, and from contemporary dance to stand-up comedy. There are workshop and studio sessions, behind-the-scenes tours, and free daily performances on the foyer stage. Also in demand are the pre-show touch tours, which explore the building's intentionally varied use of tactile materials and reliefs – which make the centre as memorable to the touch as it is to the eye. You may come here to see the Welsh National Opera or the BBC Orchestra of Wales, but another resident organisation is Touch Trust, which provides creative touch-based music, art, and dance activities for people with profound and multiple disabilities. Most importantly, WMC is a truly public building, where people can come and go, enjoy a free art exhibition, meet, eat, and enjoy.

The centre has eighteen disabled parking bays, all under cover, and bookable in advance. There are automatic doors at all entrances, lifts, and level access to all areas. Accessible toilets are distributed throughout and the auditorium has accessible seating and wheelchair access at all levels. Hearing-impaired patrons will find induction loops (in all key public areas), BSL-signed performances, and captioned performances. And touch tours and audio-described performances are available for the visually impaired. Signage and directions around the building are given in large clear type, in raised text, and in both Welsh and English Braille.

Wales Millennium Centre

SCOTLAND

- Cairngorm Funicular Railway and Ski Centre
- Cairngorm Sled-Dog Safaris
- Callander to Strathyre Accessible Walk
- Culloden Battlefield Visitor Centre
- Culzean Castle and Country Park
- Dundee Repertory Theatre
- Falkirk Wheel
- Glasgow Science Centre
- Loch Insh Watersports
- National Gallery of Scotland
- Nevis Range Mountain Experience (Aonach Mor Gondola)
- Pitlochry Festival Theatre
- The Royal Yacht Britannia
- RSPB Loch Garten Osprey Centre
- Scottish Football Museum
- Scottish Parliament Building, Edinburgh
- Steamship Sir Walter Scott
- Titan Crane Clydebank
- Walking on Air – Gliding near Kinross

IDEAS ▶▶ Festivals

SCOTLAND

Support for devolution from the rest of the UK comes and goes, but Scotland has highlights enough to stand out regardless. Handsome Edinburgh plays on its history but is also a vibrant modern city whilst Glasgow bubbles with energy and vigour. The Highlands' often jawdropping beauty can be easier to reach than you think – while the likes of the Falkirk Wheel and Dundee Repertory Theatre remind you there's life away from the classic draws.

CAIRNGORM FUNICULAR RAILWAY AND SKI CENTRE

Address: Cairngorm by Aviemore PH22 1RB **Website:** www.cairngormmountain.org.uk
Telephone: 01479 861261 (Ptarmigan Restaurant tel 01479 861341) Dedicated access tel:
01479 861 272 (www.disabilitysnowsport.org.uk) **Hours:** Disability Snowsports UK daily 9am–4pm
Dates: DSUK's Cairngorm Ski School 2 Jan–end Mar **Entry fees:** funicular only [D]£9.25 [H]free
[A]£9.25 [5–15s]£5.85 [C]£8; for ski school lesson prices enquire through website

Cairngorm Mountain Railway and Ski Centre is literally the pinnacle of Scotland's tourist industry – a fully wheelchair-accessible visitor centre with viewing decks, shop and bar-restaurant – in the heart of the Highlands, at almost 1100m (3600ft).

Thanks to climate change, the centre has had to reinvent itself as a year-round attraction. The fully accessible funicular whisks you up in eight minutes with ever-changing views, and the vistas and sunsets from the restaurant and viewing decks are simply spectacular – you might even catch sight of some of the resident reindeer. Have a look at the exhibition recounting the mountain's history, enhanced by tactile exhibits, including fur samples of the local wildlife and audio description accompanying the film show. The *Ptarmigan* bar-restaurant serves wholesome food all year round and in summer plays host to "Sunset Dining", bringing together talented local chefs (booking essential) and, on Thursdays, the highest of Highland Flings, accompanied by an extensive buffet. If you can tear yourself away from the mountain-top, the all-abilities trail around the Wild Mountain Garden, back at car park level, is also worthwhile, with plants indigenous to the area. In season, the mountain is home to Disability Snowsport UK, who specialise in getting people onto the pistes, with a full range of adaptive equipment. They offer all levels of instruction, usually one-to-one, from complete beginner onwards, to enable people with almost any disability to ski and board.

There are eight allocated parking bays at the bottom station and a lift to the ticket hall. Bear in mind that the weather can be very changeable in the Highlands and regardless of the time of year you should always be prepared with warm clothing. Even in mid-summer it can snow at the summit. In winter you should call ahead to check on conditions as the

SCOTLAND

Cairngorm Funicular Railway

car park can be snowed-in and the funicular subject to reduced or cancelled services. The four floors of Top Station are fully wheelchair-accessible.

CAIRNGORM SLED-DOG SAFARIS

Address: Moormore Cottage, Rothiemurchus, Aviemore PH22 1QU **Website:** www.sled-dogs. co.uk **Telephone:** 07767 270526 **Hours:** daytime or evening (arrange when booking) **Dates:** trips available between October and April, centre open year-round **Entry fees:** prices vary by length of trip but 30-minute tasters start from £60 per adult and £40 per child in a minimum group of six (weight limit 15 stone/95kg)

Based in the Cairngorms National Park, the Cairngorm Sled-Dog Centre offers dog-sled safaris, on winter snow or muddy track. This is once-in-a-lifetime experience, but you'll need to be fairly robust to do it. Even in good weather, it's no countryside jolly, but a true wilderness experience, with little specific provision made for people with disabilities.

The safaris are undertaken on a two-seater or six-seater sledcart. The dogs sense the excitement in the air when they're going out and their rising anticipation brings the noise level up correspondingly. Before you know it you're hurtling along forest tracks at speeds of up 40kph (24mph) – pretty impressive for dog-power. Alan and Fiona Stewart, who own and run the centre, are totally committed to their sport and their dogs – some of which have competed in the 2000 kilometre Alaska Iditarod. The Stewarts live in the beautiful forest of the Rothiemurchus Estate and have 33 dogs – all competitive, working animals but also friendly and affectionate. The Stewarts' passion for their dogs is matched by their passion for the environment: not only will you have a truly memorable day, but you'll come away enriched by, and more knowledgeable about, the world we live in.

The Stewarts will do everything they can to include anyone who wants to take part in this unique adventure, though you may want to take an experienced helper, to assist you with transfers and the like. You invariably get very wet and muddy, so warm, water-proof clothing is a must. If you're up for being cold, wet, thrown about and completely exhilarated, you'll love it.

CALLANDER TO STRATHYRE ACCESSIBLE WALK

Address: Callander, Perthshire FK17 [no full postcode available, but this pinpoints the car park] **Website:** www.incallander.co.uk **Telephone:** 01877 330342 **Hours:** no closures **Dates:** no closures **Entry fees:** free

Because of the spectacular environment, the strenuous push from Callander to Strathyre – a fourteen kilometre stretch of Sustrans' NCN Route 7 – is particularly recommended to fit and experienced wheelchair-users, with splendid scenic contrasts between Loch Lubnaig and the Strathyre Forest, set off by the more distant mountain peaks.

The small, pretty town of Callander lies on the edge of the Trossachs, 24km west of Stirling. From the car park at the western end of town, follow the *NCN Route 7* signs towards Strathyre. Continue for about 1.5km, until you come to the A821 at Kilmahog, which you need to cross with care, remembering to shut the gate behind you. The trail now follows the old railway line and, after 4.5km, you reach the southern end of Loch Lubnaig, and the trail then stays close to the west shore of the six kilometre-long loch. Towards the north end of the loch, the path begins to climb gently and then goes more steeply uphill. The surface remains good but manual wheelchair-users are likely to need strong assistance After two hairpin bends, you get to a wonderful loch viewpoint. About one kilometre further, you cross a narrow, twenty-metre-long wheelchair-accessible, suspension bridge and a kilometre or so later you reach Strathyre.

Along the largely traffic-free trail, there are accessible toilets at Callander's large car park (six disabled spaces); after eight kilometres at the Strathyre Forest Cabins visitor centre; and finally after thirteen kilometres at Strathyre forest commission car park, at the northwest end of the loch, whose RADAR-key toilet, however, is not always very clean. The whole trail, which is part of the National Cycle Network's *Route 7: Lochs and Glens: Glasgow to Inverness* (www.sustrans.org.uk) is wheelchair-passable in dry weather. As noted, you will need a fit assistant for some of the steeper sections.

CULLODEN BATTLEFIELD VISITOR CENTRE

Address: Culloden Moor, Inverness, Highland IV2 5EU **Website:** www.nts.org.uk/Culloden **Telephone:** 0844 493 2159 **Hours:** 9am–6pm Apr–Oct; 10am–4pm Nov–Mar **Dates:** closed 25–26 Dec **Entry fees:** [D]£10 [H]free [A]£10 [under 18s]£7.50 [C]£7.50

April 16, 1746 was a decisive day in British history – the date on which the British army bloodily defeated Bonnie Prince Charlie's Jacobites in the last battle fought on British soil. The centre is a Highlands must-do and a gem, one of the most fascinating attractions of its kind and accessible to all.

The new centre's natural building materials and sympathetic architecture ensure it

SCOTLAND

blends with its environment. Inside, browse the well-stocked shop, or sample the offerings in the bright, spacious café. The staff are very helpful, doling out advice, directions and tickets, and some giving historical talks in period costume. Hand-held electronic guides (included in ticket price) enhance the experience, particularly while touring the battlefield outside. Using GPS, the guides beep when you arrive at points of interest to give you the background detail. You won't need a beep to notice the Cumberland Stone – the giant boulder that's supposed to mark the spot where the Duke of Cumberland took up his position to direct the battle.

There are ten dedicated parking spaces for Blue Badge holders. It's a short stroll or push to the entrance to the centre, which has level access throughout. The well-crafted displays are presented through vocal and tactile description, as well as by traditional glass-case presentation. There's a rooftop viewing area accessed by an external ramp, which is not too steep (1:21) but rather long, so some chair-users may need assistance. It's worth the effort of getting up here, however, for the best view of the battlefield. The battlefield's hardcore paths are pushable but undulating; again, some chair-users may need assistance in places. Accessible toilets are just inside the visitor centre entrance and there are wheelchairs for loan.

SCOTLAND

CULZEAN CASTLE AND COUNTRY PARK

Address: near Maybole KA19 8LE **Website:** www.culzeanexperience.org **Telephone:**
0844 493 2149 **Hours:** castle daily late Mar–late Oct 10.30am–5pm; country park daily all
year 9am–sunset; check website for details **Dates:** castle closed late-Oct–late-Mar **Entry fees:**
[D]£12 [H]free [A]£12 [5–15s]£6 [C]£12

Culzean Castle – ancestral seat of the Kennedys who claim the lineage of Robert the
Bruce – clings to the rocky Ayrshire coast and commands some of the finest views in
the west of Scotland. The park has plenty of good paths for a woodland stroll, with deer
to look out for and sea air to fill your lungs.

As you enter the castle, you won't miss the obvious statement of power and wealth on
display, in the shape of Britain's largest collection of pistols and swords outside Windsor Castle. This armoury collection was bought from the Royal Family in the early
nineteenth century. The current castle owes much to the efforts of Robert Adam, one of
Scotland's most innovative and influential architects of the late eighteenth century. He
designed the stunning oval staircase, which you can only look upon in wonder, and the
Round Drawing Room, another fine feature, with panoramic views across to the Isle of
Arran. The castle is steeped in history – it was General Eisenhower's preferred accommodation during World War II – and the visitor centre tells its story well.

You're advised to be dropped off at the front door as the car park is about 400m away
along undulating hardcore paths which some wheelchair-users may struggle with. Once
at the castle, however, the ground floor is fully accessible. Upstairs is a different matter:
although there's a lift to the first floor, unless you can get down the staircase yourself, or
with the help of a carer, health and safety regulations state you aren't allowed up in case
of emergency. There are accessible toilets in all the main buildings and the accessible shop
and café are easily accessed for visitors with disabilities.

Culzean Castle

DUNDEE REPERTORY THEATRE

Address: Tay Square, Dundee DD1 1PB **Website:** www.dundereptheatre.co.uk **Telephone:** 01382 223530 (café tel. 01382 206699) Dedicated access tel: textphone 01382 342611 **Hours:** box office Tues–Sat 10am–7.45pm, Sun & Mon 10am–6pm (no performances Sun & Mon) **Dates:** all year, call or check website **Entry fees:** free entry, performance prices vary

Dundee, situated on the banks of the River Tay on Scotland's North Sea coast, was once known for the three "J's" – Jute, Jam and Journalism. It also has the dubious honour of having been Britain's last whaling port. Much has changed since those days. It's now a bustling University town with a thriving arts scene, at the centre of which is the Dundee Rep. With 450 seats the auditorium is a generous arena for a provincial theatre and it has many regular devotees.

The only full-time repertory theatre surviving in the UK, with six permanent acting staff, Dundee Rep is also home to the Scottish Dance Theatre, many of whose recent performances have included dancers with a disability. Commissioning new works and adapting the classics, the productions here are widely acknowledged to be among the finest in Scotland. The theatre has received several prestigious TMA (Theatrical Management Association) awards in recent years, including two in 2007 for the musical *Sunshine on Leith*. In 2009, the ensemble are booked for performances as varied as Ibsen's surreal five-act *Peer Gynt* to the dazzling celebration of the life of legendary performer Al Jolson in *Jolson & Co - the Musical*. As well as regular productions by the Repertory ensemble cast and the Scottish Dance Theatre, there's also stand-up comedy, touring productions and seasonal favourites like panto. And to complete the picture, you'll find a very good, unpretentious bar-restaurant on the ground floor and an upstairs interval bar, both fully accessible.

Parking can sometimes be a problem: there are two dedicated bays near the front doors, so it's best to arrive early to make sure you get one. Access to the theatre – purpose-built and opened in 1982 – is generally very good, with ramped access from the front, a lift to the upper bar and auditorium, and disabled toilets in the upper bar and restaurant. In the auditorium, the dedicated seating areas afford excellent views of the stage, and all abilities are well catered for, with audio-described and BSL-signed performances and pre-performance touch tours available before audio-described matinées.

FALKIRK WHEEL

Address: Lime Road, Tamfourhill, Falkirk FK1 4RS **Website:** www.thefalkirkwheel.co.uk **Telephone:** 08700 500 208 **Hours:** seasonal variations (check website or call for trip times) **Dates:** closed 25–26 Dec **Entry fees:** [D]£8 [H]£8 [A]£8 [3–15s]£4.25 [C]£6.50

The world's first and only rotating boat lift, built in 2001, the Falkirk Wheel replaces eleven locks at the junction of the Union and Forth & Clyde canals, allowing vessels to move between the two waterways and cross Scotland from east to west. Visiting is, for once, a genuinely unique experience.

The Falkirk Wheel

> *Where else in the world can you take a boat trip floating in mid air? As far as I know, only at the Falkirk Wheel. The first view of the wheel is a surreal and breathtaking sight – it looks like a piece of modern art. Disabled access is not a problem and you can comfortably board the boat as it sits in the gondola of the wheel.*
>
> *Our tour guide was amusing and explained the engineering that created the wheel as we experienced a thrilling fifteen minutes while the boat floated up from the Forth and Clyde Canal to join the Union Canal 35m above. On the ascent, we had a bird's-eye view of the surrounding land, and we soon found ourselves at the top, sailing along the Union Canal. The boat passes through the open countryside before returning to make the descent via the wheel to the basin by the Visitors Centre.*
>
> *After the trip, I urge you to try the delicious soup or home baking available in the easily accessible centre. Thanks to the glass roof, as you eat you can watch the spectacle of the wheel rearing up into the sky above you.*
>
> *Reader Review from Vicki McKenna*

The visitor trip, which lasts about an hour, starts as you roll off the boardwalk to board a wheelchair-accessible boat. This slowly motors into the lower gondola of the wheel and is then gently lifted 35m (115ft) up to the Union canal, where it floats off again. The views as you rise are magnificent – on a clear day at least 80 kilometres – with Fife to the east, Argyll to the west, and gorgeous vistas of the Forth Valley between. The rotating wheel itself looks like a double-headed Celtic Axe: a twenty-first-century innovation that links two essential elements of the industrial revolution. What adds to the fascination is that the linkage happens via the Roman era as, once you're at the top, your boat crosses an aqueduct, passes through the 180m (590ft)-long Roughcastle Tunnel, and then sails beneath the Roman Antonine Wall and into the upper basin. It then descends back to your starting point. There's on-board commentary with video, which allows both hearing-impaired and partially sighted visitors to enjoy the trip.

On entering the arc-shaped glass and aluminium complex from the level car park, you're immediately struck by the stunning scale of the operation. The bottom basin appears to be a natural amphitheatre – in fact it was once a quarry – and the paved area all around is level and allows for comfortable pushing. There's also plenty of picnicking room and a café.

GLASGOW SCIENCE CENTRE

Address: 50 Pacific Quay, Glasgow G511EA **Website:** www.glasgowsciencecentre.org
Telephone: 0871 540 1000 **Hours:** mid-March–Oct daily 10am–6pm, Nov–mid-March Tues–Sun 10am–5pm; closed Mon **Dates:** closed 25–26 Dec **Entry fees:** [D]£7.95 [H]free [A]£7.95 [5–15s]£5.95 [C]£5.95

Looking like a segment from a giant orange, Glasgow's stainless-steel-and-glass Science Centre occupies a dominating position amid reclaimed dockland on the south bank of the River Clyde. Opened for the millennium, the centre forms part of a wider group of attractions including an IMAX cinema and the (unfortunately wheelchair-inaccessible) Glasgow Tower, with the new BBC studios next door.

Enjoyable at any age, the Science Centre is above all an exceptional place to take children. Their enquiring minds are allowed almost total freedom here, with visitors encouraged to touch and explore virtually every exhibit. The centre looks at all aspects of science, with the emphasis on making it fun and comprehensible. Highlights include frequent live shows and explosive lab demonstrations, "smell the body part" (sure to get them giggling) and recognisable favourites – like the large pile of K'nex in one corner, for some stealthily -instilled engineering instruction. In fact the interactive exhibits are so entertaining and engaging that you barely realise you're learning something at the same time; they even manage to make the explanation of Pythagoras' theorem seem fun. Whether it's optics or radio, gravity or density, you'll find a cunning exhibit explaining it. While you're here don't miss the Planetarium, which for an additional £2 gives an amazing display of the Glasgow night sky – first with and then without light pollution.

There's a large car park and a drop-off point outside the main entrance. With exhibits over three floors, all of them fully accessible, the centre is well worth a lengthy visit. Each floor is linked by lift and there are accessible toilets on the ground and second floors. The planetarium has space for six wheelchairs.

LOCH INSH WATERSPORTS

Address: Kincraig, Kingussie, Inverness-shire PH21 1NU **Website:** www.lochinsh.com
Telephone: 01540 651272 **Hours:** watersports all year, daily 8.30am–5.30pm; wildlife boat tour, May–Sep 11am, 1pm & 4pm (plus 6pm Jul & Aug); other activities year-round; restaurant daily 9am–5pm low season, 8am–10pm rest of the year **Dates:** no closures **Entry fees:** dependent on activity

Set on the shores of an idyllic loch amongst the sugar-lump peaks of the Cairngorms, Loch Insh Watersports is perfectly positioned. Out of the loch pours the River Spey, tumbling into the Cairngorms National Park and into bottles of whisky. If you enjoy watersports or just messing around on the water, you could easily entertain yourself and the family for days here.

At Loch Insh, you can enjoy the adrenaline of some adventurous activities, especially in good weather, or just relax with a "nip" in the café-bar-restaurant. Just a few minutes' drive from the main A9 artery the loch is easily reached, and has accessible accommodation (excellent-value chalets from 4-berth upwards), plenty of facilities and a host of activities on offer. The Cairngorm Canoeing and Sailing School offers sailing, canoeing, kayaking, windsurfing and fishing from April to October (fishing from February), guided walks, mountain-biking and archery all year round, and snowsports too. They've been operating here for nearly forty years, and make full use of their location and reputation. If you only have time for a short visit, you can do their one-hour wildlife tour on the loch, visiting the RSPB's Insh Marshes Nature Reserve on the hunt for osprey, goldeneye duck and others in the School's motor launch

Both the main entrance at the Boathouse restaurant and the craft shop, a short distance across the car park, have ramped access, with spacious areas for moving around, and the Boathouse has an accessible balcony overlooking the loch. There are disabled parking spaces beside the door of the Boathouse, plus accessible toilets just inside the entrance. The jetties and loch shore are all accessible by wheelchair, via a sloping, hard-surfaced path which runs down to the beach. The team at Loch Insh will happily assist with boarding any craft, including the boat for the wildlife tour.

NATIONAL GALLERY OF SCOTLAND

Address: The Mound, Edinburgh EH2 2EL **Website:** www.nationalgalleries.org **Telephone:** 0131 624 6200 Dedicated access tel: disabled parking tel. 0131 624 6550 **Hours:** daily 10am-5pm (Thurs to 7pm); 1 Jan opens noon **Dates:** closed 25–26 Dec **Entry fees:** free

Right in the heart of Edinburgh, just off Princes Street, lies the National Gallery of Scotland. The Scottish national collection of fine art housed here is, for its size, the equal of any in the world and worth devoting a good half-day visit to.

Masterpieces from Raphael, Titian, El Greco, Velázquez, Rembrandt and Rubens vie for attention with Impressionist works by the likes of Monet, Cézanne and Degas and Post-Impressionists including Van Gogh and Gauguin. The Gallery also houses Antonio Canova's stunning sculpture *The Three Graces*. And above all there's a comprehensive display of Scottish painting, with all the major names, including Allan Ramsay, David Wilkie and William McTaggart represented. Perhaps the best-known painting is Sir Henry Raeburn's *The Reverend Robert Walker Skating on Duddingston Loch*, popularly known as *The Skating Minister*. The whole collection is superbly displayed in an impressive Neoclassical building, whose recent refurbishment involved the bold use of colour. The deep maroon walls might sound dark and dreary but here clever use of light creates an airy, luminous atmosphere.

Parking can be tricky in the city centre but there are four dedicated Blue Badge bays in a pedestrianised area right outside the gallery. If you wish to take in the National Portrait Gallery and the Dean Gallery as well, there's a regular, free, accessible bus that links all three. Since its refit the National Gallery is fully accessible over all levels and is connected by the modern Weston Link to the Royal Academy Building. The link houses a bar-restaurant and café, with views over Princes Street Gardens. Contact the Education department for information on BSL and touch tours.

National Gallery of Scotland

NEVIS RANGE MOUNTAIN EXPERIENCE (AONACH MOR GONDOLA)

Address: Nevis Range, Torlundy, Fort William, Inverness-shire PH33 6SQ **Website:** www. nevisrange.co.uk **Telephone:** 01397 705825 **Hours:** daily, summer 10am–5pm, longer in Jul–Aug; daily, ski season 9am– 4.30pm **Dates:** no closures except in strong winds **Entry fees:** return ticket [D]£9.50 [H]£9.50 [A]9.50 [5–15s]£5.50 [C]£8.25

Aonach Mor, situated in the Nevis Range and a short distance from Scotland's highest mountain Ben Nevis, is the location of Britain's only mountain gondola, taking visitors to 655m (2150ft), and to magical views of the dramatic mountain landscape with its lochs and glens.

The gondola is open year-round, and takes you to the *Snowgoose Restaurant* and Scotland's highest snowsports area. The slopes are abuzz with skiers and boarders in winter, and offer options for both beginners and experts. An adaptive ski instructor is available for anyone with a disability interested in skiing, though this should be arranged in advance. The upper chairlifts above the gondola don't operate in summer, to protect the sensitive vegetation. The site also has world-cup mountain-biking trails, and forest tracks which are navigable by the more adventurous disabled visitor, if they're not too muddy. Beneath the restaurant, the Mountain Discovery Centre has information about the Nevis range's flora and fauna, but access is via a flight of stairs.

The gondolas are able to accommodate wheelchairs up to 60cm wide, but if yours doesn't fit, a ramp is available and transfer onto the gondola seat is quite easy. They also have a narrow chair, which can be wheeled into the gondola by the helpful staff (your own chair can go up with you). The restaurant is accessible by a steep ramp from the outside of the building, just fifty metres from the gondola arrival point, though in winter this may mean a short journey through snow. Its balcony-cum-viewing deck has one small step down to it. There's also a café at the base station, and there are accessible toilets at both the gondola base-station and the restaurant, though this latter one has limited space.

PITLOCHRY FESTIVAL THEATRE

Address: Pitlochry, Perthshire PH16 5DR **Website:** www.pitlochry.org.uk **Telephone:** 01796 472680 **Hours:** theatre and box office daily, summer 10am–8pm, winter 10am–5pm; restaurant and café daily, summer 10am–9pm, winter 10am–5pm; garden 10am–5pm **Dates:** no closures **Entry fees:** free entry to foyer, restaurant and garden; performance prices depend on seats and show (helpers are free)

The Pitlochry Festival Theatre offers more than just performances. Visit the venue for backstage tours, a gallery, a café-restaurant, and seriously extensive gardens on the banks of the River Tummel that will delight keen horticulturalists.

This modern theatre is a walk across a suspension footbridge from the attractive centre of Pitlochry town, a step-free route, albeit steep in places. If you prefer to avoid the hills, it's better to drive to the theatre, where plenty of accessible parking is available, with striking views across the valley. The theatre offers year-round evening perform-ances, and matinées twice a week, but even without seeing a performance, you could spend a few hours here enjoying a tour, the gallery, or simply the beautiful setting. The gardens are a feature in themselves, with a network of tarmac paths, steeply graded in places, but step-free. There's a stone outdoor theatre within the gardens which is rarely used for performances, but it's an interesting spot to visit. Garden tours are offered if you'd like more information about the trees and plants. They last about ninety minutes, but you need to book ahead, and let them know if you have any particular requirements – they'll try to accommodate your needs.

The venue welcomes disabled visitors, with disabled parking by the main entrance, good access into the theatre, four wheelchair spaces in the auditorium and free tickets for carers. Tours of the backstage area, including the Green Room, are available, and can be conducted as a "touch-tour" for visually impaired visitors. A hearing loop is fitted in the theatre, and audio tours can also be arranged with advance notice. The art gallery is mostly accessible, though some twenty per cent of the display is upstairs, and there's no lift. The café-restaurant has level access and is quite spacious.

THE ROYAL YACHT BRITANNIA

Address: Ocean Terminal, Leith, Edinburgh EH6 6JJ **Website:** www.royalyachtbritannia. co.uk **Telepone:** 0131 555 5566 **Hours:** Jan, Feb, Mar, Nov, Dec: first admission 10am, last 3.30pm Apr, May, Jun, Sep, Oct: first admission 10am, last 4.30pm July, Aug, first admission 9.30am, last 4.30pm **Dates:** closed 25 Dec and 1 Jan **Entry fees:** [D]£9.75 [H]free [A]£9.75 [5–17s]£5.75 [C]£7.75

Permanently berthed at Ocean Terminal in Edinburgh since going out of service, the Royal Yacht *Britannia* is one of the city's newest tourist attractions. Having played host to kings, princesses and heads of state, it's now open to the hoi polloi to follow in their footsteps – for a rather hefty fee.

Whether you're a fan of royalty or things naval, *Britannia* is a very interesting ex-perience and much has been done to make it a barrier-free attraction, with ramping installed where necessary. Once you're on board, from the bridge to the engine room, you can access everything, and the running commentary brings the ship to life, telling stories of its crew through the years. Although it was only decommissioned in 1997, it's surprising how dated the fittings and décor are: far from splendid luxury, *Britannia* is really rather frugal by what one presumes are the standards of modern luxury yachts.

Ocean Terminal is a modern mall, and from the ample accessible car parking on multiple levels, you have a level push (and a lift) to the *Britannia* ticket office. A 21-lan-guage audio description device can be set for sight-impaired enhanced description and for those with learning difficulties. If you can manage stairs, there is straightforward access to other decks, while if you have more restricted mobility, there are ramps back into the building, where you take the lift to the next level. The maintenance staff on board will happily assist, for instance if you require a push up a ramp.

RSPB LOCH GARTEN OSPREY CENTRE

Address: off the B970, 10 miles from Aviemore **Website:** www.rspb.org.uk/reserves/guide/l/
lochgarten **Telephone:** 01479 831476 **Hours:** daily 10am–6pm ("Caper watch" 5.30–8am 1
Apr–21 May) **Dates:** closed Sep–Mar **Entry fees:** [D]£2 [H]Free [A]£3 [under 16s]£0.50 [C]£2

The RSPB's Osprey Centre – near the spot, nestling in mature pine forest, where these stunning raptors returned to breed in Scotland – is a mecca for birdwatchers and a favourite with Bill Oddie. You're greeted on arrival at the car park by acrobatic red squirrels appearing as if on cue. Most visitors are enchanted and find the sights, sounds and smells of the wilderness stay with them long after the visit.

The small, well-appointed Osprey Centre teems with viewing slots and equipment, with some binoculars and telescopes set low for wheelchair users. You get great views of the osprey nest through these, as well as good opportunities to scan for the myriad small birds feeding nearby, including, if you're lucky, chirpy Scottish crossbills, and punk-headed crested tits. While the centre doesn't have facilities for people with sensory impairments, enthusiastic staff are happy to describe the action, and numerous audio and video feeds from the osprey nest bring the atmosphere close up. Further afield in the surrounding Abernethy forest, you can see highly endangered capercaillies, roe deer, common lizards and even otters.

Arriving at the car park, you find two dedicated parking bays, but staff will allow you to drive the last 300m to the door if distance is a problem. A gentle ramp into the centre takes you to another world. The centre is all on one level and all wheelchair-accessible. The unisex adapted toilet is by the car park. If you need to borrow a wheelchair, they have one at the Osprey Centre – call ahead to book.

SCOTTISH FOOTBALL MUSEUM

Address: Hampden Park, Glasgow G42 9BA **Website:** www.scottishfootballmuseum.org.uk
Telephone: 0141 616 6139 **Hours:** Mon–Sat 10am–5pm, Sun 11am–5pm
Dates: daily, except when international matches are played **Entry fees:** [D]£3 [H]£3 [A]£6
[5-16]£3 [C]£3

Housed within Hampden Park Stadium (home of Queen's Park FC and the Scottish national side), the Scottish Football Museum – or the Hampden Experience as it likes to bill itself – is a must for football lovers. It's also interesting from the perspective of social history; Glasgow is inextricably linked to the beautiful game and all the highs and lows of Scottish football are recorded here.

From the moment of your arrival at the imposing front of the stadium you're drawn deep into the world of Scottish football. There are numerous items of tactile statuary and full-size artefacts, like old turnstiles and seating. It's not all dusty museum fare, however – far from it. There are audiovisual displays throughout, recounting anecdotes and telling the story of the game, with the stories of players, pundits and fans all given

IDEAS ▶▶ Festivals

You can immerse yourself in festivals of all shapes and sizes in the UK, from the elegance of Glyndebourne, to the eccentricity of cheese-rolling at Cooper's Hill.

There are as many variations in music festivals – some are huge commercial affairs and some small independent gatherings – and with all that mud, it's hard to be sure a festival weekend is for you. **Attitude is Everything** (020 7383 7979; www.attitudeiseverything.org.uk; suzanne@attitudeiseverything.org.uk) improve deaf and disabled people's access to live music by working with audiences, artists and the wider music industry to implement a Charter of Best Practice. The organisation has worked with many UK festivals and has achieved great improvements for both visitors and artists.

Their top accessible festival picks are the increasingly recognised **Reading & Leeds** (www.festivalrepublic.com); independently run **Guilfest** which takes place at Stoke Park (www.guilfest.co.uk); **WOMAD** (World of Music, Arts and Dance; www.womad.org) and the long-established **Cambridge Folk Festival**. All four of these events offer an accessible camping area, viewing platforms, accessible toilets and showers, comprehensive access and transport information available on the web and in different formats well ahead of the event, where applicable a '2 for 1' ticket deal for disabled customers and availability of electric scooters and wheelchairs. Attitude is Everything also suggest checking out **Glastonbury** and **Latitude** in Southwold, both of which are focusing on improving access from 2009 onwards.

Away from music and the work of Attitude is Everything, the Hay Literature Festival is an internationally recognised gathering of authors, writers and book-lovers set just outside the town. All events have wheelchair access, but beware the aged buildings that house the secondhand bookshops.

exposure. Memorabilia from each era of football is everywhere, from the origins of the game in the Corinthian clubs of the nineteenth century to the present day. There are daily guided tours of the stadium at 11am, 12.30pm, 2pm and 3pm (Nov–Mar) and 3.30pm (Apr–Oct) except when there is a match on.

The seamless ease of access makes the museum a real pleasure to visit. A straightforward and level push from the four Blue Badge parking spaces to the base of the lift makes getting inside easy. Once in, the site is level throughout. It's a bit of a tardis too, with more to discover around each cleverly constructed corner, which adds unexpected twists to the visit. The staff live and breathe football and are happy to inform and assist in any way they can. There's a comfortable and spacious café, with the shop incorporated in the same large area, while accessible toilets are situated in the corridor outside.

SCOTTISH PARLIAMENT BUILDING, EDINBURGH

Address: opposite Holyroodhouse, Edinburgh EH99 1SP **Website:** www.scottish.parliament.uk
Telephone: 0800 092 7500; Textphone 0800 092 7100; Text 07786 209888 **Hours:** business
dates Tue–Thurs 9am–6.30pm; business dates Mon & Fri, plus recess dates 10am–5.30pm (4pm
Oct–Mar); Sat & public holidays 11am–5.30pm; Sun closed **Dates:** recess dates 14–22 Feb, 4–19
Apr, 27 Jun–30 Aug **Entry fees** guided tour only [D]£3.60 [H]free [A]£6 [5–16]£3.60 [C]£3.60

It took more than three hundred years but Scotland finally got its own parliament. On a
groundswell of popular support, self-rule over most domestic affairs was devolved back
to Edinburgh in 2002. The designer of the legislature building, the Catalan architect Enric
Morales, died before its completion but left a formidable legacy. You don't need to count
yourself a politics or architecture buff to really enjoy the experience of a visit.

Occupying a prime site at the foot of the imposing rocky outcrop of Arthur's Seat and
right next to the Palace of Holyrood, Scotland's Parliament building is a remarkable realisa-
tion of Morales' vision and of Scotland's view of itself as a nation. The plan of the building
resembles tree branches and leaves to symbolise the growth of Scotland, and the lines of
the building's footprint are evident as you move around. As well as incorporating various
Scottish architectural traits, such as the crow-step feature of Edinburgh tenement gables in
the windows in the MSPs' offices, Morales doffs his cap to Charles Rennie Mackintosh in
adopting his style in several places. Extensive use of glass bathes the entrance hall in light,
which enhances the concrete vaulted ceiling, replete with the abstract Scottish saltire or
diagonal cross motif. Where possible, too, local wood and stone have been used to enhance
this unique structure. Superb guided tours are available and, if prebooked, BSL interpreters
can accompany you.

The whole Scottish parliament facility is accessible throughout, with the debating cham-
ber alone capable of accommodating sixty wheelchair-users. Six dedicated parking places
across from the front door of the building immediately make you feel good about the
whole place though, on entering, be prepared for an airport-style security shakedown. The
public gallery, committee rooms, café and crèche are all fully accessible for all abilities. Of a
slew of accessible toilets, one even has an adult changing facility. Communication facilities
are excellent, and the parliament staff welcome calls using the RNID Typetalk service.

STEAMSHIP SIR WALTER SCOTT

Address: Trossachs Pier, Loch Katrine, By Callander FK17 8HZ **Website:** www.lochkatrine.com
Telephone: 01877 332000 **Hours:** departs Trossachs Pier 10.30am, 3pm; departs Stronachlachar
pier 11.30am, 4pm (voyage duration 1hr); short scenic cruise departs Trossachs pier 1.30pm (arrives
Trossachs Pier 2.15pm). **Dates:** daily, late June to late Sept **Fares:** Trossachs to Stronlachlar or vice
versa [D]£8 single, £9.50 return [H]£8 single, £9.50 return [A]£8 single, £9.50 return [5–15s]£6
single, £7 return [C]£7 single, £8.50 return; scenic cruise same price as single

Turn the clock back to the days when Victoria was on the throne by boarding this delightful little ship and marvelling at the stunning scenery of Loch Katrine and the surrounding

SCOTLAND

peaks. It's an opportunity for a short cruise aboard a piece of marine history – and you can enjoy a glass of something, or a cappuccino, as you drink in some of Scotland's finest scenery.

Set amidst the stunning lochs and mountains of the Trossachs, and only an hour from Glasgow, the SS *Sir Walter Scott* now carries tourists the ten kilometres length of Loch Katrine – which has been the source of Glasgow's drinking water since 1900 – from its home port of Trossachs Pier in the east to Stronachlachar Pier in the west. Built at Dumbarton, and named after the writer Sir Walter Scott (whose poem "The Lady of the Lake" was set around the loch), the ship was then dismantled and transported overland to the loch – a serious feat of logistics in 1900. If you're a fan of machinery, you'll find the engine room is visible from windows on deck level. The ship, no longer coal-fired but running on bio-diesel, today plies the same route it has chugged over for more than a century.

From the seven dedicated parking spaces in the tarmac car park it's an easy push to the booking kiosk, the separate toilet block and, on the other side, the lift-accessed bistro, which also has an accessible toilet. Once you're booked, you'll find level access all the way to the gangplank which has a small, 6cm step on and off. Once you're on board, you'll find a level deck. For the opening of the 2009 season the ship has been converted to include an accessible toilet on deck as well as a bar and the seating plan improved for access.

TITAN CRANE CLYDEBANK

Address: Garth Drive, Queens Quays, Clydebank G81 1NX **Website:** www.titanclydebank.com
Telephone: 0141 952 3771 **Hours:** Fri–Mon, 10am–4.45pm **Dates:** May–Oct **Entry fees:**
[D]£3 [H]free [A]£4.50 [5–16s]£3 [C]£3

The Titan Crane helped build world-famous ships, including the *Lusitania*, HMS *Hood* and the *Queen Mary*, survived the blitz and industrial decline, and is now a visitor attraction. Its viewing platform provides unrivalled views over the Clyde and beyond and a steam-age learning experience that's hard to beat.

The Titan, like a colossal toy crane, has a box-girder construction and is nearly 50m tall. From its viewing platform, it offers a stunning panorama up and down the river Clyde as well as views of the comings and goings at Glasgow airport. Video presentations play inside and outside the crane's winding house, and sepia-tinted photos and films of a bygone age tell the story of the yard in good times and bad. The guide on the 45-minute tour offers a running commentary on the shipyard's past, pointing out the remains of the slipway, down which the likes of the *QE2* and *Britannia* were once launched, which is now little more than a few rotting planks sticking out of the river.

There is a single, free, disabled parking space at the booking office with gently ramped access to the ticket office and shop. Hot drinks are available and a video presentation on the history of the yard plays in the waiting area where there's an accessible toilet. The bus which takes you on the short tour to the base of the crane is accessed by platform lift; you then disembark and are transported in a couple of minutes by glass lift to the viewing platform. Up on the viewing platform, there are sets of fixed binoculars, two of them at a lower position which are ideal for wheelchair-users. The site is exposed, so it's best to wear warm clothes, even on a fine day.

WALKING ON AIR – GLIDING NEAR KINROSS

Address: Scottish Gliding Centre, Portmoak Airfield, Scotlandwell, Near Kinross KY13 9JJ **Website:** www.walkingonair.org.uk and www.scottishglidingcentre.co.uk **Telephone:** 01592 840222 **Hours:** by prior arrangement, usually weekends **Dates:** all year, but most frequently in spring and summer **Entry fees:** 15–30-minute trial flight £65

Walking on Air is a charity, set up to allow people with disabilities and a sense of adventure to soar the thermals using a modified glider. The club uses the Gliding Centre facilities at Portmoak Airfield, and the clubhouse has panoramic views of Loch Leven and around.

The Chairman of Walking on Air, Steve Derwin, is passionate about flying and the opportunities it offers for integration, enabling people with disabilities to participate on equal terms with the rest of the community. Go along for a trial flight and experience the adrenaline rush of the launch and landing, the almost spiritual experience of being up high as you soar quietly above the mountains, and the mesmerising views of the peaks' powdered summits and the lochs far below, sparkling like jewels. Gliding seems to make everyone a bit poetic. The club welcomes visitors and new members, and even if you're not sure about actually flying yourself, you're welcome to come along to meet the enthusiastic members, watch others fly and enjoy a very relaxing day out. For flying, they have a two-seater K21 training glider, known as "WA1", with hand controls fitted front and back. The Scottish Gliding Union have converted one of their gliders, as well, in case WA1 is out of action.

The Scottish Gliding Union have gone all-out to support Walking on Air, both with willingness and enthusiasm to incorporate disabled people into its membership and with specific, accessible facilities. There's plenty of accessible parking on a hard-packed cinder car park and the clubhouse has ramped access, with a café-restaurant and overnight accommodation (accessible though not specifically adapted). There's also a converted caravan at the launch point, with ramped access and a disabled toilet and shower.

Walking on Air

NORTHERN IRELAND

- Castlewellan Forest Park
- Glenariff and Somerset Forest Parks
- Grand Opera House, Belfast
- Laganside, Belfast
- Murlough National Nature Reserve
- The Museum of Free Derry
- The Odyssey Arena, Belfast
- Peatlands Park
- Quoile Countryside Centre and Castle
- Ulster Transport Museum

IDEAS ▶▶ Action and adventure

NORTHERN IRELAND

Northern Ireland has many areas of lush and immensely beautiful countryside. Its main outdoor attractions – such as the Giants Causeway – are dotted around the coastline, while inland are the spectacular, rugged Mourne Mountains. The largest city is the swiftly developing Belfast, a spruce and high-energy place full of grand public buildings, as well as trendy shops, restaurants and bars.

CASTLEWELLAN FOREST PARK

Address: Castlewellan, Co. Down BT31 9BU **Website:** www.forestserviceni.gov.uk **Telephone:** 028 4377 8664 **Hours:** daily 10am–sunset, café daily 10am–6pm Easter to Sep and weekends only 10am–4pm Oct–Easter **Dates:** no closures **Entry fees:** free, parking £4

Set in the rolling wooded northerly foothills of the Mourne Mountains, Castlewellan Park is host to a Peace Maze, which is in fact the world's largest and longest hedge maze. The park also has a Scottish baronial-style granite castle looking impressively over the mile-long Castlewellan lake and surrounding parkland.

The forest park is grandly laid-out, and has a variety of trails and gardens, and natural and artificial attractions. Amongst the conifer and broadleaf woodland are three marked trails. The blue Lake Path (four kilometres), labelled as a family cycling trail, is suitable for walkers, cyclists and wheelchair-users. Next to the castle, former home of the Annesley family and now a conference centre, is the attractively walled Annesley Garden, which provides a focal point for the National Arboretum, with its magnificent collection of trees and shrubs, planted among fountains, ponds and ornamental greenhouses. The Grange Yard and Grange Coffee House, where Castlewellan's facilities and main car park are located, is based around eighteenth-century farm buildings. Above this, at the upper end of the main car park, is the Peace Maze, the most recent addition to the park, funded as a Peace and Reconciliation project. It has 3.5km of accessible paths, and a spectacular view from its centre, which is also accessible via a bridge from a graded path around its perimeter. The hedge is taller than a wheelchair-user, however, so unless you really want to get lost, get an assistant to go with you.

Accessible parking is found in the main car park at Grange Yard, where there are disabled parking bays at the bottom, beside the building, and at the top next to the Peace Maze. From here, you can follow the 300m driveway down to the lake, though lakeside parking is also available. The Lake Path is relatively level, but it's best to follow it anticlockwise to avoid one steeper gradient.

GLENARIFF AND SOMERSET FOREST PARKS

Address: 6 Forest Road, Garvagh, Co. Londonderry BT51 5EF **Website:** www.forestserviceni.
gov.uk **Telephone:** 028 2955 6000 **Hours:** daily 8am–5pm **Dates:** park, exhibition, interactive
display and toilets open all year; café, shop and camping & caravan site open Easter–Oct **Entry
fees:** [D]£1.50 [H]£1.50 [A]£1.50 [5–15s]£0.50 [C]£1.50

Glenariff, the Queen of the Glens, is considered by many to be the most beautiful of the
nine Antrim Glens. A scenic looped driveway with panoramic views over the forest and
the Antrim Hills is the picturesque entrance to the Glenariff Forest Park, situated amid
the famous Glens of Antrim.

The visitor area has impressive views over the scarped Antrim hills, dissected by two
beautiful rivers; the Inver and the Glenariff. The rivers have carved steep-sided, wooded
glens with spectacular waterfalls, though these can only be seen by walking down into
the forest. A gently graded path leads from the large car park to the visitor area, with
its exhibition, interactive display, café, shop, toilets and a patio and picnic area offering
tremendous views. The interactive display gives plenty of information about the glen
habitats, where red squirrels and shady woodland plants flourish.

Glenariff is appealing for its views, but if an actual walk or push is what you're after,
then Somerset Forest Park, about a 45-minute drive west of Glenariff (1.5km south of
Coleraine) has been designed by the Forest Service to BT Millennium Mile standards. In
contrast to Glenariff, Somerset Forest Park has wheelchair-accessible trails throughout,
and includes a sensory trail and Braille displays. Following the spectacular Causeway
Coastal Route is an appealing – though longer – drive to Coleraine from Glenariff.

Glenariff Forest Park

The woodland walks at
Glenariff are fairly challenging to access by wheelchair.
The one kilometre Viewpoint
Trail is step-free, with a tarmac surface, but it's very steep
in parts, and the surface is
broken by tree roots so you'll
need assistance. Views of the
lower falls can be accessed
from Laragh Lodge, a right
turn a few kilometres down
the main glen road from the
Forest Park. A ramped patio-
cum-eating area here gives a
limited view of the falls, and
the 1.5km waterfall walk from
the lodge, which is step-free
but steep, might be tackled by
the more adventurous wheelchair-user, but again only
with assistance.

GRAND OPERA HOUSE, BELFAST

Address: Grand Opera House, Great Victoria Street, Town Centre, Belfast BT2 7HR **Website:** www.goh.co.uk **Telephone:** (028) 9024 1919 Dedicated access tel: Textphone: 028 9027 8578 **Hours:** box office Mon–Fri 9am–8pm, Sat 10am–6pm (Sat 3pm–6pm counter sales only) **Dates:** closed bank holidays **Entry fees:** ticket prices vary with performance and seats (free entry for helpers)

First opened in 1895 and extended in 2006, the Grand Opera House is one of Belfast's oldest and best-loved venues. With performances throughout the year, whether you're going to see a show, a stand-up night or the annual Christmas panto, the Opera House is the place to go. The bill for summer 2009 includes the stirring Wuthering Heights, and later in the year Irish folk singer Cara Dillon will be returning following a sold-out 2008 performance.

The theatre closed at the height of the troubles, and only reopened in 1980 when it became the focus of city centre renewal. Today, the overall experience of attending a show here makes for a truly grand evening. With all its cafés, bars and restaurants accessible you can start with a pre-show meal or drink. The auditorium is magnificent in its surroundings, maintaining its original décor and providing for an intimate and relaxing atmosphere. Seating is spacious and comfortable with ample legroom. The acoustics during a show are not too intrusive, which is useful if you have an assistance dog with you. Staff offer excellent and reassuring one-to-one customer service and will record your access requirements to ensure they're appraised of your needs the next time you visit. They can also allocate special seating to meet your needs, for example near to

Grand Opera House

the front if you have a visual impairment.

Accessible parking is available in the multi-storey car park opposite the side entrance and approximately two hundred metres away, although some paths on the approach are uneven in places. There is level access at the main entrance and fire lift access to all levels along with wheelchair access to most areas of the auditorium and all the bars and restaurants. There are accessible toilets on each level which are fitted to high standards, complete with appropriate grab rails. Colour contrast is excellent throughout, particularly helpful if you have a visual impairment.

LAGANSIDE, BELFAST

Address: Belfast **Website:** www.laganside.com **Telephone:** 028 9027 7643 **Hours:** vary depending on venue **Dates:** most venues open all year round but closed 25 Dec **Entry fees:** free to public spaces

Belfast first grew on the banks of the River Lagan, and the now revitalised Laganside represents what's great about the vibrant Belfast of the new millennium. This vast area of waterside redevelopment takes in the Odyssey Arena (see p.182), Lanyon Place, the Cathedral Quarter, Custom House Square, Donegall Quay and the famous St George's Market.

The historical significance of Laganside is characterised by the magnificent Cathedral Quarter, with the accessible St Anne's Cathedral at its heart, but the area is now best symbolised by the increasingly iconic Waterfront Hall, which hosts concerts, sporting events and international conferences. The recently pedestrianised Custom House

Laganside

Square has open-air events like the Proms, and Laganside has a multitude of other public arts spaces. Indeed, right across this showcase regeneration zone there's always a long list of events and attractions taking place, activities to participate in and addresses to see and be seen at. Pubs in the area have music and entertainment to suit practically any taste, ranging from contemporary at the *John Hewitt* to traditional Irish at *The Duke of York* or laid-back dining at *The Edge*, right on the waterfront. Alternatively, you could take a stroll along the waterfront at Donegall Quay or pick up the best of Belfast's fresh food at St George's Market.

Laganside doesn't have one central car park: there's parking near each main site and designated street parking is also available. Access is very good throughout the area, as you'd expect in a modern redevelopment: most paved areas have level access, though there's a bit of a gradient as you approach the waterfront at Donegall Quay and exit Lanyon Place towards Belfast's main railway station. Many venues have level access and nearly all provide accessible toilets, while staff are invariably helpful. Venues such as the Waterfront and St George's Market are particularly accessible, each of them having level access throughout. The cobbled streets of the Cathedral Quarter make it more difficult to negotiate, but it's well worth doing so.

MURLOUGH NATIONAL NATURE RESERVE

Address: Dundrum, Co. Down BT33 0NQ. **Website:** www.ni-environment.gov.uk/nature_reserves **Telephone:** 028 4375 1467 **Hours:** café and toilet daily 10am–5pm Jun–Aug and weekends through the rest of the year **Dates:** no closures **Entry fees:** free, parking £3

The views of the Mourne Mountains from Murlough National Nature Reserve (NNR) make the visit well worthwhile. The conical peak of Slieve Donard – Northern Ireland's highest mountain is a stunning backdrop to the six-thousand-year-old sand dunes and shingle beach within the rich habitat of the reserve.

The Murlough NNR is a Site of Special Scientific Interest or SSSI, and the reserve's 280 hectare (700 acre) sand dune system supports a wide variety of plant and animal life – it's carpeted in flowers in spring and summer, abundant in butterflies and moths, and internationally important for wintering wildfowl and waders. It is also home to common and grey seals. A network of boarded walkways can be accessed from the main car park, with information points along the paths for self-guided rambles. Two boardwalks twist through the dune heath to the impressive seven kilometre-long shingle strand of Dundrum Bay: make the effort to go the extra five to ten metres from the end of the boardwalk and you'll get a spectacular view of the beach, and a real sense of space and wildness.

Car parking is on grass, with no designated disabled parking, though there is space for two cars on tarmac near the café, up to which there's a single small step. Murlough has no visitor centre, but year-round facilities include parking, a picnic area, a café and toilets. In the summer a National Trust information caravan is parked by the entrance and they occasionally offer guided walks and other activities. Unassisted wheelchair access is possible at Murlough, but can be challenging as the gate onto the boardwalk is difficult to open, and there's a lip up onto the boards. The boardwalk itself is a bit of a roller-coaster through the dunes and, although step-free, is quite steep in places.

Murlough National Nature Reserve

THE MUSEUM OF FREE DERRY

Address: Bloody Sunday Centre, 55 Glenfada Park, Derry BT48 9DR **Website:** www.museumoffreederry.org **Telephone:** 028 7136 0880 **Hours:** Mon–Fri 9.30am–4.30pm, Sat 1–4pm (Apr–Sep only), Sun 1–4pm (Jul –Sep only) **Dates:** closed 25–26 Dec **Entry fees:** [D]£2 [H]£2 [A]£3 [5–15s]£2 [C]£2

Established in 2006 in the heart of the Bogside, the Museum of Free Derry brings together more than 25,000 artefacts focusing on a key period of the city's history. Recently refurbished, it now attracts visitors from all over the world and provides an engaging and informative visit in this historic city.

You can work your way gradually around the displays and exhibits at a pace which suits you, and spend anything from an hour to most of the day here. Don't forget to look round outside, however, at the many murals which define this part of Derry. The interactive tour of the museum starts with the history of the emergence of the Bogside in the 1600s, to the civil rights era and internment and Bloody Sunday itself. Along with plenty of factual detail, touch-screen computers allow you to look at many private collections of photographs, never seen in public before. The journey through the period of most recent upheaval is accompanied by the audio soundtrack from amateur footage taken between 1968 and 1972, which you can watch as you approach the end of the tour. Staff are on hand for questions.

Parking is difficult owing to the museum's proximity to a residential area, with the approach pavement slightly uneven in places. More parking, but without any designated disabled spaces, is available on the main street adjacent to the museum. With level access throughout and an even floor, the museum allows for easy and independent viewing. The displays tend to be very visual, but staff can escort people with visual impairments.

THE ODYSSEY ARENA, BELFAST

Address: 2 Queen's Quay, Belfast BT3 9QQ **Website:** www.odysseyarena.com **Telephone:** 028 9076 6000 Dedicated access tel: textphone 028 9073 9174 **Hours:** box office 10am–7pm Mon–Saturday (reduced hours in Jul & Aug) **Dates:** closed 25 Dec **Entry fees:** Belfast Giants [D] £8 [H]£8 [A]£14 [5–15s]£8 [C]£8; game day less than 24 hours before game [D]£8.50 [H]£8.50 [A]£15 [5–15s]£8.50 [C]£8.50

Belfast's "Millennium Project", the Odyssey Arena, has quickly gained a reputation as one of the city's main entertainment venues. Home to the Belfast Giants ice hockey team, it also stages frequent events, from sports competitions and exhibitions to concerts by some of the world's biggest acts.

There is no such thing as a bad seat at the Odyssey Arena: great views of the ice rink or stage are guaranteed. Designed by Marshall Haines & Barrow, it's the largest indoor entertainment venue in Northern Ireland, with a range of events and facilities in the wider complex that attracts people of all ages and caters proficiently for people with disabilities. This is a venue with activities and events which will fill many days. With seating for up to 10,000, unlike many open-air concert venues the enclosed and compact nature of the venue provides for a more intimate, yet still electrifying atmosphere during sporting events and concerts. Adjacent to the arena, within the Odyssey complex, is a range of other facilities, including an indoor bowling arena, restaurants and bars, all of which are fully accessible.

Designated parking bays are within fifty metres of the entrance, with just one crossing and no steps to negotiate. There is lift access to the two upper levels with level access throughout the ground-floor area. Accessible toilets are on all levels and the recently improved signage is clearly defined throughout, making it easier for people with visual impairments. Low-level counters at the box office and many of the retail outlets on the main concourse make for a more enjoyable and independent experience. And event stewards are briefed with the details of visitors with disabilities who have notified the Odyssey in advance.

PEATLANDS PARK

Address: 33 Derryhubbert Road, Dungannon, Co Armagh BT71 6NW **Website:** www.
ni-environment.gov.uk/peatlands **Telephone:** 028 3885 1102 **Hours:** park gates open daily
9am–9pm Easter Sunday–30 Sep, 9am–5pm Oct–Easter Saturday; facilities and attractions
open weekends and bank holidays noon–5pm Easter–31 May plus Sep, and daily noon–5pm
Jun–Aug **Dates:** closed 25–26 Dec **Entry fees:** free entry, train [D]£1 [H]£1 [A]£1 [5–
15s]£0.50 [C]£0.50

A leafy driveway leads into the woodlands and wetlands of Peatlands Park, the first of its kind in the British Isles, offering a network of waymarked walks and visitor exhibits about the 10,000-year-old peatland habitat.

The area is home to a wide variety of wildlife including waterfowl, butterflies, moths, lizards, newts and frogs. Much of the park is protected as a National Nature Reserve and an SSSI (Site of Special Scientific Interest). Peatlands Park is also the venue for the annual International Bog Day on the last Sunday of July, with its bizarre bog-snorkelling competition – the current world record was achieved here. Accessible paths connect the car park to the central area of the park, where a visitor centre, an education centre with an interesting low environmental-impact design, a railway, shop and toilets are located. Immediately around the centre is grassy parkland with picnic areas, an orchard and a small lake. The narrow-gauge railway associated with the original turbary, or turf cutting, now has a visitor train, which makes for an ideal way to view the open bog area. There are some 16 kilometres of way marked trails.

The train is fully accessible to wheelchair-users. The mile-long (1.6km) Parkside Walk is the only tarmac trail, but a boardwalk loop around the Bog Garden is also wheelchair-friendly. The other trails have mixed surfaces of wood chip, boardwalk and gravel, so would be strenuous for unassisted wheelchair-users, though they're just about suitable for mobility scooters. If you want to reserve one of the park's electric scooters, you should call in advance, particularly in winter when visitor facilities are normally closed. If your mobility is restricted, you can also arrange vehicle access into the park area by calling in advance.

IDEAS ▶▶ Action and adventure

This guide features many suggestions for action-packed outdoor activities from dog-sledding in the Cairngorms to sailing on Rutland Water. There are a wealth of organisations and charities in the UK who provide specialist facilities for adventurers with disabilities. If you want to take to the skies, see p.36 for the work of the **British Disabled Flying Association** and p.174 for **Walking on Air** in Scotland, which provides specially adapted gliders. The **APT Charitable Trust** (www.disabledflying.org.uk; 01722 410744; admin@disabledflying.org), based at the Old Sarum airfield in Wiltshire has microlight aircraft with modified controls, and has been operating for fourteen years. **Flyability** (www.flyability.org.uk; contact@flyability.org.uk) is the disability initiative of the British Hang-Gliding and Paragliding Association. Tandem flights are available with Flyability, but the charity also encourages people with disabilities to train alongside able-bodied students.

Back on the ground, the **Disabled Ramblers** (www.disabledramblers.co.uk) is a group of like-minded people who enjoy being in the countryside. Rambles on a sliding scale of challenge levels are organised across England and Wales, mainly for people with limited mobility, and so far the group has traversed over one thousand miles of off-road trails. A programme of rambles is available from the website. Sister organisation the **Forth & Tay Disabled Ramblers** hires accessible transport to take members to venues where all the paths have been previously checked and risk-assessed in advance. If you'd prefer to venture out on trails in Scotland, the guide to wheelchair-friendly trails in Scotland - Walking on Wheels - has handy maps and tips for fifty scenic routes.

If you're more at home away from dry land, **Sailability** has clubs (two of which are featured on p.44 and p.71) all over the UK. And for even less gentle water pursuits, try the **British Disabled Water Ski Association** (www.bdwsa.org) which has seven centres across the UK, including Yorkshire and Scotland, or contact Wiltshire-based Scuba Diving trainers **SabreScuba** (www.sabrescuba.co.uk/about.php) which offfers underwater diving experiences to disabled people.You can train for a PADI certificate that you could make the most of in more exotic locations than the British Isles.

QUOILE COUNTRYSIDE CENTRE AND CASTLE

Address: 5 Quay Road, Downpatrick BT30 7JB **Website:** www.ni-environment.gov.uk/quoile
Telephone: 028 4461 5520 **Hours:** daily 11am–5pm Apr–Aug; Sat & Sun only, 1–5pm Sep–Mar **Dates:** closed 25–26 Dec **Entry fees:** free

This pleasant and relaxing countryside area has accessible riverside walks and an abundance of wildfowl and other birds. A National Nature Reserve, with a countryside centre and castle tower at its heart, it has a fantastic bird hide on its eastern fringe.

The river banks have been transformed from tidal inlet to freshwater grass and woodland since a tidal barrage was constructed in 1957, to prevent flooding of the area. A 2.5km path with a hard surface runs through woodland along the riverbank, from the floodgates at the Downpatrick end of the reserve to steps climbing to Steamboat Quay, once a busy port with a paddle-boat steamer to Liverpool. The reserve is a haven for wildfowl and you'll see large numbers of ducks, swans and geese. The countryside centre has displays on the wildlife and history of the area, an attractive, small garden with raised organic beds, and a picnic area beside the stream. They also offer introductory birdwatching courses – call them for dates. Also worth a visit for views of the seashore and Strangford Lough is the four kilometre drive to the Castle Island Road, where the large and attractively constructed Castle Island bird hide overlooks the reserve from the south and offers ornithologists wonderful viewing opportunities.

Quoile Countryside Centre is just north of Downpatrick, on the road to Strangford (signposting is poor), and effectively situated on both sides of the Quoile River. The paths and buildings within the nature reserve are all ramped and suitable for wheelchair access, though it's best to park at the countryside centre to avoid steeper ramps up to the other two car parks further along the river. Steps lead up to the castle tower, and to Steamboat Quay. Castle Island bird hide has ramped access.

ULSTER TRANSPORT MUSEUM

Address: Cultra, Holywood, County Down BT18 0EU **Website:** www.uftm.org.uk **Telephone:** 028 9042 8428 **Hours:** opens 10am Mon–Sat, 11am Sun, closes 4pm winter weekdays, 5pm winter weekends and spring weekdays, 6pm spring weekends and summer all week. **Dates:** closed 25–26 Dec (call to confirm) **Entry fees:** [D]free [H]free [A]£5.50 [5-18s]£3.50 [under 5s]free [C]£3.50 [F]£11–15.50

Tram carriage at Ulster Transport Museum

Part of the Ulster Folk and Transport Museum (separate admissions), this award-winning collection of all things vehicular is huge fun for transport buffs and a great place for a family day out. You can travel from the steam age to the jet age, testing your skills in the latter on an impressive flight simulator.

Voted Irish Museum of the Year, this is one of the largest transport collections in Europe. Over the centuries, Ireland was a major pioneer and innovator in the technology of rail transport, and the railway section demonstrates this with an impressively restored collection of historic locomotives, carriages and wagons from standard and narrow-gauge railways. There is a great deal more to see, with displays of aircraft, boats, horse-drawn carts, old Belfast trams, motorcycles, bicycles, and a world-renowned exhibition about the Belfast-built *Titanic*. The museum is also the only one in the world to feature a collection of Irish-built cars. Many of the exhibits are unique – the only surviving examples of their era. The exhibits are ranged chronologically and the physical displays, photos and audio work seamlessly together to create a compelling experience for any visitor.

The museum is split across two sites, separated by the main Belfast–Bangor dual carriageway. You can drive from one car park to another as you visit the museum. If you want to borrow a wheelchair, they have a few available. The ramp system is very wheelchair-friendly and only two areas are inaccessible to wheelchair-users. In both cases, though, the provision of viewing areas allows you to see the exhibits. There's a small, wheelchair-friendly café, and in good weather, the grassy areas and picnic tables make the beautiful grounds perfect for a picnic.

USEFUL CONTACTS

Useful contacts features the Rough Guide pick of the specialist organisations and independent companies that provide advice, assistance and services to help disabled people with holidays and day-trips in Britain. **Getting Around** has the lowdown on practical services for your day-to-day travel needs. **Travel Advice** flags up the disability charities and organisations that, in addition to their everyday work, provide travel and leisure advice and aid. This section also champions specialist providers of UK travel and holiday information. **Holiday Services** is a great place to get started when researching accessible accommodation or finding a specialist holiday operator. And finally, **British Tourism** highlights the regional and national tourist boards and keepers of national heritage whose information stands out from the rest.

GETTING AROUND

BBNav – Blue Badge enhanced GPS navigation ⓦwww.bbnav.co.uk Sat-Nav system with all the usual functionality as well as coverage of Blue Badge on-street parking bays, car park access and local council parking rules for over 150 major UK cities and towns.

Blue Badge Parking Map ⓦwww.blue badge.direct.gov.uk Online interactive UK map with locations of Blue Badge parking, car park access, accessible toilets, railway stations etc. Click on points of interest to get further details, such as allowed waiting times. A very helpful tool for research but sadly the map is not printable.

Bus pass scheme – England Free off-peak travel on the whole English local bus network is now available for over 60s and disabled people. Passes are usually available from your local council. Some councils offer additional benefits such as peak-time travel. Further information available at ⓦwww .direct.gov.uk or ⓦwww.dft.gov.uk.

Bus pass schemes – Wales and Scotland Wales and Scotland operate independent bus pass schemes. In Wales, contact your local council for a pass you can use on buses at any time of day. The scheme in Scotland is run by Transport Scotland ⓦwww.trans portscotland.gov.uk and requires a National Entitlement card.

Changing Places ⓦwww.changing-places. org England, Wales and Northern Ireland: ⓣ020 7696 6019 ⓔchangingplaces@ mencap.org.uk Scotland: ⓣ01382 385154 ⓔ pamischangingplaces@dundee.ac.uk This consortium campaigns for toilets for people who require non-standard access features, including hoists and height adjustable changing benches. Site includes a map of current and future Changing Places toilet locations with details of opening hours.

Disabled Person's Railcard ⓦwww.dis abledpersons-railcard.co.uk ⓣ0845 605 0525 Textphone 0845 601 0132 ⓔdisabi lity@atoc.org Concessionary railcard that allows 1/3 off most standard and first class rail fares for those with a disability, plus an adult companion if train travel presents difficulties. Site also has useful links to station accessibility details and contacts for booking assistance.

Door to Door ⓦwww.dptac.gov.uk/door -to-door ⓔdptac@dft.gsi.gov.uk Site run by the Disabled Persons Transport Advisory Committee (DPTAC) providing transport and travel advice for disabled people. A great starting point for basic information on all forms of transport if you can get beyond the sometimes obvious advice.

Mobilise (incorporating Disabled Drivers Association) ⓦwww.mobilise.info ⓣ01508 489449 ⓔenquiries@mobilise.info Charity campaigning for improvements in access. Members receive a monthly magazine and can access information officers who advise on individual transportation needs. Check the website for updates on disability schemes and legislation.

Motability ⓦwww.motability.co.uk ⓣ0800 923 0000 ⓣ0845 675 0009 (minicom).Car and Scooter Scheme for disabled people.

National Express ⓦwww.nationalexpress .com/coach/OurService/disabled.cfm ⓣDisabled Persons Travel Helpline 08717 818179 Textphone 0121 455 0086 Aiming to run a 100 percent accessible coach network by 2012, wheelchair-accessible vehicles are being steadily rolled-out. To check serviced routes see the website or call the travel helpline. Adapted coaches have a wide entrance with a floor lift and a large toilet. Reduced fares for disabled passengers of up to half price are available on some services.

National Federation of Shopmobility ⓦwww.shopmobilityuk.org ⓣ08456 442446 ⓔinfo@shopmobilityuk.org Most towns and shopping centres have a Shopmobility scheme that lends manual wheelchairs, powered wheelchairs and scooters. Schemes operate differently from place-to-place with some charging and others free. The site has a searchable database of affiliated schemes.

Need a Loo? ⓦwww.needaloo.org Online directory of publicly accessible disabled toilets. Whilst not totally comprehensive, there are a lot of loos listed. Locations displayed via Streetmap and Google Maps.

TRAVEL ADVICE

Ableize ⓦwww.ableize.com Online directory of services that includes listings for travel, recreation, sport, holidays and accommodation. Not the easiest site to navigate, but it is worth digging out the particularly nice section on accessible gardens.

Arts Access UK ⓦwww.artsaccessuk.org Venue and events database detailing access to arts and culture in Britain. Search by region and/or type of art form including film, music and visual arts for a summary of services as stated by the venue itself. An events calendar lists performances relevant to visitors with specific disabilities.

Contact A Family ⓦwww.cafamily.org.uk ⓣ0808 808 3555 Publishes a guide to 'Holidays, Play and Leisure' containing advice on available facilities for children with disabilities and details of holiday providers along with possible sources of funding. Download it free from the website or order by phone.

Direct Enquiries ⓦwww.directenquiries.com ⓣ01344 360101 ⓔcustomerservices@directenquiries.com Online directory with a great London Underground accessible route planner that has platform-to-platform and platform-to-street-level information for every station. Access reviews for many services (hotels, shops etc), are available, but solely for companies that have registered. Check out the detailed photograph guides of accessible nature reserve trails.

Directgov ⓦwww.direct.gov.uk/en/disabledpeople Government site for public services with an area dedicated to people with disabilities. Contains background on the National Accessible Scheme for accommodation in England, the Blue Badge parking scheme and advice on places of interest, leisure and accessing the arts.

Disabled Go ⓦwww.disabledgo.info ⓔinfo@disabledgo.info Heavily detailed access information for restaurants, hotels, cinemas, tourist attractions, pubs and train stations etc. All sites are researched in person with invaluable minutiae detail on points such as the transfer side in an adapted toilet. The only issue is that they haven't yet covered the whole country.

Disabled Holiday Info ⓦwww.disabledholidayinfo.org.uk ⓔinfo@disabledholidayinfo.org.uk Useful site with advice on accessible attractions, transport, accommodation and activities in selected regions – most comprehensively for Shropshire. Factsheets are available on subjects including accommodation with wheel-in showers and accessible accommodation with fishing.

Disabled Information from the Disabled ⓦwww.disabledinfo.co.uk A website where disabled people can share their experiences and expertise with others by submitting 'articles' on various subjects – the result of which is a diverse mix of informative pieces and some obvious promotion. Features some useful advice for drivers.

Disability Now ⓦwww.disabilitynow.org.uk Magazine published by Scope with some travel articles. The website has a listings section for accessible hotels, cottages and B&Bs.

Good Access Guide ⓦwww.goodaccessguide.co.uk ⓣ01502 566005 Essentially an online directory of services, businesses and venues that advertise themselves as accessible and disabled-friendly. Far from a comprehensive list but definitely a good starting point.

National Autistic Society ⓦwww.nas.org.uk Features some advice on planning days out when you have a child with autism, plus lists of holiday providers and accommodation suitable for adults with autism. Also features the extensive Autism Services Directory which lists organisations providing play and leisure services.

National Blind Children's Society ⓦwww.nbcs.org.uk Organise days out for children with visual impairments at many attractions in the UK. They also run a holiday home in

Somerset that can be booked by families with a child with visual impairment.

Ouch! ⓦwww.bbc.co.uk/ouch BBC site concerning disability issues with news, blogs and an active forum. There isn't a specific message board for travel but posting a question on the general board is likely to gain a good response.

RADAR ⓦwww.radar.org.uk ⓣ020 7250 3222 ⓔradar@radar.org.uk Campaigning network of organisations and disabled people who operate the National Key Scheme for accessible toilets. Key and toilet locations are available from their website and they also publish an annually updated guide to Holidays in Britain & Ireland that covers accommodation, activity holidays and specialist care centres.

RNIB ⓦwww.rnib.org.uk Advice on leisure activities and holidays for those with visual impairments, including a list of accessible museum and gallery events plus links for rambling, cinema, theatre and spectator sports with audio description. The RNIB also run vacation schemes for children and provide a guide to over 100 recommended places to stay.

RNID ⓦwww.rnid.org.uk Check the 'Entertainment' section for details on signed theatre, subtitled and audio-described cinema, and BSL-signed gallery and museum tours.

Special Needs Kids ⓦwww.special-needs -kids.co.uk The Fun & Leisure section on this site has some useful suggestions for days out for families with children who have special needs. Also has details of disabled sporting organisations and children's activity clubs.

Tourism For All ⓦwww.tourismforall.org.uk ⓣ0845 124 9971 Holiday Care, the Tourism for All Consortium and IndividuALL merged several years ago to form Tourism For All, a national charity dedicated to making tourism welcoming for all. They publish 'Easy Access Britain', a guide to accommodation assessed under the National Accessible Scheme, in conjunction with Visit Britain. The site has lots of info on places to go.

Youreable.com ⓦwww.youreable.com Online community site with a travel section offering advice on planning a trip. Also has links

to providers of holidays and accommodation suitable for the disabled. They also have a travel forum for questions.

Your Level Best ⓦwww.yourlevelbest.com Searchable database of accessible pubs, restaurants and snackbars. Minimum criteria for inclusion is disabled-accessible with an adapted toilet with grab rails. All venues have either been visited or have taken part in a phone questionnaire.

The Wheel Life Guide ⓦwww.thewhe ellifeguide.com Useful directory specialising in leisure and lifestyle, in association with thewheellife.com (a social networking site). Other useful organisations, accommodation, activity holidays and tour operators are listed and there is a particularly good section on disabled sporting associations.

HOLIDAY SERVICES

Accessatlast ⓦwww.accessatlast.com ⓣ01772 814555 Database of properties (UK and international), searchable via requirements such as hoists, grab rails or BSL interpreters. Many properties have been visited on behalf of accessatlast.com and/or reviewed by users. Those with full assessments have a good level of access detail.

Action for Blind People ⓦwww.action forblindpeople.org.uk/holidays This charity runs four hotels, specifically adapted for those with visual impairments fitted with talking alarm clocks, facilities for guide dogs, Braille books and audio-described videos.

All Go Here ⓦwww.allgohere.com The hotels and accommodation listings on this site are generally not aimed primarily at disabled customers, but have accessible rooms nonetheless. Lots of group hotels are listed, and all properties have been checked out over the phone by a wheelchair-user on a 'mystery-shopper' basis.

British Tour Plans ⓦwww.britishtourplans. com/disabled-tours.php ⓣ01623 511210 ⓔinfo@britishtourplans.com Bespoke road-trip planning service that can cater for disabilities. Send details of where you want to go, any specialist interests and what the nature of your disability is and they will supply an itinerary with places to visit, accommodation and turn-by-turn driving directions. They check access for all accommodation and any recommended attractions.

Can be Done Ⓦwww.canbedone.co.uk Ⓣ020 8907 2400 Ⓔholidays@canbedone.co.uk Disabled holiday company providing a bespoke tailor-made service for destinations worldwide including the UK. There is also a rather limited database of accessible hotels on their website.

Caravanable Ⓦwww.caravanable.co.uk Ⓔinfo@caravanable.co.uk Founded by a couple whose son is a chair user, providing detail on camping and caravan sites offering a minimum of ramped access shower, basin and loo facilities. All sites have been vetted by the couple or recommended by other campers and caravaners. Also has a great guide to accessible beaches.

CaRE Ⓦwww.careinthecountryside.net Ⓣ01952 815335 Ⓔenquiries@careinthecountryside.net National network of accommodation providers (mostly B&B or self-catering) in rural areas that can cater for disabled people and those with specialist needs. An easily navigable online database lists member properties. Whilst there aren't huge numbers listed, those included appear to be excellent.

Chalfont Line Ⓦwww.chalfont-line.co.uk Ⓣ01895 459540 Ⓔholidays@chalfont-line.co.uk Escorted holiday service for slow walkers and wheelchair-users. Among other services they offer door-to-door transport, assistance with baggage and a Personal Assistance service. They run coach tours specialising in British History and tailor-made holidays can be arranged in London and the surrounds.

Holiday Access Direct Ⓦwww.holidayaccessdirect.com Ⓣ01502 566005 Holiday Access Direct pulls together links and advice. The main focus is overseas holidays and flights but they do cover accommodation and services in the UK. A team of disabled travel experts can help you with specific queries.

Holidays For All Ⓦwww.holidaysforall.org Ⓣ0845 124 9973 Website of a consortium of leading disability charities and specialist tour companies offering a variety of services from fully supported residential centres to accessible sailing holidays. Some of the members have their own listings in this chapter.

Livability Holidays (formerly Grooms Holidays) Ⓦwww.livability.org.uk Ⓣ08456 584 478 Ⓔinfo@livability.org.uk. Own and operate two hotels and several self-catering properties around the UK, all fully accessible with hoists, wheel-in showers etc. Demand for their properties is high so booking is via a ballot system: every 1–4 Oct they take telephone bookings for the following April to Sep.

Matching Houses Ⓦwww.matchinghouses.com Ⓣ01736 361871 Home swaps based on the premise that if your access needs match another members then their home will be accessible to you. Online sign-up is free but required even to do a preliminary search.

Phab Ⓦwww.phabengland.org.uk Ⓣ020 8667 9443 Ⓔinfo@phab.org.uk Aside from supporting a network of over 200 inclusive activity clubs, Phab also runs a number of summer camps and festivals for physically disabled children to enjoy alongside able-bodied peers. They operate two accessible holiday homes in Weymouth and publish an annual Holiday Guide full of accommodation listings and places to visit.

Responsible Travel Ⓦwww.responsibletravel.com Ⓣ01273 600030 Responsible Travel have hand-picked accommodation in England, Scotland and Wales that is not only accessible, but also ethical. Go to the 'Special Interest' section and select Disabled Travel from the drop-down menu.

Vitalise Ⓦwww.vitalise.org.uk Ⓣ0845 345 1970 Ⓔinfo@vitalise.org.uk Providing group holidays in the UK and overseas for people with visual impairment. Sighted guides provide assistance throughout the trip and tours offered range from gentle sightseeing to theatre trips and outdoor activities. They also run five holiday centres in the UK offering respite care and hire out two accessible self-catering lodges in Cornwall.

BRITISH TOURISM

Accessible South West ⓦwww.accessible southwest.co.uk A site produced by South West Tourism with a directory of accessible services and places. The accommodation directory is useful but places to eat are harder to find as they are listed with laundry services etc. under 'businesses and services'.

Disabled Cornwall ⓦwww.disabled cornwall.co.uk Not an official tourism site but worth a mention nonetheless. Although limited in content at present this site has some listings for accessible restaurants, cafes, tourist attractions and activities in Cornwall. As it is run by a disabled person, you can feel confident that the inclusions will actually be accessible. Accommodation listings are said to be appearing later in 2009.

English Heritage ⓦwww.english-heritage. org.uk ⓣ0870 333 1181 ⓔcustomers@ english-heritage.org.uk Owners of over 400 historic properties, English Heritage operates an 'Access for All' policy. They publish an Access Guide that features properties with good provisions for visitors with limited mobility and those that have services for sensory needs. However as heritage sites, even those that are more accessible inevitably have inaccessible parts. Access information for individual properties is listed on the website, though sadly you can't use accessibility as a criterion in the 'search for a property' function.

Enjoy England ⓦwww.enjoyengland.com The accommodation search function on the Enjoy England website allows you to search by type of disability (physical, visual or hearing). However information for disabled visitors on the rest of the site is limited to one page – for the whole of England they seem only able to recommend six accessible places to visit.

National Trust ⓦwww.nationaltrust.org.uk ⓣ01793 817400 ⓔaccessforall@national trust.org.uk The National Trust welcomes visitors with disabilities. The dedicated 'Access for All' office runs a policy that includes an 'Admit One' card scheme allowing free entry for a necessary companion. The website has further info on policies as well as access details for individual properties. An annually published 'Access Guide' has details for every property. The guide does regularly highlight steps and uneven surfaces, which can make parts of it depressing reading, but this is to warn you of problems, rather than state what is possible. Predictably with heritage sites, there are some largely inaccessible areas of certain properties – but the assessments in the Access Guide have been written by disabled people so you can feel confident of accurate, considered information.

Visit Birmingham ⓦwww.visitbirmingham. com/information/access_for_all ⓣ0121 202 5115 Undoubtedly the most useful regional tourist board website. It's not perfect, but the 'Access for All' section has tips on getting around Birmingham, including a link-up with Direct Enquiries to provide 'photo journeys' of getting to tourist destinations from the nearest public transport. Birmingham City Centre Partnership run two great schemes – 'meet and greet' to help people get around (call 0121 616 2259) and Wayfinder talking signs (www.birmingham.gov.uk/wayfinder) for the blind and partially sighted.

Visit Britain ⓦwww.visitbritain.co.uk Britain's national tourism agency also run the National Accessible Scheme – a nationally recognised rating for accessible accommodation (more information about the scheme is available on the website). Disappointingly on the site you can't use the scheme's symbols as search criteria on the accommodation database. There is however a satisfactory section for 'People with physical and sensory needs'.

Visit Lancashire ⓦwww.visitlancashire. com ⓣ01257 226600 ⓔinfo@visitlanca-shire.com An online list of accessible accommodation and some access information for attractions but unfortunately the fairly comprehensive 'food and drink' listings section doesn't include access details.

Visit Scotland ⓦwww.visitscotland.com ⓣ0845 225 5121 ⓔinfo@visitscotland. com Tourism Scotland runs its own quality assurance scheme for disabled access. Accommodation and attractions are searchable on the website, using accessibility criteria making this by far the most useful of the national tourism websites. A printed guide is also available.